The Keys to Successful UNIX System Management

Robert King Ables

Prentice Hall PTR
Englewood Cliffs, New Jersey 07632

Library of Congress Cataloging-in-Publication Data

Ables, King.

The keys to successful UNIX system management / King Ables.

Includes bibliographical references and index.

ISBN 0-13-948381-0

1. UNIX (Computer file) I. Title.

QA76.76.063A26 1994 94-3453

004'.32—dc20 CIP

Editorial/Production Supervision: Lisa Iarkowski
Acquisitions Editor: Mike Meehan
Manufacturing Manager: Alexis R. Heydt
Cover Design: Whitman Studios

Prentice-Hall, Inc.
A Paramount Communications Company
Englewood Cliffs, NJ 07632

The publisher offers discounts on this book when ordered in bulk quantities. For more information, contact:

Corporate Sales Department
PTR Prentice Hall
113 Sylvan Avenue
Englewood Cliffs, NJ 07632
Phone: 201-592-2863
FAX: 201-592-2249.

Printed in the United States of America

10 9 8 7 6 5 4 3

ISBN 0-13-948381-0

Prentice-Hall International (UK) Limited, London
Prentice-Hall of Australia Pty. Limited, Sydney
Prentice-Hall of Canada, Inc., Toronto
Prentice-Hall Hispanoamericana S.A., Mexico
Prentice-Hall of India Private Limited, New Delhi
Prentice-Hall of Japan, Inc., Tokyo
Simon & Schuster Asia Pte. Ltd., Singapore
Editora Prentice-Hall do Brasil, Ltd., Rio de Janeiro

Trademarks

About the author

Robert King Ables is currently a member of the Technical Support Staff in the Network and Systems Management Division of the Hewlett-Packard Company in Fort Collins, Colorado. Mr. Ables holds a Bachelor of Arts degree in Computer Science from The University of Texas. Over the past 15 years, he has been employed as a systems administrator and software developer in both business and academic environments. Mr. Ables has published articles in several technical journals and operated his own systems administration consulting business.

for Mom and Dad

Contents

Preface

System management has long been a neglected subject. As computing environments have become more sophisticated, however, it has been receiving more attention. Several good books now exist to help with the nuts and bolts of the job ([TF89], [NSS89], and [Fri91] among others). System management is finally being recognized as an essential function for most computing environments, but little attention has been paid to the *philosophy* of system management.

The person who takes care of computer systems and computer users is generally referred to as a system administrator. Because of the neglect of the field of system management in general, the position has never been very well defined. Someone wanting to become a system administrator has probably had a difficult time finding information about the profession itself. This book attempts to remedy this situation.

How someone becomes a system administrator

Sometimes it's a surprise. You're sitting in your office, minding your own business, when a vice president (or other equally high management type) walks into your office and says "Dale has just resigned; we want you to be the new system administrator." Your first reaction is one of curiosity. Later, the curiosity changes to fear as you realize that you have no idea what a system administrator does. Your previous experience, other job responsibilities, or even the fact that you were not trained for the job won't matter. The job is yours.

Sometimes you wind up as a system administrator by working your way through a technical support organization. You're not really sure how you got there, but there you are. You know quite a bit about the machine and the people, but you have never really had any formal training in system management because so little was available.

People newer to the computer industry may have been able to identify the job early and work toward it. No matter how you came to have the job, you have it, and there are few resources, other than experience, from which to learn how to do it properly. That is what this book attempts to do.

Intended audience

If you are (or want to be) a system administrator, this book will explain the job to you. You may have some experience as a system administrator, in which case it will fill some holes in your understanding. Even if you are a "seasoned" system administrator and already know most of what is contained here, you may pick up a few new ideas by considering other perspectives. If nothing else, it will serve to reassure you that you are not the only one in the world dealing with these problems (it might also make a great gift for your boss).

If you are a manager or a system administrator (or even simply a user in a computing environment with a system administrator), this book will give you insight into the job of system management and help you better understand the constraints under which these people do their jobs. You will understand what they can and cannot do for you, and you will be better able to identify qualified and talented people for your staff.

Prerequisite knowledge

The reader is expected to have a user-level knowledge of the UNIX® operating system and be familiar with UNIX environments. This book does not attempt to provide an introduction to UNIX. It is assumed anyone who wants a deeper understanding of the job of UNIX system management is already familiar with the environment itself. Anyone who is, or is soon to be, in charge of a UNIX computing environment should be a competent user first.

What you will learn

System management has often been a job shrouded in mystery and left up to the so-called *gurus*. It isn't that the job itself requires a degree in Mystical Engineering, but the information you need to know is not available in one place and much of it is not available in any manual at all. Traditionally, a new system administrator learns the ropes by becoming a *wizard*'s apprentice to an experienced system administrator. This has worked fairly well in informal circles, but it is mysterious to managers and others not directly involved in the process. With the explosive growth of UNIX in the marketplace, this is no longer an effective solution. There just aren't enough wizards to go around. As the world moves to distributed computing, the scale of the problem is getting larger, not smaller, so the need for experienced system administrators will only increase. Many vendors have made great improvements in their training programs, but no single source exists to explain how to be an effective system administrator. This book is a good place to start.

While the primary concern of this book is system management from the point of view of the UNIX operating system, the nontechnical information contained herein applies to almost any computing environment. Users and their needs are similar whether their tools are PCs or mainframes. Anywhere you find users with problems to solve, disk space to fill, or e-mail to send, this book should help.

This is not a how-to book. Instead, it addresses the more fundamental questions of *what* and *why*? What does a system administrator do, and why is the job so important in a modern computing environment? The answers to these questions will provide a better overall understanding of the field. They will help the new or aspiring system administrator be more effective when performing the job. And they will give the manager a better insight into what the job is really all about.

This examination of the philosophy of managing computer systems and helping the people who use them, will help you learn what tasks are necessary and where to find more detailed technical information. You will learn about the typical activities performed by and expected of system administrators, operators, programmers, and the other people who support computer systems and their users. Most importantly, you will learn about dealing with the needs of the people using the computer system, "the users."

Without a grasp of the big picture, a system administrator may wander blindly through a seemingly endless sea of random problems. It is difficult to do a job well when you do not know what is expected of you. It is also difficult to perform to everyone's satisfaction when they have unrealistic expectations. As you read this book, you will note that the point is not to educate you in great detail about any particular technical subject. The references provided are capable of that. The objective is to make you aware of available resources and to give you an overview of the technical issues involved in system management. Rarely is the system administrator an expert in all these topics, although he or she may have special knowledge in some of them. Some see the system administrator as a "generalist," whose expertise includes some knowledge of almost every aspect of the computing environment. This grasp of the "big picture" and the ability to learn more about specific pieces are a system administrator's most valuable traits. Don't worry that you do not (and indeed will probably never) know as much about any one topic as other people you may know. You should only worry if you feel completely lost in a topic (and this book should help eliminate that).

Organization

The first part of the book is somewhat technical in nature. The job itself and the myriad of services provided by system administrators are examined. These include the software, hardware, and environmental aspects of the "care and feeding" of computer systems. After we have convinced you why these services are important, you can find more detailed information in the provided references.

Once the basics are covered, the next chapters are devoted solely to networking and security. These topics involve both hardware and software issues and are thus best covered by topic rather than split between hardware and software. Networking and security are closely related to each other since the majority of security problems result from the connection of your computers to external networks. Networking is fast becoming the most critical part of a computing environment, and it is difficult to find an environment where it does not exist in some form. As networks expand and the number of people using computers grows, the informal, friendly, open environments of the past come under even more attack. More organizations are storing vital and sensitive data in their computer systems, and many could not function if their systems were inoperable for more than a few hours. The dangers include Mother Nature as well as the *cracker* trying to break into your system(s). These chapters will make you more aware of the risks that face almost any computer site and how you can minimize these risks.

The next two chapters examine the administrative and personal skills necessary to be an effective system administrator. Good organizational and communication skills are essential. In any environment where you support the people who use the systems, communicating effectively with them is the system administrator's most valuable skill.

The final chapter is aimed at both the person hiring the system administrator and the person aspiring to be a system administrator. This chapter discusses the career of the system administrator and should provide both parties with some new perspectives on each other that may lead to a better understanding for both.

Notes throughout the text

References to other publications that will give you more detail about the topic being discussed appear throughout the text. All referenced documents available on the Internet® were verified at the time of printing, but their availability is not guaranteed. Of course, any documentation shipped to you with your computer should be your first source of valuable information. While all the references provided represent some of the best information available, there is no substitute for the expertise of the people who built your computer.

Terms that might be new are italicized the first time they are used and are defined in the Glossary. You will also come across the famous

Internet "smiley" `:-)` used to convey humor, irony, or any number of other emotions that do not always come across in print.[1]

> Occasionally, you will encounter text set apart from the regular text, like this paragraph. These are personal stories from the author's experience, or that of a colleague, which are intended to illustrate the point made in the preceding text.

While this book is intended to be read in the order in which it is presented, this is by no means a requirement. For those with little or no experience, the later information will build on what is presented earlier. If you are already experienced in one or more of the aspects of system management, you may wish to jump directly to the section that interests you the most.

Most of this book is based on the personal experience of the author. The opinions expressed are my own. If you are an experienced system administrator, you may not agree with everything expressed here. If you are a new system administrator, not everything you read should be noted in gold ink on parchment. It is simply information that my experiences, and the experiences of some colleagues, have proven to be useful. I hope you will find it useful as well. It is not a *complete* guide to the job of system management, but it is a good place to start.

[1] If you're not familiar with this, tilt your head to the left and you should "get the picture."

Acknowledgments

I have always enjoyed reading about the people who influence someone who writes a book, regardless of the subject. I used to be amazed at how many people were involved in a project in one capacity or another. Having now seen it from the author's end, I am no longer amazed.

I must thank Bertrand duCastel, Doug Bordner, Gina Mundy, and James McLaughlin at Schlumberger in Austin for their flexibility and helpfulness while I worked on this book. Thanks to Bill Leddy, Jim Moore, Jim Sullivan, Sid Hayes, Jim Wiley, Paul Tuthill, Don Strickland, Mike Strong, and Pamela Hanes for information, feedback, and helpful discussions during the early stages. Those who reviewed the various incarnations of the manuscript—Bob Paver, Laurel Ives, David Carver, Mona Carver, Judy Ashworth, Karen Morgan, Jim Knutson, Charles Sandel, Nate "Woodstock" Hess, Kathy Holle, Chris Garrigues, and Dave Brennan—provided unique insights, with amazingly little redundancy. Reviews from Steve Blair, Sherry Moe, and Ed Guy were particularly detailed and helpful.

Thanks to Stephen Lundstrom, who thought enough of me and my ideas to put me in touch with the fine folks at Prentice Hall. Karen Gettman, Paul Becker (who always seemed to know when I needed some encouragement), Mike Meehan, Sophie Papanikolaou, Lisa Iarkowski are great to work with.

Thanks to Bob Paver for giving me my start in User Services when he had very little reason to believe it was a good idea.

Thanks to my friends, some of whom must feel I moved to another planet. Special thanks to Ken and Lori Wisian and my goddaughter Danielle, who let me "hide out" with them from time to time to escape the diversions of real life and work in peace.

Lastly, and most importantly, I must thank my parents, to whom this book is dedicated. This is because of you.

R. K. A.
Austin, Texas

Chapter 1

Introduction

The strange and seemingly magical evolution of UNIX and UNIX-based environments has lead to a somewhat distorted view of UNIX in general, and especially of UNIX system management. UNIX has acquired an image of mysticism, where only a "wizard" has the power to wave his hands and restore order from chaos and only a Wizard's Apprentice is able to learn the tricks directly from the Wizard.

UNIX had its origins in the laboratory. In its early days, no one could have envisioned the impact it would have on the computer industry. Its designers had no idea how its use would spread. It solved a problem, nothing more. It provided the designers with an easy-to-use and easy-to-modify operating system for their other work [Rit84], [LMKQ90, pp. 3–8], [Bac86, pp. 1–3].

Because of its informal development, many capabilities that are associated with most modern operating systems were not originally implemented in UNIX. It was not a product, so there was no need. UNIX has not so much been developed as it has *evolved.* System management is one major area where the original designers chose to take shortcuts. Now UNIX is making its way into the business world, where users are not accustomed to "flying by the seat of their pants," as the traditional UNIX user has been willing to do.

Fortunately, in the past few years, many people have set out to correct this situation by publishing articles and books on the intricate details of UNIX system management. In addition, vendors are attempting to provide more consistent and usable tools to help manage systems. System administrators are no longer tolerant of the baroque traditions surrounding the care of a UNIX system, and these publications have significantly helped to remove some of the mystical perceptions UNIX has acquired over the years.

However, many who are new to UNIX and system management are also new to computing and are not aware of the generic functions necessary to maintain the smooth operation of a computer system. Before getting detailed help with UNIX system management, these people need some background in general system management issues.

Even at sites where sophisticated computing environments already exist, the hiring managers who search for a system administrator often do not know much about the job itself. They take a "shot in the dark" when hiring someone, hoping that as long as they get a technically competent candidate, all will be well. Sometimes this works, but often it backfires.

Every site is different and the needs of a site vary as widely as the user community and the hardware and software. The intent of this text is to provide you with information about needs, expectations, and options. You will solve your own problems in the way best suited to your local computing environment and its users. Your solution will not be exactly the same as anyone else's, but it should be an informed decision.

1.1 Who is the System Administrator?

The term "system administrator" conjures up different images in the minds of different people. No one-and-only definition for a system administrator has ever been found. Only an examination of the job from the broadest possible perspective will provide a model that is close to reality.

A system administrator is the person (or a member of the group of people) responsible for the proper operation of the computing environment in any organization. For our purposes, this job will cover every possible level of support and maintenance from clerk to operator, from programmer to executive. The entire function is usually called "system management." Some choose to view system administrators and system managers differently (the "system manager" might be thought to have some additional managerial responsibility). Others use the terms interchangeably. Some also use the plural "systems administrator" since, in modern computing environments, there are usually many systems. This sometimes causes an unfortunate miscommunication between people. The choice is largely a matter of taste. This text will refer to the job itself as "system management" and the person performing the job as the "system administrator."

> A company where I once worked assigned titles somewhat arbitrarily. System administrators within departments were given the title Systems Analyst, but the system administrator for the company MIS department was a Systems Manager. All the various system administrators of the departments worked independently of each other (including the MIS system administrator). When we asked someone in personnel why this one title was different from all the others, the answer was "because you all work for him, right?" It was obvious at this point that the titles meant nothing since they in no way reflected reality!

Many different functions and responsibilities fall into the category of "system management." How they are divided up between people, and what titles are assigned to these people, is up to the individual site. In a small organization, a single person may do all of these jobs. In a large organization, no one person could do even one of these jobs alone. No two sites will use the same division of labor or number of people to support their computer systems and users. The number and expertise of the people involved depends on the number and type of computers as well as the number of users, their expertise, and the tasks for which they use the computers. Some sites may find that twenty users per system administrator to is optimal for providing the needed services, while a site with self-sufficient users may be able to support hundreds of users per system administrator.

The "system administrator" might be anyone—from an extra-bright high school student earning money in a part-time job all the way up to a multi-degreed technical person who is responsible for an entire computer center. It is up to each site to decide which functions will be assigned to which personnel in a way that makes the greatest use of available talent.

Your site might have several people employed, each managing a different aspect of your computing environment. The following list of traditional computing center jobs exemplifies the responsibilities that fall under the heading of "system management." Each title represents a different job function. In any particular organization, one person may perform more than one function.

Clerk

The *clerk* usually fields requests from users and directs them to appropriate members of the support staff. The clerk also processes forms and paperwork such as purchase requisitions and maintenance contracts.

Operator

The *operator* is generally thought of as a junior-level technical person, possibly in training to advance. Typical operator duties may range from mounting tapes and filing printer output to performing regularly scheduled support and maintenance tasks such as daily backups, account management, the running of daily production jobs, or performing preventive maintenance on computers and printers.

Technician

The resident hardware expert, the *technician*, diagnoses hardware problems, replaces defective components, and performs periodic preventive maintenance. In a large installation, spare parts may be maintained on-site so that the technician(s) can solve the immediate problem. In this case, the technician may also coordinate the repair and restocking of spare parts with the hardware service provider.

Systems analyst/programmer

The *systems analyst* is the resident programming expert and does specialized programming to customize local software and possibly fix problems in the system software. Traditionally, the *systems analyst* designed software systems, whereas the *programmer* simply implemented them, but in recent years, this division has become blurred since the same people often do both jobs. The resident UNIX expert may also help the user community with their own programming problems from time to time.

Operations manager

The *operations manager* oversees the operators (in a large organization) and acts as the focal point for dealings with other groups, management, and users. The operations manager may work with the site manager (see below) when dealing with equipment and service budget issues.

User services consultant

Many sites provide a contact person to assist users in the use of the computers and applications they run. The person who provides these services to the user must have a strong technical background and be experienced in using any of the tools and applications with which the users might have problems or questions. In large organizations, several people with overlapping expertise make up the user services group.

Network administrator

In a computing environment with a complex local network, configuring and managing the network may be a full-time job in itself. The *network administrator* manages the operation and growth of the local network, as well as the interfaces of any external networks that connect to the local network. This is usually a technical position since the protocols and routing mechanisms involved must be well understood. It often also requires manual skills such as climbing in ceilings or through tunnels to string cable.

In modern computing environments, the network is becoming the most critical single aspect of system management. Without a local network, distribution of information and communication between users is impossible. Many applications and tools are dependent on the infrastructure provided by the network in order to function.

Site manager

The *site manager* has ultimate responsibility for the entire computer site: hardware, software, and support personnel. She will supervise the operations and user services managers to ensure the correct operation of the computer environment so that all user needs are being met. The site manager takes care of the overall budget and other high-level administrative tasks such as conveying the needs and accomplishments of the department to upper management.

1.2 What Does the System Administrator Do?

The function of any computing environment is that of a tool. The users may use this tool to generate financial reports, produce programs that the company sells, track information important to the organization, or simply communicate information between people and places.

Many system administrators and their managers find it hard to quantify the work of a system administrator. It is unlike most jobs because it is difficult to establish a well-defined set of goals to be achieved. "Keep the users happy" is a pretty vague workplan, but to some degree, that's exactly what the system administrator does. Since a great part of the job is reacting and adapting to situations that were not predicted, the definition of the job must reflect this. Ideally, all changes are anticipated and prepared for, but it never quite works out that way.

Some system administrators believe that upper management has no concept of the job they do (and in many cases, this is true). Some managers think system administrators unpack computers, plug them in, and then sit back and relax. Of course, those of us who have done the job know that nothing could be farther from the truth.

The bottom line is, if your users are happy with your service and it has helped them accomplish *their* goals, then you've done a good job. Of course, not everyone will always be happy and there may be some valid reasons for some user unhappiness (not everything everyone wants is always possible). But over time, you (and perhaps your manager) will be able to differentiate between a spoiled user who is looking to blame someone else for a missed deadline and a user who truly thinks more or different services should be provided by the system administrators.

How the system administrator is perceived can run the gamut from totalitarian czar to overly helpful mother. Users will resent the "czar" who keeps all the secrets to himself and only hands them out to those deemed worthy of the knowledge. At the other end, if the system administrator "mothers" the users and is so helpful that nothing else gets done, they will be happy in the short term, but the overall health of the computing environment will suffer. A good system administrator falls somewhere in between these two extremes. You have the authority as well as the responsibility to make the computer environment a useful tool for your users. This means enforcing policies that are for the good of all, without unduly hindering people from accomplishing their tasks. A system administrator should be cooperative, but if he is so helpful that the last request received is the one that always get serviced, no one will ever get the full help they need. One of the system administrator's primary tasks is to determine the priority of pending services and requests for new services.

Most activities performed by system administrators can be grouped into several broad categories. These are high-level tasks every computing environment needs performed by somebody somewhere. If your site doesn't have a system administrator, look around and see who is taking care of these things for you, because someone is doing it.

1.2.1 Daily operations management

The term *operations* refers to the day-to-day running of the computer environment. This includes maintaining the availability of system services, performing necessary routine maintenance, and performing regular administrative tasks.

This also involves keeping a watchful eye out for problems. Even a well-established and smoothly running computing environment will develop problems from time to time. Disk space and other resources can become exhausted. Configuration files can become outdated if every equipment change isn't fully documented. These are just two of the many things that can cause a problem later if not caught early. Entropy is a strong force, even in the electronic age.

A system administrator must maintain the ever-changing information that defines the environment. This means keeping the network information tables up to date as people add and remove devices. It means keeping the list of valid users accurate (making accounts for new users and deleting accounts of users who no longer require access). It means doing a complete set of backups in case some disaster occurs. It means monitoring the environment to watch for unauthorized accesses and identify and stop them if and when they occur.

Examination of event logs kept by the system may show security or hardware problems before you might see any other indication. For example, a failing disk drive may start to show a few bad sectors long before completely failing. If you identify the problem early, you can replace the disk before losing data, and diagnose the problem off-line or send the unit to the manufacturer for diagnosis and/or repair. This is *much* easier than waiting for the disk to fail and having to replace it and restore the data from backup tapes.

Often when a new employee arrives or a current employee departs, you will be asked to read or write a tape so that the user may keep his files with him in his next position. Of course, you should remind a terminating employee that company-confidential material should not be included on the tape, but this is ultimately up to the employee making the request. It is usually not your place (nor your right)[1] to inspect all the information you might write on a tape for someone. That is an issue better left to to the employee and his manager or other responsible party.

Typical operations activities include:

- doing backups
- keeping printers filled with paper, changing ribbons or toner cartridges
- managing accounts
- managing file systems and disk space
- monitoring performance
- monitoring accounting data
- monitoring event logs
- maintaining security
- managing the network
- managing information services
- maintaining the computing facility

1.2.2 Hardware and software maintenance

As with all complex machinery, some components of the computing environment will fail from time to time. Enter the system administrator. While far from being the system administrator's only role, "repairman" is the most visible one. When things go wrong, a great many people are usually waiting for the "tool" to be repaired. Think about how helpless you feel when your car breaks down. Many of your normal activities are put on hold until you have it back in running order.

[1] That is, unless company policy explicitly requires you to monitor certain kinds of information. This usually happens only in extremely high-security environments where the user has acknowledged the need for such measures and is aware that they take place.

The system administrator is the person responsible for maintaining the usefulness of the computer environment and restoring that usefulness when a failure occurs. This can be a double-edged sword. It is a highly visible job, but that visibility usually comes when something is wrong. When everything is working well and all the users are busy working, some will wonder why they bother to have a system administrator. Everything runs so well all by itself! Some system administrators find the job thankless since the blame for problems lands on them but often the praise for smooth operation lands elsewhere. If you do this part of the job perfectly, you are invisible.

Much of your time will be spent improving the computing environment. No environment ever reaches a point of being static; something is always changing. As time goes by, the need for new software, faster hardware, more disk capacity, or higher quality printers will always keep a system administrator busy. You will coordinate the ordering and installation of new software and hardware. You may even need to connect your site to new networks.

Common activities related to hardware and software maintenance are:

- booting and halting machines
- installing new equipment
- installing, upgrading, and modifying software
- diagnosing hardware problems
- dealing with utility failures

1.2.3 User support

Depending on the environment, a large part of a system administrator's role may be in supporting the users of the computer equipment. This usually involves being a sort of on-site technical support contact for some or all aspects of the computing environment (which means being more versed in its use than the average user). It might also include writing programs and documentation to address specific local needs not met by operating system or applications software.

Being able to effectively deal with people on an interpersonal level is a critical skill for interacting with users.

1.2.4 Administration and planning

Not all of the system administrator's activity is technical in nature. Administrative concerns and planning for the future are two of the most critical areas of activity performed by a good system administrator. Without planning and organization, a computing environment will become disorganized.

The administrative duties required of a system administrator vary greatly from one site to the next. Some of the most common are:

- attending meetings
- generating reports for management
- documenting the local environment
- dealing with hardware, software, and service vendors
- learning about new technologies and products
- moving to a new site
- downsizing and merging departments or groups

1.3 Why is the System Administrator Needed?

Lately there has been a debate over whether or not the need for system administrators is decreasing. Many feel that since operating systems are becoming increasingly user-friendly, computers will one day run themselves and the need for a system administrator will vanish.

Let me assure you, the job is here to stay. This is not to say that it will remain exactly as it is (not that anyone has been able to come up with a clear and completely appropriate definition for it anyway).

The job will continue to evolve, but it will remain essential for any computing environment to have a resident expert to solve problems, maintain security, do routine maintenance, and generally be available for user assistance and in case of emergencies.

How do you know if you need to hire someone? The only way to know "if" is to understand "why." Why does a site need someone devoted to the care and maintenance of computer equipment? If you can answer "why," then you will also have a task list to use in a job description and a beginning for your search.

1.3.1 Not everyone can be an expert

Some will argue that as computers become easier and easier to use, users will administer their own systems and the system administrator will become unnecessary. Remember the old saying, "He who represents himself has a fool for a lawyer"? The same could be said of system administrators, even in the PC world. Hidden costs of setting up equipment, installing new programs, and customizing environments add to the cost of purchasing and operating computers. A recent study estimated the typical five-year cost of a personal computer for a large corporation to be $40,000.[2] Much of this cost is attributed to employee time spent working *on* the computer rather than *using* it. Some PC users believe they "fiddle" with their PCs as much as 20-percent of the time. This is 20-percent of their time *not* spent doing the job the computer is supposed to help them do *faster*. A UNIX machine often requires even more "fiddling" than a PC. It is not cost-effective to require each employee to become a computer expert. It is much more efficient to centralize the problem-solving function in a staff of system administrators. By concentrating the expertise in a few people, users' problems can be solved much more efficiently. The system administrator will benefit from having seen the same problems with other users and will be able to quickly replicate the fixes.

System suppliers are working to make the system administrator's job easier, but it will never be so simple that someone with no interest

[2] This estimate comes from William Kirwin, an analyst with the Gartner Group, a consulting company in Stamford, Connecticut.

in performing the function can be effective. To perform effectively as a system administrator, one must understand the concepts of system management and be at least somewhat technical. Most users still are not at that level, and indeed often do not need or wish to be there. Do you take your car to a mechanic or do you fix it yourself? Just as some of you like to work on your own cars, there will be some users who will wish to tinker, but many more will not. It is much more efficient to centralize that expertise (as with the mechanic) than to duplicate it among an entire group of users.

1.3.2 Increasingly complex computing environments

Computing environments, like cars, are growing more complex, not less. People have less of a tendency to fix their own cars today than they did even ten years ago. UNIX machines are far more complicated than single-user personal computers (PCs) and will probably remain so. UNIX system suppliers continue to try to make UNIX more and more friendly (and great progress has been made in recent years), but UNIX and UNIX-based operating systems will never be as simple as MS-DOS®[3] or any other uni-processing operating system because so many more tasks are being performed. UNIX is a multi-processing operating system, which means that more than one program can be active at the same time. With all this activity, even if no user is logged in, potential for failure exists (log files can fill up or necessary network connections can fail, rendering some automatic processes unable to function). A UNIX machine can *crash* (i.e., fail in such a way that the operating system cannot continue to run) without a user even using it.

The modern computing environment is a distributed environment. Unlike the historical mainframe computing environment where a single large computer sat in a computer room and provided all the services, the modern environment is made up of interconnected servers and workstations located in offices throughout a building, a group of buildings,

[3] I know MS-DOS environments are far from simple, but as a uni-processing, single-user operating system, MS-DOS is still relatively simple when compared to UNIX. However, as MS-DOS evolves and becomes more powerful, it also becomes more complex.

or even in several locations across the city or country. In the old centralized environment, making changes to the operating system or the hardware provided a service to all users. Today, a system modification may need to be made on many computers, not just one, in order for all users to benefit from the change.

No one user needs to understand a UNIX machine or the complex environments in which it operates to the degree necessary to recover from all possible failures. Individual users do not need that level of expertise to get their job done. However, when a failure does occur, they *do* need someone who can help them get their machine back in working order so they can get on with their work. Whether that person is called the system administrator or "the woman in the office next door who just happens to know all about the machine," the necessity for some qualified "problem solver" will always exist. If this is understood and acknowledged from the start, the individual doing that job will be able to do it much better.

1.3.3 Greater user productivity

The service provided by the system administrator is critical. You will have people "sitting on their hands" when a problem stops their work, and until the problem is resolved the organization will suffer a loss of productivity. (Have you ever been standing in line at the bank while their computer is down?)

It is tempting to make cuts in personnel in a system management group (or not hire anyone to fill that specific job) because this function usually fits into the corporate structure as "support" (i.e., overhead, the dreaded category that no one can ever justify). Unfortunately, because some managers do not know how to justify the need, these and other kinds of support positions are often the first to be cut or go unfilled. The negative effect on the rest of the workforce is so obscured in the day-to-day routine of the employees (barring any crisis where it becomes more obvious) that no one explicitly sees the loss of employee productivity. It is there, nonetheless.

At a site of any size, it is almost always better to have one person who will not only devote a full-time effort to becoming an expert in the care of the computer systems, but who will also be *responsible* for doing so. Someone doing it as a sideline will never put it high on their priority list, unless something is actually stopping them from performing their primary task. If your list of milestones (what you must accomplish to get your year-end bonus) includes finishing a report that isn't done yet, but does not include fixing the disk crash in Bill's PC, which one are you going to do first? What effect does that have on Bill's milestones?

> In my first system management job, I was supposed to be half-time system administrator and half-time programmer. This was done to better justify the position because the hiring manager didn't think a full-time system administrator was required. I wanted to do some programming, so it seemed like a fine deal to me. You can probably already guess the end of the story. I never got to do much programming, and as the site grew, we had to hire additional system administrators to cover the existing workload. The job always seems to require more effort than is apparent to those looking at it from the outside.

1.3.4 Someone is already doing it

Even in organizations where no one is designated with the responsibility of managing systems, someone is still regarded as the resident expert and is the person to whom people look when something in the computing environment goes wrong. Though these sites "officially" have no system administrator, someone is still performing the task. Because there is no position for a system administrator on an organizational chart, many will claim they do not have such a person and do not need one.

However, this resident expert that everybody looks to for help when things go wrong also has a full-time job, a job that doesn't get done in times of crisis. Performing even day-to-day activities "for the general good" takes time away from regular responsibilities (though rarely will this be acknowledged on a status report or annual review). Not only is it unfair to the employee, it is unfair to the company because they aren't getting 100-percent productivity from that employee at the job he is supposed to be doing.

In fact, this sort of job sharing only works in small shops. Once a site grows to significant size (often this means as few as a dozen computers), the job of the system administrator can drain more than 50-percent of an employee's time. At this point, something has to give. Either the employee's job description must be changed so she is acknowledged to provide support services half or more of the time (and half of her other duties must be reassigned), or a "real" system administrator must be hired.

1.4 Where is the System Administrator Needed?

Many different kinds of computing environments exist. Even if I listed every one I have seen, worked in, or imagined might exist, someone somewhere would still be able to tell me about another one and how it is different from all of them. Different kinds of sites require different kinds of support. A big part of the job of system management is knowing what is important at the local site and making sure that needed support is provided.

No two sites are exactly alike; however, there are three major types of sites that exhibit unique characteristics: academic, small business, and large business sites. Your site probably falls into one of these categories. Some sites may have a combination of attributes from different categories. For example, a research lab, depending on how it is funded, may be more like an academic site, especially if the users and managers were previously employed in academia. If the funding comes from corporations and the majority of the employees come from corporate backgrounds, it will probably *feel* more like a corporate site. Don't be insulted or feel misunderstood if your site doesn't fit neatly into these categories. They are designed mainly to give you an idea of potential needs and the different levels of support that might be necessary.

Academia

An academic site, such as a college department, is sometimes made up of users who are self-taught and eager to jump into any problem on their own. They may require less "hand-holding" because they not only wish to solve their problem, but also to understand what it takes to do so.

Academics often integrate research tasks into the day-to-day tasks associated with teaching courses, working with students, and fulfilling other departmental responsibilities. If a failure causes them to be without service for a few hours, they can often find other duties that demand their attention (so they aren't standing over you every minute while you work on the problem).

If your users are the type that stand over you while you work on a problem, this sign, found in one variation or another in many system administrator's offices, might help:

Hourly Rates	
$30.00	standard
$35.00	if you watch
$45.00	if you help
$60.00	if you worked on it first
$75.00	if you laugh

This isn't always the case, however. Sometimes an academic client may be fighting a publication deadline for a paper they haven't finished (or maybe even *started*) yet! In general, people in the academic world are usually more relaxed than those in the corporate world because the deadlines they have aren't as tied to product releases or end-of-quarter revenue statements.

Academic departments aren't known for having a lot of money to spend on computer systems, software, or support. Therefore, there will likely be less commercial software in such an environment and fewer software support contracts to administer. However, public-domain, freeware, or shareware software is often found in these environments, and these can often be at least as complex to administer and support as commercial software products. Sometimes public-domain software and freeware involves even more work to install because it may need to be compiled (possibly debugged) and tailored to the local environment.

Departments may also have student users who are working on specific assignments. If you, as the system administrator, get pulled into helping students do their homework, you'll never do anything else. Academic departments (or some other entity on campus) should provide this sort of student support, or at least make it clear that you are not the person to provide that service.

Small business

A small business site is one where the business depends on the use of the computers, be they PCs or UNIX machines, and as many as fifty people regularly do some work on a computer. This type of site often has no system administrator and support is done on an as-needed basis by anyone willing to pitch in and help. At most, these sites will have a single system administrator.

This kind of site will run on deadlines. When a machine or network is down, people will be waiting for it to come back up so they can continue with their work. Until then, they will have nothing better to do than to call you and ask when it will be fixed (and as long as you're answering that question, you're not fixing it).

This site is likely to have more commercial software (accounting packages, spreadsheet programs, etc.) than an academic site. The system administrator may need to be more experienced in the use and maintenance of these software packages in order to help users and talk knowledgeably with the vendors about problems.

Large business

A large business site will have all the needs of the small business site, plus other unique needs because of its size. A large site should have a staff of support personnel rather than just one person. Additional problems are brought about by the size of the computing environment and the need for communication among the system administrators.

A new administrative problem encountered at large sites is how to best divide the labor and responsibility between the members of the support staff and how to notify the appropriate individual when a problem comes up. The complexity of the computing environment usually increases dramatically over that of a small business site. A large site might have dozens of different kinds of machines connected to different kinds of networks spanning floors in a building, buildings on a campus, cities, or even countries.

In the small-site model, the system administrator can get to know all the users and have a good grasp on what they know and what they don't know. The one-on-one attention it is possible to give in that situation is more helpful to the user and more satisfying to the system administrator who derives pleasure out of helping individuals. In a large site, the problem reports are usually sent in via electronic mail or some other on-line mechanism so that they may be quickly directed to the appropriate staff member. Often, that staff member may or may not be acquainted with the user and, therefore, won't have the intuitive knowledge of how best to help the user that the system administrator in a small site might have. The issue in this environment is to solve the problem as best you can and get on to the next one. You trade some personal attention for volume of service. At some point, a support organization may decide it is best to divide up and service a smaller segment of a user community to provide more personal and effective service to the users. On the other hand, in these days of cutbacks, it often is just the opposite. Different support groups merge together to eliminate redundant services and maximize efficiency.

Chapter 2

Software

The system administrator is generally a fairly technical person despite the nontechnical appearance of the title. A solid understanding of all aspects of the system is necessary to effectively manage its use and help users achieve their goals.

You will most likely start your tour of duty as a system administrator in a computing environment that already exists, so dealing with the arrival of all-new equipment will not be your first task.[1] Your first concern will most likely be with software, so that is where we will begin our examination of system management.

As with any situation, some functions are absolutely essential and others are merely nice to have. We will deal with the essentials first and work our way down in approximate order of importance (of course, specific needs at your site could make your priorities different).

While all of these topics are important, you should make sure you cover the "critical" ones before dealing with some of the others that might be more interesting. Nobody cares if your kernel is tuned ideally for a specific application if your disk crashes and you don't have any backup tapes!

[1] While this does happen, it is rare. No one thinks to hire a system administrator until they have already built up somewhat of a "mess" thinking they could take care of it themselves. By the time they realize they need someone to take care of it, the environment and the problems already exist.

When you make changes to your software or its configuration, always save original copies of the files you change. This will guarantee you the option of *backing down* to what worked before if the new version doesn't work or has some unforeseen side-effect.

2.1 Backups

If you get nothing else out of this book, get this: *do regular backups.* Performing regular *backups* is the single most neglected duty in computing. No words can sufficiently emphasize the importance of this one task. Besides, it is one of the easiest to accomplish! Still, people often put it off, intending to get around to it, in favor of more interesting and challenging problems. The importance of developing and following a sound backup procedure is impossible to overstate [Bra90, pp. 25–26].

The loss of your data costs much more than the effort to back it up. Think of the effort you spend doing backups as the premium you pay on an insurance policy. We all buy insurance and hope that we have wasted our money because we hope we never need it (but the one time you do, it more than pays for itself). The same applies to doing backups. You feel like your time is wasted making copies of your data on tapes that you never read. However, few system administrators can claim they have never had to replace a disk drive because of a failure. Most would envy anyone who had never had to restore an entire disk. That would be payment enough for the "wasted" effort!

2.1.1 Tools

Every version of UNIX includes some kind of utility to back up the files on your system. Some of these tools are easier to use than others. Rarely does any one tool satisfy all your needs for backups across your entire environment.

Some sites choose to purchase a commercial backup application. The advantage to such software is that it is supported by the vendor and usually ported to most of the popular UNIX versions and platforms. The disadvantage, of course, is that it is not free.

Many of the various backup utilities (both commercial utilities and the basic UNIX tools) do not write information in compatible formats. Be sure to identify at least one alternate computer and tape drive pair in your local environment that is capable of restoring each type of backup format you use. If you use a certain method on one machine and no others, and that machine fails, it will be difficult (or impossible) to restore files from it onto another machine.

If you choose to make use of one of the utilities included in your UNIX system, you have several options.

`dump` and `restore`

One of the most widely used programs for doing backups is the `dump` program (and its counterpart `restore`), which was originally contained in the BSD (Berkeley Standard Distribution) versions of UNIX from the University of California at Berkeley [NSS89, Chapter 18], [Fri91, Chapter 9]. In recent years, this program has made its way into other versions of UNIX as they are made BSD-compatible. The name of the program may vary from one version to another (it is sometimes changed because another program was already called "dump"). For example, under the AIX® operating system (the version of UNIX distributed by IBM®), it is known as `backup`, and under SVR4 it is known as `ufsdump`. The corresponding file restoration program is still called `restore` in AIX but is called `ufsrestore` in SVR4.

When doing your backups with `dump`, there are issues surrounding dumping an active file system that should be considered [Fri91, p. 277]. An active file system is any file system that is mounted and being accessed by users. Traditionally, `dump` only guarantees to back up every file correctly if the file system is not active. To make the file system inactive requires that it be unmounted (except for file systems like `/usr` or `/`, which must be present for the system to run normally). Taking your system down each time you need to perform a backup may not be a reasonable option in your environment. A file system that is mounted read-only (such as a source tree) can be safely backed up at any time, however.

Many sites choose to take the system down for a monthly *full backup* (a backup of every file), but do their daily and weekly *incremental backups* with file systems active. Thus, they accept the slight risk of a few files not being backed up during a particular backup. If a file is missed, it is because the user was modifying it at the time the backup was done. If it was being modified, it will usually be backed up during the following day's backup. Regardless of what backup program you decide to use in your environment, you should investigate the potential risks of active file system backup and be sure you understand them.

The `dump` command accesses data on disk by directly reading the raw file system (`dump` understands the file system structure). An advantage of this is that it is faster than going through the file system access system calls. It also does not alter the last access time associated with each file the way other utilities that use regular file system access system calls do. The major disadvantage is that it can only back up file systems it understands (which means Berkeley file systems or file systems a vendor has added to its version of `dump`).

tar

The `tar` command (which stands for "**t**ape **ar**chive") is included in most versions of UNIX [TF89, pp. 83–101]. Because `tar` can be found in most versions of UNIX and the format of a `tar` tape is independent of any specific architecture (unlike the format of a `dump` tape), it is frequently used to write tapes to send to other UNIX sites.

As a full-dump mechanism, `tar` works well, but it is cumbersome to specify only certain files to be backed up.[2] This makes it difficult to perform incremental backups using `tar`.[3]

[2] This is because `tar` requires that files or directories to be written be listed on the command line. Depending on the number of files or directories being written, this command line could overflow the shell's command buffer.

[3] Some versions of `tar` improve on some of these deficiencies. For example, AIX `tar` can span media volumes and GNU `tar` (see page 41) allows filename exclusion and inclusion lists.

cpio

The `cpio` command (which stands for "**co**py **i**nput to **o**utput") is also included in most versions of UNIX. This command is similar to `tar` but allows the list of files to be supplied on the standard input. Thus, combining the `find` command with the `cpio` command, it is possible to do an incremental backup [TF89, pp. 101–126].

2.1.2 Media

The whole point of doing a backup is to store your data on another medium from which you can retrieve it if the primary storage location (the disk) becomes unusable. Therefore, duplicating files on another part of the same disk drive is not a backup.

Usually, backup media are slower (and less expensive) than the disk drives attached to your computer. The speed of access provided by a local disk is not necessary for a backup copy of data. Tape drives are most often used to back up data on disk. Depending on the volume of data being backed up, other types of portable media, ranging from diskettes to a WORM[4] disk (see page 70), may also be used. When the volume of data was small, diskettes, 9-track tapes, or cartridge tapes served the purpose. As sites increase their disk storage capacity, higher capacity media, such as 4mm or 8mm tapes, or WORM CDs will be necessary.

It is also possible to maintain an active copy of a file system on another disk. Disk *mirroring* or *shadowing* allows you to define a file system on two different physical devices. If one device fails, you still have the data on another usable device. This is an effective protection against hardware failures because the odds of *both* disk drives failing are low. It is also extremely important in sites where high availablity is a requirement. However, if your building floods and all your disk drives are damaged, you had still better have good backup tapes, and they had better be someplace else. As a sole means of backup, disk mirroring is not the best use of resources.

[4] WORM drives are rarely used for backup purposes because of the cost involved, but it *is* possible.

With today's distributed networks, it is no longer necessary to have a tape drive connected to each machine that contains a disk to be backed up. Most versions of backup programs have the ability to write data onto a tape drive or other device on a different host via the local network. With any machine where a large volume of data will be written regularly, it is still best to have a backup device directly connected to the machine, as this will speed the backup process and reduce traffic on the local network.

Since high-capacity tape drives are now available, it is common for sites to run unattended backups overnight. User activity and network traffic is usually lowest outside of regular business hours. Before these high-capacity media were available, an operator changed tapes during the backup, and therefore backups were run during regular work hours—or the operator came in very early or stayed very late. Now the operator simply changes the tapes the next morning and verifies that the backups ran to completion.

2.1.3 Schedules

The typical backup schedule involves doing a full backup followed by one or more incremental backups [Fri91, pp. 276–289]. An incremental backup is performed by copying all files that have been modified since the full backup was done.[5] A common backup schedule is to do a full backup once per month and incremental backups on a daily and/or weekly basis.

Depending on the site, daily backups are usually required. If your users aren't modifying information very often, you could get away with doing your backups less frequently. Think of it this way: how many days' worth of work can your organization afford to lose at any moment? That's the longest time you want to go between backups.

You will probably *cycle* your incremental backup media (reuse the tapes or disks), so this information will not be available forever. Once

[5] Some backup programs, such as the Berkeley `dump` program, have the concept of backup "levels." In this case, an incremental dump copies files since the last lower-level incremental dump (or full dump if no lower-level incremental dumps were done). This allows more flexibility to back up only files that have changed since the last backup was done.

the next full backup is performed, the incremental backup information is not needed. Whether or not you cycle your full backup media is up to the individual site. Some sites maintain a permanent archive of their monthly full dumps as a way of providing a complete history of work. Other sites don't care about history and want to save tape storage space, so they cycle their full backups as frequently as every six months.

2.1.4 Off-site storage

If your data is critically important to your operation, then you should strongly consider keeping your backup media at another location, an *off-site storage* location. If your business has multiple locations, simply arrange with another site to swap tapes on a regular basis. If you're a small business site, keeping a copy in a safe at your home will probably suffice. Yes, it's a hassle, but if some natural disaster (earthquake, flood, etc.) strikes your site, not only are you liable to lose your equipment, but your data, both on the machine and on the backup media. If the disaster destroys your "insurance policy" along with what you're insuring, there wasn't much point in having the "policy" to begin with.

If you can arrange a media swap with someone in another city, that's even better. The more geographic distance you can achieve, the better. Of course, there is a tradeoff between the safety of distance and the effort required to retrieve the media when it's needed. You will probably keep your most recent backups in town and store the older ones at an out-of-town site. The odds of needing the most recent full backup are much higher than that of the earlier month's backup.

2.1.5 Restoring data

Once in a great while, you will actually lose an entire disk drive and have to rebuild the file systems that were on that disk. You will have to *restore* the last full backup and any incremental backups that were done after that full backup.[6]

Technically, you do backups for only one reason: to protect the user community (and yourself) from losing data files because of some catastrophic failure of hardware or software. You may think of the effort involved in doing backups as "data insurance." However, as a side-effect, you also protect users who mistakenly delete the wrong file during a late-night editing session or when they're in a hurry to make a three o'clock meeting. UNIX, unlike many operating systems, has no "undelete" feature. When you delete a file, it's gone. It is possible to define aliases which cause the `rm` command to move the file to a temporary directory rather than deleting it, thus simulating an undelete function, but in practice this won't always save you. You can count on receiving requests for file restorations from users. If you have done good backups, it will not be a problem.

Not only should you perform backups, you should read your backup media on a regular basis, just to make sure you will be able to restore from it if that becomes necessary. It does no good to make the backups if you can't read them later! In fact, the most reliable way of proving to yourself that your backup tape is valid is to read it on a different tape drive than the one on which it was written.

[6] One method of arranging incremental dumps is known as the "Towers of Hanoi" sequence, which strikes a nice balance between minimizing the number of separate backup tapes used and maximizing the amount of data that is backed up [NSS89, pp. 379–380].

> I once had to restore a file from a backup tape, but the tape drive on the machine had recently failed and was in the process of being repaired. No problem, I could just take the tape over to another tape drive and read it there. Well, the other tape drive wasn't able to read the tape. It turned out that the heads in the first tape drive were slightly misaligned and the tracks of data on the tape were not written correctly. The first tape drive could read tapes it wrote since the misalignment affected both the reading and the writing of a tape. However, no other tape drive could read the tape. Fortunately, we got the tape drive fixed and read the backup tape successfully. Then we realigned the heads in the tape drive. At the next opportunity, we did a full dump of that machine since all previous dump tapes were rendered unreadable when the drive heads were realigned.

Even if you do verify your tapes periodically, that doesn't guarantee that they will always be readable.

> At one site, seemingly random backup tapes turned out to have nothing but garbage data recorded on them. When they started keeping detailed notes about the disposition of backup tapes, a pattern emerged. All the unreadable tapes were stored on the bottom shelf of the tape cabinet. It turned out that the janitors were coming into the computer room on the weekends and polishing the raised floor with an electric floor polisher. The magnetic field generated by the floor polisher was corrupting the tapes close to it!

2.2 User Accounts

One of the first tasks you'll have to perform as a new system administrator is adding a new user to the system: yourself. When other new employees join the organization, you'll have to add accounts for them, too [Fri91, Chapter 4], [NSS89, Chapter 6], [TF89, Chapter 2], [Uni90b, Chapter 17]. When employees leave, you will need to remove or disable their accounts.

Once mastered, this will seem like a mundane and boring task, but it will always be an important one. Depending on the turnover rate of employees in your organization, it may be a subject you deal with on a daily basis.

2.2.1 Creating new accounts

How a new user account is set up varies from site to site. At a small site, someone may stop you in the hall and say "Joseph Jackson is starting next Monday and will need an account." If you're lucky they'll tell you before it happens; if you're unlucky they'll say "Meet Joseph Jackson, he just started and needs an account."

At a larger site, there may be a New User form that the hiring manager fills out and gives you that contains all the necessary information with which to make the new user's account. If your organization doesn't have such a form, creating one should be your second task. Your life will be much easier if you receive all the information you need at once and in advance.

The basic steps required to create a valid user on a UNIX system include:

- add an entry to the password file
- set a password for the account (don't leave it null, see page 189)
- create the home directory (owned by the new account)

Without a home directory, the `login` program will have no directory in which to leave the user when the login process is completed. Early versions of UNIX would just leave the user in the root directory. Some newer versions of UNIX consider an invalid home directory to be an error and do not allow the user to login until the problem is resolved.

In newer versions of UNIX, encrypted passwords are not stored in `/etc/passwd`, but in a "shadow" password file which users cannot read directly. This is a security enhancement. While the encrypted strings cannot be reversed to obtain a password, the same process used by the `login` program could be used to test possible passwords against those encrypted in the password file. Though a more tedious task, it is possible to "crack" passwords in this manner. Eliminating user access to the encrypted strings eliminates this risk. Educating users about how to pick "good" password will also help (see page 195).

Some additional steps are often taken to more completely define a user. These are not required by the operating system for the user to be able to login, but they are things that are usually necessary for the user to effectively use all the local functions available:

- define an electronic mail alias for the user
- add the user to appropriate mail aliases
- give the user a set of default initialization files
- define a disk quota for the new account
- set an expiration date for the password (if applicable)
- send a "welcome" message to the new user with essential information every user needs to survive

Users should have a single location where they read their mail. This will most likely be their workstation or the server that serves their files to their workstation or PC. If a single location is not defined, it is possible that the mail could be delivered to a machine that the user never accesses and the user may never see the mail.

Some versions of UNIX provide a capability known as *password aging*. The system administrator may specify an expiration date after which the password will not be valid if it has not been changed. This forces users to change their passwords on a regular basis.

On many UNIX systems you must perform the steps of creating a new account manually. However, recent versions of UNIX feature commands and menu-driven interfaces which can be used to create accounts. These utilities often perform more steps than what is obvious, so before skipping them and editing files manually, be sure you understand what the "generally accepted" method of adding users to your version of UNIX does before choosing to do it another way.

If your version of UNIX does not include automated tools to build accounts, you can write your own program or shell script after you have created a step-by-step procedure for doing it manually. Including standard "init" files (files to initialize shells and window systems, such as `.cshrc`, `.login`, or `.xinitrc`) also gives a new user a base environment that can be easily customized.

2.2.2 Removing accounts

It is also important to remove (or at least deactivate) accounts of users who no longer need them (usually accounts of ex-employees). Leaving unused accounts active creates a security hole that someone might one day use to gain unauthorized access to your system.

If other users need to access files owned by the terminated user, it may be useful to deactivate the account by setting an impossible password (set the encrypted password field to "`*`" or "`nologin`") but leaving the files available. Be sure to remove the user from mail alias lists, however, so the account doesn't continue to receive mail.

When removing accounts (and their associated files), be careful not to remove system accounts, such as `bin`, especially when their home directories are set to `/`. If an automatic account removal program is used, it might also try to remove the account's home directory. You can imagine the result of removing an account whose home directory is the top node of the UNIX file system (`/`)!

Unless you have a foolproof procedure for removing accounts that are not being used, it is advisable to perform a yearly review of all accounts on your system to validate their need and use.

2.3 The General Health of Your Systems

Once you get your network of systems in stable condition and cooperating, they will seem to run themselves. However, entropy being what it is, that will not last. Log files fill up, disks develop bad sectors, hundreds of different things can happen to undermine your nice, stable environment. That's why you can't just turn your back and walk away from it even though all seems to be well.

However, you don't have to *wait* for something to go wrong, either. You can monitor any number of conditions in your systems which can let you know a problem is brewing before it actually becomes a problem for a user [NSS89, Chapter 23]. Doing so will help you stay ahead of requests from users to fix problems. It is always easier to fix a problem before it becomes a problem to a user.

2.3.1 Booting and halting

The two fundamental computer operations are starting and stopping processing. These operations are generally known as *booting* and *halting* the machine [Fri91, pp. 60–92], [NSS89, Chapter 2], [TF89, Chapter 5], [LMKQ90, Chapter 13].

The word *boot* comes from *bootstrap*, which is used to describe the process of loading the operating system. To oversimplify, the hardware of a computer is built so that it knows just enough to automatically read a single block of data from a specific location on the disk whenever power is supplied. This block contains a small program, which can then go out to another location on the disk and load a larger program into memory and transfer control there. That program is then large enough and has enough capability to load the rest of the operating system.

When a UNIX machine boots, the kernel (the operating system) is loaded into memory in this step-wise manner and execution begins. The kernel probes the system *bus* (the hardware inside the computer to which all devices are attached) to find out what devices are present so that the appropriate device drivers can be loaded. Then the file systems are checked for corruption by initial boot scripts (also called startup scripts) [NSS89, Chapter 20] and the network and service *daemons* (see page 38) are started. These boot scripts can be modified by the system administrator to start up any local programs in addition to system daemons that need to run.

When you first set up a computer, if the operating system does not come pre-loaded on the hard disk, you will need to boot it from a tape, a diskette, a CD-ROM, or from another host on your network. In this case, a special installation program will run which helps you install the complete operating system on your local disk drive. After successfully installing the operating system so that your computer will boot correctly, it is often tempting to discard this initial boot media. *Do not do this!* You should keep at least one copy in case your disk becomes unreadable or the boot information becomes corrupted and the computer will no longer boot.

> Once a user switched his workstation with another belonging to another user who was on vacation (because the other user's workstation was a more powerful model). However, he didn't know what was necessary to make the network think the machines had been switched. The boot information on the disk was left in an inconsistent state and the other user's system would no longer boot. The system administrator was able to boot a smaller version of UNIX from a diskette and repair the information in the boot files (and then switch the systems back the way they were).

Halting is the opposite of booting. Unlike a PC, to *halt* a UNIX machine involves more than simply shutting off the power. UNIX machines have daemon processes that run continuously in the background whenever the computer is running. UNIX computers are meant to run twenty-four hours a day. Services not directly related to user activity (like remote file system access or electronic mail delivery) can be needed at any time. However, it is sometimes necessary to stop the machine to add or remove components or make repairs. Simply turning the computer off would interrupt running processes which might have files open and might be in the middle of work. These background processes need to be instructed to clean up their affairs and terminate properly. The act of halting a UNIX machine sends a signal to all running processes to terminate their processing. The operating system must also flush information from disk buffers to the disk. Once buffers are flushed and processes have terminated, the operating system exits. The power may then be shut off.

> You should also explain to your users the importance of orderly shutdown on a UNIX computer. I once had a problem with a workstation exhibiting file system corruption problems most mornings. After a few days of this, I asked the user if anything unusual was happening before he left in the afternoons. He said no, that he finished his work just fine, and then turned off the machine. Then, in the morning when he turned it back on, it would have problems! Before his UNIX workstation, he had a PC in his office.

2.3.2 Fault management and problem diagnosis

During normal operation of your UNIX computers, events will occur that will require either your immediate attention or your attention at some time in the future. These may be errors from which the operating system can recover and continue, or errors which cause the operating system so much confusion that it terminates (this is known as a system *crash* [Fri91, pp. 92–94]. These problems may have many different causes.

Hardware failures will almost always represent a serious problem. When a disk drive fails to write the data to a disk block, the operating system will usually log the failure in a system log file and attempt to continue. The process may return a failure to the user. The operating system may retry using another disk block, succeed with the next attempt, and return success to the user. Even so, information about the failure will be logged and the system administrator should investigate.

Software problems can also cause system failures. A bug in the operating system software may be responsible for a system crash or some other anomalous behavior. It is important for the system administrator to be observant of the system's behavior. Much like a human illness, a serious problem will often start out as a series of small and fairly innocuous symptoms before becoming a major problem.

Check log files on a regular basis (either manually or via an automated process) for indications of problems. Many drivers and software packages will log extraordinary occurrences as a form of passive notification to the system administrator [GS91, Chapter 7], [Fri91, pp. 240–242].

When you encounter a fault or failure, you may not immediately know the cause. If it is a problem you have seen before or something obvious (like the printer being out of paper), you will have no trouble. But what if everything appears to be in working order but something still won't work?

The first step is to narrow the problem down to a software or hardware problem. Eliminate all the components you are confident *are* working properly. Though it is often tempting, don't make assumptions when verifying proper operation of hardware and software. Often, "the obvious" is not so obvious.

This is one area where the expertise of the hardware or software vendor can help. If you have a support contract with them, you can get some diagnostic help. Even if you do not have a support contract, you can often call your sales representative and get some clues to help you identify the problem. It never hurts to ask.

If you know other system administrators with the same hardware or software, ask them if they've ever seen the problem. There's no shame in admitting you have a problem for which you don't immediately know the solution. If someone else has seen it before, they might save you a lot of time trying to figure it out for yourself. If you have Usenet or Internet access, you have access to discussion groups and mailing lists for certain software and hardware vendors, as well as for generic UNIX questions, where you can take advantage of thousands of man-years of experience.

This is not to say you should run for help at the first sign of trouble, but if you're really stumped, don't slam your head against the brick wall any longer than necessary. Ask for help. A good system administrator doesn't necessarily have all the answers, but knows how to find them.

2.3.3 System accounting

Most versions of UNIX come with system accounting software which can keep track of resource usage. In environments where the computing center charges its users for use of the computing resources, running accounting is a critical function. Even if you don't bill for service, accounting statistics can be useful to justify the purchase of additional resources by showing where and by whom the resources are being consumed. You can also use this data to spot trends and forecast future needs for equipment.

The accounting daemons are started when a UNIX machine is booted, and they run as long as the machine runs. They can monitor resources like disk usage, user logins, pages printed, and network usage. The specific commands used to gather and display the accounting data vary greatly from one version of UNIX to another. It is best to consult the documentation for your particular version.

Accounting statistics can also be used to bill back to other departments for usage of computer time and resources (like printer paper or disk space). In a large organization where each department is responsible for its own computing costs, a centralized computing center often charges the department for resources used. Sometimes these costs are covered through the use of what is affectionately termed "funny money" (money on paper, but provided throughout the organization more as a quota mechanism to prevent any one department from using more than its fair share of computing resources). Sometimes "real" money is transferred.

Even if billing is not a requirement, accounting statistics can give you valuable information about who is using how much of what in your computing environment. Over time, this information can be used to identify trends and forecast future requirements.

2.3.4 System services

Whenever UNIX is running, programs called *daemons*[7] are also running in the background and waiting for work [NSS89, Chapter 20]. The names of these running programs usually end with a "d" (such as `ftpd`, `nfsd`, or `updated`). They provide a myriad of services to local and remote users. Use of specific service daemons can be controlled by the system administrator, and daemons providing some local service can be added to the system.

2.4 Third-party Software

The installation, configuration, and update procedures for third-party software (software that comes from some source other than your operating system vendor) always provide new and exciting experiences. Each vendor has its own idea of how to install software, where to put the code, and how to update the code. Not only are these methods different from each other, they are usually different from the standards already in use at a local site.

2.4.1 Evaluation

You cannot always be sure if a software product will solve your problem. Unlike most products in our consumer-based society, if you don't like software after you have opened it, you may not be able to exchange it. The vendor cannot assume you haven't made a copy for yourself that you will continue to use. Most software comes with a license agreement stating that once you open the package, you own it. Some products enforce the terms of the license by only allowing it to run on machines for which it was licensed.

However, most vendors allow you to evaluate software without having to buy it to find out whether or not it will work in your environment. Often the vendor will ship a "stripped-down" version of the software (where only some of the features work). You may receive a fully oper-

[7] Often drawn as childlike devils (complete with pitchforks), daemons are viewed as "good" entities that run around inside a UNIX computer helping provide services for users and programs.

ational version of the software containing a "time-bomb" (that renders it useless after a certain date). This allows you to use the software long enough to get the feel of how it works and what it can do, but still protects the vendor from the possibility of your using it indefinitely without paying for it. At the end of the evaluation period, the software becomes unusable (although you are usually still asked to delete it and you are still required to return any media and documentation).

With recent improvements in licensing technology, the production version can be sent with a license code that will become invalid over time. The customer can send payment for the software and get a new, permanent license code, thus eliminating the need to reinstall the package when the "real" one is delivered.

Even in instances where a vendor sends you the production version of software for evaluation, it is important not to take advantage of that trust. Software vendors survive on the business their software generates. If they don't have mechanisms in place to prevent you from abusing the evaluation procedures, it may be because they do not feel the need to account for every single potential loss of sale. More likely, it is because they do not have the resources to devote to the problem and must depend on the honesty of their customers. This, of course, is more typical of small software shops, but this is often where the most ingenious software is born.

2.4.2 Installation

Different sites have different policies about where in the file system local software should be installed. Nearly everyone has a different philosophy on where to keep local software and why to name the directories a certain way. For the most part, this should be up to the local site, although adhering to some unofficial standards used by other sites with whom you exchange information may make the process simpler at times.

You should keep your local software (whether public domain or commercial third-party) separate from your operating system. If you put local software programs in system directories, you will lose track of what came with the operating system and what you installed locally. This can cause small problems—like embarrassment when calling a vendor to report a software bug only to find that it isn't the vendor's software. It can also cause bigger problems—like upgrading the machine only to have the installation program "blow away" all your local software when reinstalling a system directory. Keeping your local software on a physically separate disk drive, if possible, simplifies matters when a drive must be replaced for any reason.

Newer software installation mechanisms have improved and standardized the system administrator's control over installation locations. AIX and SVR4 include package installation software that third-party vendors are encouraged to use as well. AIX uses the `installp` program and SVR4 uses `pkgadd` to read a software package from a distribution medium and install it in the same fashion as all other packages. The vendors provide software publishers with the format requirements and the software providers create their installation media accordingly.

However, in many parts of the UNIX world, you will still find that the "standard" format for an installation tape or diskette is a `tar` or `cpio` file containing shell scripts that control installation. In any "home-grown" installation procedure like this, the system administrator should carefully check the script to make sure it will have no unforeseen side-effect in the local environment.

2.4.3 Types

Special cases of third-party software are *public-domain software*, *freeware*, and *shareware*. Software that has been explicitly placed in the public domain is freely accessible and modifiable without restriction. Freeware is freely available, but it may not have been placed in the public domain so as to retain certain restrictions on its use, redistribution, or modification. Shareware is publicly available and may be evaluated for some period of time, but then the author usually asks that you register it and pay a nominal fee for its use (which is usually an order of magnitude or two lower than what commercial software for a similar purpose would cost). Shareware is most prevalent in the PC world, but it does exist in the UNIX world.

One extra precaution that should be taken when dealing with any software obtained from dubious sources is to check for possible security problems. If you are getting source code versions of software, this is a simple, although not very interesting, task. Installing executable versions directly can be risky, but since UNIX isn't quite ready for the world of shrink-wrapped software, you will probably find more public software in source-code form. The explosion of viruses in the PC world is largely due to people running binary executable programs on their computers and not being able to know what the program is doing.

This is not to say that because your software comes from a reputable company means it is totally safe. Programming errors occur that cause security breaches. Also, just like your computers, the vendor's computers can, themselves, become infected with a virus through some means local to the vendor's operation. A vendor with a good communications network with its customers can notify them and provide a fix for the problem in short order.

> Recently a large software vendor shipped thousands of copies of a program to customers before realizing that a virus had unwittingly been included in the program. The machine which created the software package had become infected with the virus and it dutifully passed it on to each copy of the software.

GNU software

The most famous example of third-party software in the UNIX world is the GNU software. GNU, standing for "GNU's Not Unix," started out as a collection of useful utilities written by students and others interested in sharing useful software without having to pay large amounts of money for it. As it grew, more UNIX utilities were rewritten (from scratch to avoid licensing problems) and added to the collection. Some UNIX utilities even run under MS-DOS.

Richard Stallman, who began the GNU project, later founded the Free Software Foundation to administer funding and distribution of GNU software. While not strictly public-domain, the GNU software is freely available on the Internet[8] in source code form with only a few restrictions on its use and modification. (See page 138 for more information on the Internet.)

2.4.4 Maintenance

Commercial software is usually supported by the vendor, possibly free of charge for some amount of time after your initial purchase. By purchasing a maintenance contract from the software vendor, you usually receive the right to call the vendor for technical support and receive future new releases of the product. As bugs are fixed and new capabilities are added, you can keep using the "latest and greatest" version of the software. You can also report bugs if users at your site find them and have a reasonable expectation that they will be fixed in the next release, or the vendor may send you an updated version to fix a major bug.

The decision whether or not to purchase maintenance varies for each site. Over time, you can wind up spending more for the support than for the software. If your organization depends on the software for critical functions, then this expense is usually worth it. If only a few users use the software, then an unsupported version may be sufficient.

Software upgrades

How you choose to upgrade your software depends on your environment. If you have one machine that many people use, then everyone must make the move at once. Even in a distributed environment, the least painful decision may be to decree that over a weekend, *everybody's* machine will be upgraded. Sometimes certain groups have specific deadlines. In these cases, it may be more prudent to upgrade one group or department at a time. If you upgrade different machines to different levels of the operating system, be careful to ask the vendor about any potential problems involved in running different versions on the same network. Normally this is not a problem, but if the upgrade is

[8] One of the *many* sites is `ftp.uu.net` in the `/pub/gnu` directory.

significant enough, or if you have not performed the last few upgrades and now you're skipping several levels at once, it could pose a problem.

Kernel upgrades

A special case of a local software modification is modifying some attribute of the UNIX *kernel*. The kernel is the heart of the UNIX operating system which always runs on the computer and services requests of programs (like command shells or application programs). While you rarely change code within the kernel, many configurable values can be changed depending on the user's need. For example, a user may complain that her machine won't do something that she believes it should be able to. Say she tries to run a program and gets an error telling her the process table is full (meaning she is trying to create a new process and no more process slots are available). One answer might be to tell her not to do so much at once, but this is not always a good response. It may become necessary to reconfigure the kernel so that it has a larger process table.

2.5 Device Management

The processing power of the computer system is what most people think of as the important part of any computer. But that is only one piece of a complex interaction that allows users to get the information they need to do their job.

The devices attached to a computer are equally important. What good is being able to process your data quickly if you cannot get the information out of the computer after it has been processed? The words I am typing now would do no one any good if I did not have a printer, diskette, or network device attached to my computer. The words would sit on the local disk of my computer forever.

When dealing with devices, hardware and software are closely related. This section will examine the aspects related to the configuration of the software used to control the devices.

2.5.1 Device drivers

Device drivers are the programs that communicate directly with the device or with a controller which, in turn, communicates with the device. UNIX device drivers use logical devices represented by special files called *nodes* in the `/dev` directory to allow application programs access to devices [Fri91, pp. 47–52], [NSS89, Chapter 7]. Though not what one normally thinks of as a file (of information), these nodes are entries in the file system and may be manipulated as if they were disk files. This abstraction makes it simple to access different physical devices or disk files interchangeably.

A node entry is created with a name (which will be used to reference the device), the major and minor numbers (used by the kernel as an index to identify the proper device driver and unit to be accessed [LMKQ90, pp. 225–234]), and information about whether it is a block or character device. A block device is one that allows the operating system to buffer data for it so that data is transferred in blocks. A character device is a device where no buffering is done by the UNIX kernel. Either single character I/O is required (such as for a terminal device), or the application will do its own buffering and having the operating system do it again would be wasteful.

The files in `/dev` do not contain data, they are simply place holders for device driver access. When a user process accesses a logical device, the kernel intercepts the request and connects the user data to the proper device driver for handling.

Even though the `/dev` directory contains these special files (usually created with a tool such as `/dev/MAKEDEV`), nothing will *prevent* you from creating regular files there since it is just another directory in the file system. However, files created there are sure to lead to confusion since the convention is that no regular files belong in this directory.

> We once had an operator doing backups who mistyped the name of the tape drive. He typed `/dev/rtm0` as an argument to the `dump` command, rather than `/dev/rmt0` as he should have. The `dump` program did exactly what it was told and wrote the entire dump to the disk file `/dev/rtm0`. We had two problems because of this. The first was that the tape on the tape drive did not contain that day's backup after the command was finished, even though we thought it did (had someone been in the computer room to watch the tape, they might have noticed that it never moved, but our operator did backups between several computer rooms). The second problem, and the reason we noticed the error, was that the root file system had completely filled up. When no one could create a file in `/tmp` (which was also in the root file system along with `/dev`), we went looking for a problem. After deleting the new file, we ran the backup again.

2.5.2 Disk devices

Disk devices are the most common devices you will be required to maintain. Almost every computer has some kind of local disk, even if it gets most of its files from a file server.

Adding a type of disk drive already known by your version of UNIX is simple, but adding a new type of drive can be a complex operation [Fri91, Chapter 8], [NSS89, Chapter 12].

The typical steps necessary to make a disk drive usable by a UNIX system are:

- create appropriate device entries in `/dev`
- add the driver to the kernel
- format the disk drive
- label the disk drive

- define the partitioning and/or volume information (see page 48)
- create the file systems
- add file system entries to mount tables
- add file system to export table if it is to be mounted via a remote file system by other machines

Adding the driver to the kernel may only be necessary if this is the first disk drive of this type to be added to the system. Some disk drive manufacturers now ship disks already formatted, labeled, and partitioned, as well. You might be lucky and be able to plug it in and create file systems. In that case, these other steps were done for you.

When you add file systems into your environment, be sure to add them into your backup scheme as well.

2.5.3 Tape devices

Tape devices are usually used for backing up files or writing files onto a tape so that they can be taken to another computer. Access to the tape devices is provided through entries in the `/dev` directory, but the names used may vary depending on your version of UNIX.

When moving tapes between a UNIX site and a non-UNIX site, in addition to data format (because few non-UNIX sites can read a `tar` formatted tape), you may also have to worry about the representation of the characters on the tape. Today, most computers use the ASCII (American Standard Code for Information Interchange) character code to represent characters so there is no conflict moving data between like computers. If you are moving data between a UNIX machine and a mainframe computer, then you will have to deal with translating between different character representations, as IBM hosts use the EBCDIC (Extended Binary Coded Decimal Interchange Code) character code. In this case, you will also need to worry about other tape attributes like blocksize, logical record length, and tape labels. You should always contact someone at the site where you plan to send a tape and find out what formats and types of tape they can most easily read.

2.5.4 Terminal devices

Before workstations and personal computers became popular, most users had a terminal on their desk which was connected to a mainframe or minicomputer in the computer room. Today, this is less common, but you will still deal with "dumb" terminals from time to time [NSS89, Chapter 9], [Fri91, Chapter 10].

Terminals may be connected to a UNIX system via serial ports on the back of the machine (sometimes terminal servers provide access to hosts via the network). Terminals are another type of device and also require an entry in the `/dev` directory for each terminal to be used. Modems are also connected to the computer in this same fashion.

For terminals that have the ability to display graphics and other special screen functions, UNIX provides a method of defining how these screen operations are performed so that a user program doesn't have to build in the capability to deal with every kind of terminal that may be used. The `/etc/termcap` file is used by BSD-based versions of UNIX. A new method of providing this data is known as the `terminfo` database, which was introduced in System V Release 3.

2.5.5 Printer devices

Printer devices are often a special case of a terminal device since they may be connected via a serial port. Some printers can be connected directly to the local network and accessed by all computers on the network.

In addition to connecting the printer to a machine, you will create and maintain the printer queue used by the printer spooler software [Fri91, Chapter 11], [NSS89, Chapters 10–11]. On Berkeley-based systems, defining a printer consists of creating the spool directories and adding a definition for the printer to the `/etc/printcap` file, whereas on SVR4-based systems, the line printer administration commands (commands beginning with "lp") are used to define printer information. One or more of the `lpc`, `lpadmin`, and `lpstat` commands are used to administer the printer queues, depending on your particular version of UNIX.

2.6 File System Management

For a user to store information on the computer, there must be disk space available in which to create files. UNIX disk space is divided into *file systems* [TF89, Chapter 4], [NSS89, Chapter 4], [LMKQ90, Chapter 7], [Uni90b, Chapter 5].

In the past, each hard disk was divided by the device driver into *partitions*. Each partition coincided with a device node in the `/dev` directory and thus could be accessed as a single unit of disk space. Generally, the partition boundaries were defined by explicit numbers in the device driver code. A file system could then be built in this disk space, but the size of the file system was limited by the size of the partition.

Later, as disks grew larger and customer needs changed, vendors began providing ways to customize the partition sizes so that you did not have to modify the source to your device driver and rebuild your kernel just to alter your partition sizes. The label on the disk contained the partition map and software was provided (sometimes as a command in the `format` program) to allow the customer to modify the sizes specified in the label. Even this became cumbersome as a file system would become full and increasing the partition size meant changing the sizes of other partitions on the disk as well (if you expand the length of one partition, that eats into the space used by the following partition). This usually meant moving entire file systems around, possibly relocating some physically onto other disk drives.

Today, the system administrator has several types of file systems to choose from and several management issues to consider.

2.6.1 Volumes

In the past few years, UNIX vendors have been moving toward the idea of logical file systems called *volumes*. Volumes are another layer of abstraction of the file system to allow the file system to span physical partitions. The file system code behaves as if it had a single contiguous span of disk space. The volume manager underneath the file system supplies the file system code with what appears to be contiguous disk space but which, in fact, is made up of disk blocks from many different areas on the disk and even different disk drives.

This provides great freedom to increase the size of a file system simply by allocating more free disk space, whether it be on the same disk on which the file system currently resides or a new disk drive just installed in the system. Of course, at some point, this freedom can lead to chaos if it is not managed in some rational way. You can wind up with a file system that spans disks all over your computer room, increasing the chances that some part of the file system will fail and generally making everything more confusing.

Note that programs which in the past read the raw file system by accessing the entry in `/dev` cannot do this when using volumes since any single partition is only going to be a part of the complete file system [Fri91, pp. 52–58].

Managing a logical volume is conceptually a level above managing a file system on a raw disk partition. When dealing with a volume, you probably will not need to know as much about the physical extent of the partition because the volume manager will keep track of that for you. Some volume managers allow file systems to be set up as *mirrored* or *striped* file systems (see page 25 for a discussion of disk mirroring).

In *striping* a file system, the file system is written evenly across multiple physical disk drives so that more disk arms reach more parts of the data and the access speed is increased. Having twenty disk heads reading data in parallel allows a process to read data faster than if only one head was doing the job on a single disk platter.

Volume-based file systems are also being designed to do transaction-based operations. This means that a log of operations will be available and if some catastrophe occurs, it may be possible to use the transaction log to reconstruct the file system up to the time of the failure (rather than requiring you to get out your backup tapes and restore the most recent snapshot of the file system).

2.6.2 Remote file systems

Several networked file systems are in common usage today and more are being developed all the time. These are file systems that allow remote access via a network through the regular file system mechanisms so that the files appear to a user or an application as if they are on a local disk [Bac86, pp. 138–139].

NFS

The best known and most widely used remote file system is NFS® (Network File System™) developed by Sun Microsystems® [Ste92a]. NFS is a stateless file system, meaning that the file server which actually contains the disk files maintains no state data about a file being used by a remote host. As a result, the client simply requests that autonomous operations be performed on the file (read a certain block, write a certain block). If the client crashes, the file is not left open and unusable by the server or another client. If the server crashes, the file is not corrupted and when the server returns to service, the client process can continue right where it left off. One disadvantage is that there is no built-in locking mechanism since no state information is available. Sun® has maintained the statelessness of NFS and supplied a lock daemon, which, when used consistently by software, serves the same purposes. However, use of the lock daemon mechanism is purely voluntary, so the validity of the locks cannot be guaranteed in every case.

RFS

Another well known remote file system is AT&T's RFS (Remote File Sharing) [Uni90a]. RFS is a stateful file system and because of this, the advantages and disadvantages are nearly the inverse of NFS. Access to RFS-mounted files can be easily locked, but if the server crashes while the file is open, problems can result. Additionally, RFS allows remote device access (through remote access to the `/dev` directory). The two types of remote file systems were developed to solve different problems. Technical superiority has been (and will continue to be) argued on behalf of both. NFS became more popular because Sun released the code to the public, which allowed it to be easily ported to many different hardware platform (much in the spirit of UNIX itself).

2.6.3 Making a file system available

File systems are made available to the users of the system by *mounting* them as a part of the file system tree. The `mount` command connects a file system into the overall system file hierarchy as a branch. The `umount` command removes the file system from the hierarchy. This is usually done at boot time or when accessing file systems on portable media such as diskettes, but mounting and unmounting can be done (by root) at any time during the operation of the machine.[9] To make the file system available for mounting by other machines by a remote file system, it will also have to be added to export tables appropriate for the remote file system being used.

A common method of making a file system available to *all* machines on the network is to use an automatic mounting program. Sun Microsystems first developed `automount` to solve the problem caused by having many NFS file systems that all needed to be mounted on most machines on a local network. The `automount` daemon provides easier management and distribution of information about how and from where to mount remote file systems. Most vendors that support NFS file systems include `automount` in their UNIX distribution.

Sun's `automount` wasn't perfect, so Jan-Simon Pendry of Imperial College of Science, Technology and Medicine in London developed `amd` as an alternative. It is available as part of the `comp.sources.unix` archive on USENET and the Internet (see page 138).

2.6.4 Repairing a corrupted file system

The modern UNIX file system is made up of several levels of data structures which provide a system call interface to the hardware far below [Bac86, Chapter 4], [Fri91, pp. 52–58]. While file systems have undergone improvement over the years and are much more reliable today than ever before, they are still not perfect. From time to time, either because of hardware failures or system crashes, the complex system of links and pointers can become corrupted in some way.

[9] You cannot `umount` a file system which has open files or users connected to directories contained in the file system. Only file systems not currently being used by any process may be unmounted.

The fsck program is used in virtually all versions of UNIX to identify and repair these kinds of inconsistencies in the file system [Fri91, pp. 242–246]. The name fsck stands for "**f**ile**s**ystem **c**hec**k**." This command is normally run whenever a UNIX machine boots and should be run unless you have some reason to believe your file systems are fine or you intend to only do one or two commands before rebooting again. Running fsck often slows down the boot process,[10] depending on how much disk is attached to the machine, and it is often tempting to bypass this step in the interest of time. This is usually a mistake. A file system inconsistency can result in more file system corruption as the system uses it (and assumes that incorrect data is actually correct) and will probably lead to a system crash with loss of data.

Some file system maintenance commands now check to make sure that file systems do not overlap each other on the physical disk (this is especially true with volume managers). Before this was common, you had to know the size of your partitions and be sure they did not overlap because nothing would prevent you from specifying a configuration where partitions did overlap.

> I once inherited a disk where two file systems overlapped each other by a few blocks. Until the first file system was filled with data, no one noticed since the last few blocks were never used. Once those blocks were used, the second file system developed problems. When we ran fsck on the second file system to fix its errors, then the first file system developed problems because we had just written over the end of it. So, of course, we ran fsck on the first file system (not yet realizing what was happening), at which point the second file system was again corrupted. Eventually we noticed the pattern, examined the disk partitioning, and found the problem.

[10] Some newer file system implementations have the notion of whether the file system is "clean" or "dirty" (if dirty, it needs to be checked) so that fsck is only run when necessary.

2.6.5 Monitoring free space

No matter how large a file system you create, your users will eventually fill it. Short of extending the volume or building a new, larger partition, your only option is to clean up what is currently there.

One of the first culprits to look for is a large log file (usually only in the case of a system partition) that can be trimmed. Second, look for any large files that can be regenerated by the user if needed. The best known file of this type would be a memory image file from an aborted program execution. In just about all versions of UNIX, a file named `core` is created in the directory where a program is run when some unrecoverable error occurs. This file may be quite large because it will contain a complete virtual memory image of the running process (used for later debugging). Often, these are created and the users are not even aware of their existence until they happen across them and delete them later.

If a log file or some unwanted temporary file hasn't suddenly used up your disk space, you are faced with having to go through files and clean up unneeded files. In the case of user file systems, you will depend on the users to clean up their own unneeded files, since you have no way of knowing what files are important. You can encourage your users to do one of several things:

- discard old files or files that could be regenerated by a program or reinstalled off of other media
- run a file compression program (such as `compress` or `gzip`) over large or seldom-used files to minimize the disk space they use
- provide you with a list of files that can be written to tape or other portable media that they could keep as a backup (in addition to the system backups you keep)

You may wish to use the `find` command to list particularly large or particularly old (not recently accessed) files to give users an idea of candidates for removal or archival.

Most file systems now provide a quota mechanism which allows the system administrator to set limits on how much disk space each user may use [NSS89, Chapter 22], [Fri91, pp. 221–224]. Without a quota system, each file system can grow, even by the growth of files belonging to a single user, until it is full. The file system itself does not care who fills up the space, only that the space is full.

A quota mechanism allows you to put a limit on how much space each user may use, so that no one user will cause an entire file system to run out of space. Any one user should hit his own quota limit before filling the entire file system and making it impossible for other users to create files as well (unless, of course, the file system is close to being full already).

2.7 Operating System Modifications

From time to time you will need to make changes to the way your operating system is configured, sometimes to the code itself. This may be as simple as modifying a configuration file so that when a daemon starts, it behaves differently. It may be as complex as modifying the code for a device driver or other part of the kernel and then rebuilding the kernel [NSS89, Chapter 8].

Always, *always*, ALWAYS keep a copy of what was in place before your changes so you can go back to it.[11] This includes a complete copy of your root file system before an operating system upgrade. This makes backing down much easier. Nothing is more frustrating than trying to fix something and only succeeding in making the problem worse. Sometimes a fix may seem like a small matter, but after "toying" with a dozen different possible ideas, it is often difficult to remember what the original setup looked like.

Never make significant changes just before leaving for a vacation or business trip. Even seemingly small changes in boot scripts could present problems that might not be as obvious to others. When changing system configurations, you should reboot the machine to test the new settings. If you make the changes and don't reboot for a month, if the changes cause a problem, you may or may not remember all of the details of what was changed and why. The system should be tested

[11] Did I mention that you should **always** do this? :-)

as soon as possible after the change so you are back to a configuration that is known to boot properly.

After any major changes (to the operating system or any services that are started at boot time), you should reboot the machine to verify that everything will start up properly. If you think you have something installed correctly only to find a problem three months later when the machine reboots, you'll have a much harder time remembering what you did in the first place. Fix any problems now while everything is fresh in your mind.

Try to build walls around local modifications. Either locate the files in a local file system (such as `/local` or `/usr/local`) or make copies of the files in a local file system. Often, when installing an update to the operating system, the vendor's installation program will assume it can write in any system directory it pleases, not expecting you to have locally modified files there. If you've kept copies elsewhere, it is a simple matter to reinstall your modifications after the upgrade.

2.8 Performance Tuning

You can increase the power of your system in dozens of ways [Lou92]. As shipped from a vendor, the UNIX operating system is configured to provide the best service for what the vendor believes to be the most common needs of its customers. If your needs are common, then this configuration will be sufficient, but if you have particular needs that are extraordinary, you may wish to tune the settings of your operating system.

2.8.1 Swap space

The most common tuning need is increasing *swap space* [Fri91, pp. 207–221], [Bac86, Chapter 9]. Swap space is necessary for any *virtual memory* computer. Most versions of UNIX implement a virtual memory architecture. To manage virtual memory, the operating system must have a location, usually on a disk drive, where process information can be written when a process is *swapped out*.

Each UNIX process must have enough swap space available for it to be swapped out (since it will be swapped out at some point) [Bac86, Chapter 6]. The number of processes, and thus applications, that can be run depends on how much swap space is available.

The method used to increase swap space varies greatly with different versions of UNIX. Some can only swap into explicitly referenced raw disk partitions. Some systems allow swapping to a file in a file system. The advantage to this is it is easy to create and increase. The disadvantage is that since access to the swap space goes through file system access calls, it is slower than direct disk I/O usually performed in swap space. Since this file is large, you should be sure it is *excluded* from your backup mechanism, since it would be a waste of backup media space.

A virtual memory computer must have at least as much swap space as it has real memory. A UNIX process cannot be started unless there is enough space in the swap area for it to be stored when the scheduler runs a different process. Because of this, having less swap space than real memory will prevent all the real memory being used. Even having exactly the same amount of swap space as real memory will negate all the advantages of having a virtual memory machine. Depending on the applications being run, the ideal amount of swap space is usually two to three times real memory.

If you have multiple disk drives, you can spread your swap space across them. This is similar (as a performance enhancement) to striping a file system across disks. The more disk heads you have working on your swapping, the faster you can swap data in and out and the faster the processes will be run.

Several versions of UNIX also put the `/tmp` file system in memory (for faster access to temporary files). This memory space, too, may be swapped out to the swap area from time to time. If you're using a memory-based file system, be sure to add the size of the file system to the size of your required swap area.

Some swapper programs don't work as well as others. Many sites feel memory is cheap enough that it makes more sense to turn the swapper off and simply install enough real memory in the machine to support the applications. If you can afford this, the machine certainly will run faster, but it isn't always practical.

2.8.2 Number of processes

Each UNIX kernel has a maximum number of processes that it can manage at one time. The list of running processes is maintained in a process table. The larger this process table, the more processes your system can run at one time (and the larger your swap space must be to accommodate them). At some point, having this much going on in memory will affect the amount of available memory left in which to run a user process. Even though most versions of UNIX have a virtual memory architecture where the address space appears to be unlimited, the kernel itself must be resident in real memory at all times. Since the kernel is not swapped out, whatever memory is left after the kernel is loaded is what is available for other processes. So the larger the process table, the less memory is available in which to run user processes.

2.8.3 Device drivers

In a statically linked kernel, all parts are loaded when the kernel is run and they run as long as the computer functions. Newer UNIX kernels have dynamically linked parts which can be loaded when needed and unloaded when no longer needed. This helps reduce the size of the running kernel when the other parts are not needed.

If you run a statically linked kernel, you want to remove the device drivers for which you have no devices from your kernel definition files so your kernel will be smaller. After all, it makes no sense to load drivers that will never be used. Later, if you buy one of the devices, you can always reconfigure your kernel and build one a new one containing the appropriate driver(s). Methods used to build new kernels vary greatly and it is best to consult your vendor's documentation for specific information.

2.8.4 I/O efficiency

Many commands can be used to monitor the usage and efficiency of your I/O processing. This includes local disk accesses [Lou92, Chapter 5] as well as network access for remote file systems [Lou92, pp. 193–202], [Ste92a, Chapter 12]. Commands such as `iostat` can be used to gather statistics about I/O performance, and commands like `tunefs` can be used to modify a file system to improve its efficiency.

You can use these commands to identify bottlenecks in service. You will then have some idea where you need to apply additional resources to provide the level of service being requested. Balancing the workload across disks, controllers, and even physically across a disk platter, can make a significant difference in access time for applications reading and writing large amounts of data.

2.8.5 Network traffic

Just like on a highway, if the traffic on the network to which a computer is connected is too great, the progress of the machine will slow down. In today's massively distributed computing environments, most UNIX machines depend on remote computers for at least one service. If access to this service is slowed down or terminated entirely, the processing of the machine will suffer.

Monitoring traffic flow and watching for bottlenecks in your local network is a critical function. Of course, the method you use depends greatly on the type of network you have. Using whatever network monitoring software is available to you for your type of network, you can establish a "normal" amount of traffic for your network. This will allow you to identify times when traffic has increased significantly.

2.8.6 Queue volume

Often, various queue activity is not considered part of the performance of a machine (performance being viewed as machine speed, network speed, etc.). However, in the sense that if a queue is not processing correctly, the user is not able to get her work done, it can affect her perception of the machine's performance.

By monitoring the various input and output queues being serviced by a machine, it is possible to identify and correct problems before the user recognizes that the problem exists. Printer queues, plotter queues, and mail queues are the typical types of queues where a user might notice a problem if processing were to stop or be slowed down.

2.9 Dealing With Heterogeneity

Rarely will you be able to maintain an environment where all the equipment comes from a single vendor. The trials of maintaining the hardware supplied by different companies is discussed in the next chapter, but the differences in the software on these different manufacturer's equipment will also be significant.

A site where all versions of UNIX are the same and the hardware is supplied by the same vendor is called an *homogeneous environment.* Such environments are the exception rather than the rule today (especially if you take into account the various PCs that are also present in most environments). With the explosion of vendors in the UNIX marketplace, almost every site has a need for more than one kind of UNIX machine.

This may be because the different vendors excel at different specialities. You may buy one vendor's UNIX box because the graphics capabilities of the box outperform all others. Or you might need a box that performs floating-point calculations faster than any others. In these cases, you are more concerned with a specific need than with the version of UNIX being used. You choose to live with the differences in operating systems to get the graphical capability or the performance.

If your organization develops software for UNIX platforms, you may need to have one of every major type of UNIX box because you will be shipping your software to work on each vendor's machine. You may not want to reduce the market potential for your product simply because some potential customers did not buy the same kind of UNIX machines that you did.

Whatever the reason, your environment will more likely be an *heterogeneous environment*, having more than one type of UNIX machine supplied by more than one vendor. You will learn more about the workings of each operating system than you might think. While "UNIX is UNIX," to some degree, internal details can vary a great deal. For example, the order in which a hostname is obtained from local host tables or network host tables can cause all kinds of trouble (you expect it to use one value when a different value is actually being used). Most of the time, the various versions of UNIX work well together, but not always. Don't ever assume that just because it's UNIX it will understand your other UNIX machines completely.

2.10 Staying Ahead

Your goal in supporting the smooth operation of the computing environment is to be "proactive" rather than "reactive." Don't wait for a user to find a problem before dealing with it; try to find as many as you can yourself.

We have seen the sort of information that should be checked. Commands that come with most versions of UNIX provide access to most of this information, but may not allow you to trigger some event or notification based on the information. The tools provided with your system are not always sufficient to identify and solve your problems.

2.10.1 Creating your own tools

If you are one of those system administrators trained as a programmer, developing your own tools will not only be easy, it will probably be one of the more enjoyable projects you have. Even if you have had no formal programming training, you should not let the idea of programming intimidate you. Many of the tools you will wish to build can be created with simple constructs and commands you already know.

Most system management tools are written as shell scripts. People debate whether the Bourne Shell or the C Shell is better for writing scripts. The bottom line is, whatever you feel most comfortable using and are most productive with is what you should use to create your tools.

A recent addition to the world of system management is the Perl language written by Larry Wall [WS91]. Perl provides much of the power of programming in C while still maintaining the simplicity[12] of a shell script. Versions of Perl can also be found for other operating systems such as MS-DOS.

If your tool requires such complex capabilities that only a C program will suffice, then having a programming background will be more important. C is the language of choice for the UNIX environment [KR78], [KP84]. C++ (an object-oriented language created by extending C) is growing in popularity and, depending on the tool being developed, might prove useful [ES90].

Whatever method you use to implement your tool, use something with which you feel comfortable and which provides enough flexibility to accomplish the task at hand. Try to write enough comments or documentation so that other system administrators that work with you or come after you will be able to make sense out of it.

2.10.2 Automating routine tasks

Most of the tasks you perform to keep an eye out for trouble can be automated using the `cron` command [Fri91, Chapter 6], [NSS89, Chapter 23]. Either with standard UNIX commands, or with tools you have developed for your local site, you may wish to monitor:

- space left in file systems
- mail queues
- printer queues
- what hosts are up (using `ping`)
- size of log files, truncating when appropriate
- passwords so as to check for "guessability"

[12] Simple, compared to writing a C program.

- old or large user files or `core` files, so you can consult with the user about archiving old data and removing unneeded data
- date and time, so as to synchronize with another host on the network

Automate as much of this as you possibly can. Every time you find yourself checking on something a second time, write a script or a program to do it and set it up to run automatically on a regular basis.

In a distributed environment, it is possible for each of your machines to "wake up" and run these monitoring tools on a regular basis and send you output that should be checked. You could set the program up to notify you by popping a window up on your workstation or simply by sending you an e-mail message. The machines are out there running already. The more of your monitoring you can get them to do for you, the more time you'll have to chase down the *real* problems.

Chapter 3

Hardware

Once you finally have the software side of your house in order (sometimes even before you do), you can count on receiving new equipment. This may be something as simple as a printer or a modem.[1] It may be a completely new system with diskless clients to put on a new *subnet*.

It is the system administrator's responsibility to make sure all the hardware works together and is configured to perform as advertised. In the "old days," when a site bought everything from a single vendor, the site manager let the sales representative or engineer make sure the pieces fit together. Today, it is rare to find a site where all the equipment is purchased from a single vendor. A few places may still think it worth the extra cost to buy the simplicity of using a single vendor, but not many. It is, therefore, the customer's responsibility to make sure all the parts are usable together.

3.1 Equipment Components

Many more devices exist than the ones discussed here. These are only the major components of an average computer environment, the ones almost everyone will see when setting up even a small site. Certainly, many other devices *could* be added to an environment to satisfy a spe-

[1] "*Simple!?*" I hear some of you cry! Believe me, I know neither of these devices is particularly simple! It was just an example, okay? :-)

cific need. Data input devices are some of the most varied (and most troublesome) that you will find, and new ones are being developed all the time. If a company builds a device for some extraordinary use, you may well have a user in your environment who needs it.

3.1.1 CPU, memory, and device controller boards

Not long ago, the CPU (Central Processing Unit) and memory were on different circuit boards in most computers. As the size of these components has gotten smaller and smaller, more and more of them will fit on the CPU board. The old architecture of the *backplane* having a slot for each board, including the CPU, is giving way to the more modern PC-style *motherboard* which contains the CPU chip, some base amount of memory, and bus connectors into which other boards can be plugged (a *backplane*).

Either way, the same information and cautions apply to all kinds of boards. If you are going to be doing your own replacement of board-level components, there are a few points to consider. If you have never handled hardware before, it will seem intimidating at first. As you get used to doing it, the mystique fades and you feel more comfortable with it.

Unless otherwise specified by your vendor, the power to a computer should always be turned off before inserting or removing boards.

Static electricity

The main problem with handling any exposed part of a computer, like a circuit board, is static electricity in your own body. We've all shuffled across a carpet, then touched someone else and seen or felt a static charge between the two points of contact. If you allow this static charge to cross from you to a computer component, the charge might blow a chip or other component on the board, rendering it useless. Humidity levels and anti-static carpeting have a significant effect on the amount of risk static can pose to your equipment.

A simple precaution you can take to help prevent this is to wear a grounding strap on your wrist which dissipates any static buildup from your body [NSS89, p. 213]. A metal contact is in constant contact with the skin on your wrist, and the other end is grounded to the frame of the computer. Thus, there is no buildup of unbalanced charge between your body and the computer while you wear the strap. Any buildup of charge is balanced across the wire. You should wear a grounding strap anytime you are handling a circuit board or other component where you can come into physical contact with sensitive hardware (you can blow chips in disk drives this way, too, although it is more rare).

Failure diagnosis

Since you are probably not trained as a hardware technician, you may ask exactly what you are going to do if you find a board has failed. Your main option will be to replace the failed board with a working one (if you maintain your own spare parts, this is simple; otherwise you probably will have to call your vendor to have them come out and replace it for you). In most cases, you will not be making the repair yourself unless it is extremely simple, like replacing a single chip.

Sometimes the board itself will not have failed, but the connectors between it and the backplane or bus will not be making complete contact. Sometimes it is enough to *reseat* the board in its slot (to remove it and replace it again). This often fixes a transient bad connection. If some kind of oxidation or dust has built up on the connectors, reseating the board may not help. You may also want to take a pencil eraser and rub it on the board contacts carefully. This will gently rub off any debris or result of oxidation and leave the metal exposed for the connection. Transient hardware problems can sometimes be fixed this simply.

Just in case your hardware failure isn't fixed this easily, it is usually worthwhile to learn a little about the layout and the components on any board you are using in your computer. You do not need to understand the design of the circuits and the paths they use across the board, but the general purpose of the larger functional components (like the CPU, the block of memory, etc.) is helpful. Understanding what a board does, even in general terms, will help you identify candidate components or boards when diagnosing a hardware failure.

> An early CPU board of a popular vendor had a problem with the battery that powered the clock chip on the board (the battery would explode from time to time). After our server crashed and would not boot, we pulled each board to examine it and reseat it. When we pulled the CPU board, the empty space and debris around the area where the battery had been allowed us to quickly identify the problem.

3.1.2 Tape devices

Tape drives are relatively slow, sequential devices upon which data can be stored and later retrieved. Tape drives come in many different shapes and sizes and are designated for many different purposes [Fri91, pp. 273–274]. The major uses for tape drives are for backing up your disk files or transferring data to another site. Transferring data this way is becoming less and less common today because of the proliferation of high-speed data networks and the ease of access to them. Most users choose to send data over network connections rather than write a tape and mail it. Unless your organization has some specific need to send tapes to sister sites or customers, your most significant use of a tape drive will probably be to back up your systems.

9-track and cartridge tapes

Backups have changed in recent years. When you only had to backup a few hundred megabytes of data, a single 9-track or cartridge tape drive was sufficient. Today, it is not unusual for a "small" computing environment to have tens of gigabytes of disk storage. A large environment may have hundreds or even thousands of gigabytes of data that need to be backed up. A 9-track tape drive (or even a room full of 9-track tape drives!) is no longer sufficient to do the job.

The 9-track tape comes on a spool (much like the old reel-to-reel audio tapes) and is $\frac{1}{2}''$ wide. The name "9-track" comes from the fact that the read/write head has nine separate areas that are used to write bits on the tape.[2] Often, 9-track tapes must be loaded onto the tape drive by hand by winding the end of the tape around the take-up reel of the drive and spinning the reels up to the tape's load point. Newer tape drives automatically load the tape onto the take-up reel.

The cartridge tape looks somewhat like a standard audio cassette tape, except that it is twice as big. The tape is $\frac{1}{4}''$ wide and is wound around, and attached to, two spools. The cartridge tape is easier to use since you do not have to touch the tape or wind it around a spool.

The density setting of a tape drive determines how much physical tape space is required to write the data. The higher the density, the more compact the data and the less tape required. Both 9-track and cartridge tapes often offer a choice of density settings.

Helical scan tape drives

A newer type of tape drive taking the UNIX world by storm uses helical scan technology. Helical scan tape is what most of us know as video tape. Rather than a single head in contact with the tape, the tape is wrapped around cylindrical heads that read and write the data.

The big advantage of helical scan tapes is their capacity. A single tape can hold anywhere from several hundred megabytes to a few gigabytes of data. Most 9-track tapes hold less than 100 megabytes, and most cartridge tapes are limited to a few hundred megabytes. The disadvantages of helical scan tapes are that the drives are expensive and there is still confusion over the standards (hardly a new problem in the UNIX world, though!).

The two major types of helical scan tapes are 8mm and 4mm tapes. The 8mm tape is consumer 8mm video tape (which is about the size of an audio cassette). The 4mm tapes are also in a cartridge, which is a little smaller than the 8mm cartridge. Physically, the 4mm tape is the same as the Digital Audio Tape (DAT) you have probably heard so much about in recent years.

---

[2] If you remember 8-track audio tapes, you might compare the two. The 8-track tapes were $\frac{1}{4}''$ wide and had 8 tracks on them, 4 separate programs with two tracks (stereo left and right channels) per program.

Now that computing sites commonly have many gigabytes of disk space that needs to be backed up, these higher capacity tape drives are becoming more of a necessity than a luxury. You could spend your life backing up a site of any size with a 9-track tape drive.

3.1.3 Disk devices

Disk drives, unlike tape drives, are fast, random-access devices that also store data. Whereas tape drives are suited to store data that is infrequently needed, disk drives store data that is used constantly by your computer system. Disk drives can store large amounts of data and provide access to any part of it at any time.

In the past, computer manufacturers usually supplied the disk drives with the machine. Every company used its own format, its own disk controllers, maybe even its own disks. Since standards have emerged and independent companies now manufacture disk drives, it is now common to buy disk drives from a third party (i.e., not the same company that sold you your computer). This is both a blessing and a curse. You can pick and choose to get the best performance, capacity, and price, but you also must deal with the mechanics of installing, formatting, and setting up the drive yourself.

Hard disk drives

In the last decade, the size and capacity of disk drives has changed dramatically. In the 1970s, the disk drives on mainframe computers had to be rolled in by professional movers, as they came in their own racks and were extremely heavy. In the 1980s, a few hundred megabytes fit into a rack-mountable chassis which could be lifted by two people. With today's disk drives you can hold these same few hundred megabytes in the palm of your hand, and larger drives that hold 2 gigabytes can be easily carried in two hands.

While several standards for hard disk drive interfaces exist today, the most common in the UNIX world is the SCSI interface. SCSI (often pronounced "scuzzy") stands for Small Computer Systems Interface [NSS89, pp. 190–194]. SCSI disk drives can be found on everything from

PCs to small supercomputers. Many different capacities are available in such disk drives, from a few *megabytes* on up to a few *gigabytes*, and capacities are increasing every year.

Disk drives have different geometric layouts, and most formatting and file system creation programs require this information in order to format the disk drive and create a file system [Fri91, Chapter 8]. The location and use of this information varies with different versions of UNIX, but it is usually found in a file used by formatting commands (one common example is `/etc/disktab` on some BSD-based systems). Sometimes the drive will be shipped already formatted to save you that trouble. Drives not supported by your computer maker can be used if the type of interface used by the drive is supported by your computer. In this case, you must determine the geometric information required to correctly format the disk and create the file system(s). With help from the disk vendor, this is usually relatively simple.

A special form of hard disk drive is a RAID drive (Redundant Array of Inexpensive Disk). These are small disk drives (often SCSI drives) connected together in a cabinet to form a very large logical disk drive. File systems are *striped*[3] across these disks to improve access time (taking advantage of multiple disk access arms in each disk drive). File systems are often mirrored on multiple drives in the RAID architecture to allow "hot" replacement of any single drive that has failed. The RAID switches access to another copy of data on another disk while the drive is replaced and synchronizes the copies once the drive has been replaced. RAID drives are high capacity, high performance and highly reliability built using generic and relatively inexpensive component disk drives.

Diskette drives

Gone are the days of the 8″ floppy disk in the home-built computer system. These big floppy disks gave way to $5\frac{1}{4}''$ which has given way to $3\frac{1}{2}''$. These new, smaller *diskettes* are superior because they hold more information and are no longer as fragile, since they are packaged

[3] See page 49 for a discussion of disk striping.

in a hard plastic case. While the magnetic media on the inside is still "floppy," they no longer appear to be.

Diskettes are not good for storing long-term copies of important data or for doing backups (unless you really like inserting and removing diskettes in the disk drive). Being removable, they are better suited for transporting data between different machines that use the same format of diskette or transporting "just a little" data between two sites not connected by a network. Software companies often send small software updates in the form of a *patch* on a diskette or in an electronic mail message.

Optical disk drives

All the disk drives discussed to this point are magnetic in nature. They record data on a surface by magnetizing the surface in one direction or the other. While this method of recording is effective, it can be affected by magnetic fields introduced from outside influences (i.e., don't put a diskette in your shirt pocket along with a screwdriver with a magnetized tip if you care about the data on the diskette!).

Optical disks store data by setting up a reflective surface for a laser beam to bounce off of at different angles to represent different data. The information cannot be changed by the introduction of a magnetic field. In fact, on most optical disks it cannot be changed at all. Thus, this medium is well suited for making distribution copies of data, but not for updating information.

Software is often shipped on CD-ROM disks. These look exactly like the compact discs that you buy in the record store (and, in fact, are exactly the same, except that they contain digitally-encoded data rather than digitally-encoded audio recordings). They cannot be modified, but each disk can hold a great deal of information (as much as 800 megabytes [Lau86]). They are, therefore, perfect for distribution of large software packages. Only one piece of media is then necessary, and you will always be able to reinstall from the original media.

WORM (Write Once, Read Many) drives are often used to make a full backup of data that will be kept for a long time. They also can be used to store data that is static but to which users need on-line access. This saves regular disk space for data that needs to be modified. WORM optical disks were developed from the same technology as the CD-ROM, but without the large expense of manufacturing. The user may write to any sector on a WORM disk one time, after which it cannot be modified.

A newer type of optical disk drive which can be updated is coming into use at some sites. It is not strictly optical, as some magnetic recording is also used which allows the data to be changed, but the physical disk is not in danger when exposed to a magnetic field. This type of recording is known as magneto-optics, or magnetically assisted optical recording.

3.1.4 Serial devices

Entire books have been written on the ins and outs of RS-232 cabling and communication (like [NNM82]). The typical system administrator does not usually need to know this much about serial communications. Less detailed examinations (like [Fri91, pp. 307–315] and [NSS89, pp. 142–148]) are generally sufficient.

Typical devices that are connected via a serial cable include terminals, modems, and some printers and plotters.

Cables

RS-232 is a common term for a *serial cable* that implements the standard definition for communications across serial wires as defined by the Electronic Industries Association (EIA).

The old-style RS-232 connectors have up to 25 pin connectors at the end, so up to 25 wires can be connected in a single cable. These connectors are known as DB-25 connectors. Most RS-232 cables never used more than a few of these wires. Since DB-25 connectors are bulky for the amount of pin space that is generally used, smaller DB-9 connectors became popular, especially where space in the back of a machine is critical. For example, my notebook PC uses a DB-9 for its modem connector, even though my modem uses a DB-25.

If you are the system administrator in a shop that is self-sufficient, you will eventually find yourself building or buying serial cables. You can order them in bulk if you always need the same kind, but you will find that ordering one or two of a specific configuration cable will be expensive. It is usually better, as well as faster, to keep the parts on hand and make the cables yourself as you need them.

The signal traveling through a serial cable will degrade as it continues through the cable. The RS-232 standard specifies a length limit of 50 feet. In practice, almost everyone runs cables longer than this (and the slower the baud rate across the connection, the longer it can be run [McN82, Appendix A]). Using shielded cable rather than ordinary unshielded cable will increase the distance the cable can be run as well. You should be aware that you cannot run such a cable forever, and you should try to decrease the length wherever possible, but don't be afraid to try something a little "out of spec" (i.e., out of the bounds of the specification). RS-232 cable, especially unshielded cable, is vulnerable to electromagnetic interference. The longer the cable, the weaker the signal, and the more of a chance of interference by surrounding electromagnetic radiation.

> One site had continuous, but intermittent problems with a printer connected over a serial line. The printer was a "private" printer, used by a few executives on the second (and top) floor of a small company. The printer worked fine most of the time, but occasionally it would print totally nonsensical data. After several weeks of head-scratching, an employee on the second floor mentioned that it seemed coincidental that often someone arrived on the floor by elevator about the same time some useless output came out on the printer. Further investigation revealed that the RS-232 line connecting the printer to the host computer downstairs had been run through the elevator shaft (unknown to anyone on the current staff, which also points out the need for good records of such connections!). Re-routing the printer cable eliminated the problem.

Over time, the RS-232 standard has been broadly interpreted and has been used to connect all types of devices together. The result is that your connections don't always work exactly as you would expect. Terminals, modems, printers, and any other devices connected via RS-232 connections often turn out to be the source of the system administrator's most aggravating problems. Unfortunately, these cables also connect the devices that are most visible to the user, and will therefore be most noticeable when something is wrong.

Some sites (and newer devices) use RJ-11 or RJ-45 telephone jacks for serial connections rather than RS-232. The connectors are easier to build (with the right tools, of course) and to deal with, both for the system administrator as well as the user. These kinds of plugs are often used for office connections. Of course, where a device has a DB-9 or DB-25 connector, you will be forced to use the appropriate end on your cable.

These telephone jack connectors are useful when creating a patch panel (often in the computer room), which enables connections to specific computers and offices to be easily switched around rather than having to rewire an office. If you use a patch panel, be sure that you keep your documentation, cable labels, and jack labels up to date! Few things are more exasperating than trying to connect something in the patch panel only to find that the destinations are marked incorrectly!

Terminals

In many leading-edge computing environments, terminals are nothing more than historical relics. You probably will not find even one being used by a user at some of these sites (sometimes there will be a few acting as consoles on file or printer servers in a computer room). But if you go to a smaller site, a site that cannot afford to always buy the latest and greatest hardware, you may find many terminals still in use. Even data processing and order-entry locations in a large organization may use terminals for specific menu-driven applications.

UNIX has been taken over by windowing systems, the most successful of which is the X Window System® developed at the Massachusetts Institute of Technology [MP92]. To use windowing systems, a system must have a *bit-mapped graphic display* attached to it rather than a plain ASCII terminal. Today, most UNIX computers and some "smart" terminals (such as X terminals) are equipped with such a display. Terminals are mainly useful on large compute servers or other multi-user systems where users need access via other means than the console device. If the users have their own workstations, they will connect to such a host via the network, but if the organization cannot afford to supply every user with his own workstation, then terminals come into play. Most terminals connect to hosts with a serial cable which plugs into a serial port (sometimes called a *tty*).

Printers

Connecting a printer is often just an extension of connecting a terminal since printers often use the same kind of serial cable. Some printers can also connect to a computer via a parallel port or be connected directly to the network.

You might find many different kinds of printers in a computing environment. In the "old days" everybody had a line printer that was used to produce code listings, reports, and every other kinds of necessary output. For graphical output, plotters were used. Since the coming of the laser printer, the two different kinds of output can be generated on a single device. Code listings, typeset text, charts, and graphs can all be produced on a laser printer. Personally, I miss the fan-fold paper for code listings, but in every other way, laser printers are superior to the line printers and the (cheaper) dot-matrix printers of the past.

The resolution of a laser printer is referred to in *dpi* (dots per inch). This number defines how many individual dots can be put on the paper in the space of one inch. The more dots per inch that can be drawn, the finer the resolution of a line or a picture. A 300-dpi printer is common. A 600-dpi printer will allow higher quality output, but will cost more.

Another measurement used with laser printers is the number of pages per minute, *ppm*, the printer can produce. The faster the printer can produce its output, the more you'll pay for the printer. In an office environment where many people share the printer, this could be important. A 4-ppm laser printer may serve well for a single user who only prints a few pages at a time. A busy office where people are printing 50-page reports may find a 24-ppm printer well worth the extra cost.

Laser printers are usually driven by some kind of page description language which allows characters or even lines and figures to be specified in larger units (rather than having to set each dot on the page as "on" or "off"). Many printer manufacturers have defined their own printer languages for many printers. The most well-known language used by multiple vendors is the PostScript® page description language. Originally developed by Adobe Systems, Inc., PostScript has become a standard for page description. Technically, PostScript is a programming language where the output is an image on a page [Rei90]. Most printer manufacturers now have PostScript interpreters either built in or they may be added as an option so that PostScript files can be printed by their printers. While it is not necessary to be able to program in PostScript to be a good system administrator, it certainly helps to be familiar with it. One advantage of PostScript files is that they are plain text files and can be easily copied, edited, and even sent via electronic mail to another user. Even if you do not have a PostScript printer,

PostScript interpreter software can sometimes be used to drive non-PostScript printers.

Modems

The word "modem" is derived from the functions it performs, those of **mo**dulation and **dem**odulation of a signal. As with terminals and some printers, a *modem* is connected to a computer via a serial cable. A modem allows two devices to communicate data over telephone lines.

Modems send data at different speeds, specified in *bps* (bits per second). This is sometimes referred to as *baud rate*.[4]

It wasn't that long ago that 300-bps and 1200-bps modems were in common use (300 bps is close to the reading speed of many people). Since then, even 2400-bps and 9600-bps modems have become outdated. Today, speeds of 19200 bps and higher are possible with modems containing data compression capabilities. Digital transmission lines that can take advantage of the coming ISDN standard will increase even these speeds dramatically [Gul91, Chapter 4].

If you are only connecting a terminal to a modem, then these slower speeds may be acceptable (since getting data faster than you can read it is usually sufficient), but this is not sufficient for all uses. The development of X terminals (which act as X Window System display servers) has allowed an entire multi-windowed development environment to be accessed over phone lines. These terminals require a much larger amount of data to drive the display, and the higher speed modems are a necessity with this kind of connection.

3.2 Equipment Installation

At various times, you will be required to add pieces of all of these different kinds of equipment to your local environment. Generally, you can get help from the vendors with specific problems or concerns. Being familiar with the basic steps necessary to install each type of equipment

[4] While this is not totally correct usage, it suits most purposes [NNM82, p. 227].

will make you feel more comfortable, even the first time you have to do it.

3.2.1 Delivery and acceptance testing

When the equipment first arrives, you must make sure that it is what you ordered and in proper condition (i.e., not incomplete or damaged during shipping). In most cases when you have ordered equipment from a vendor, there will be a list of acceptance criteria that must be met before you will accept delivery. This list could include anything from all the pieces being present in the shipment to the machine being installed by a technician from the vendor company and verified as operating on your network. The criteria for acceptance by your organization (and thus, payment to the vendor) must be satisfied before you can move on to any subsequent steps.

> My organization once ordered a new multi-processor UNIX system and wanted to take delivery (including acceptance testing) before the end of the fiscal year. The machine arrived in our computer room the morning of December 31, which was a holiday. Knowing time would be tight, we arranged with the vendor to send a technician. Our acceptance criteria was that the machine be up and running UNIX on our network before we could accept delivery. It was up to us to make sure the machine was up and working before midnight. His incentive was our purchase of the machine. Mine was that we could spend money from that fiscal year instead of the next. We ran into a few minor problems, but the technician was good and his company provided remote assistance and we were up by early evening.

3.2.2 Computers and workstations

Installing new computers on your existing network is always a challenge. The new host must be modified to use the resources in the local environment (accounting files, printers, remote file systems), and the existing machines must have the new host added to their lists of machines authorized to access these resources [Ste92a], [AL92].

Picking a hostname

One of the first issues you'll think about is what to name a new computer. In the age of distributed systems, each system is given a unique hostname to distinguish it from every other system. Some organizations choose to simply number each host (xyz1, xyz2, and so on). This eliminates any conflict with varying opinions about the name. Generally, this is not only boring, but confusing since all the hostnames will be similar.

Some sites simply let the user pick any name that is not already in use. This allows the user to enjoy some individuality and feel like a part of what is going on. The disadvantage is that having hostnames follow users is a little more work for you when moving machines around (because they must be renamed as well). One advantage of this is you will soon associate hostnames and users and not have to look up who is affected by problems on certain machines.

Another method often used to pick hostnames is to assign a group of hosts a hostname type, such as birds. All hosts belonging to a certain department or group might use names such as falcon, pigeon, hawk, dove, etc. You, as the system administrator, can then easily identify the parent group of a machine just by seeing the hostname. When groups are functionally or financially separate within an organization, this can be a big help.

These are only two of a myriad of ways to assign a hostname. The method you use is completely up to you and is dependent on what works best for your site. Some good suggestions can be found in Internet RFC 1178 [Lib90]. (See page 143 for more information on RFCs.)

Picking a network address

Depending on the type of network you use, the format of your network address will vary. To go into any amount of detail in examples would require assuming a certain type of network. A later chapter on networking will provide an overview of the various kinds of networks that are available in today's market. The one you pick will depend heavily on the kinds of other machines to which you wish to be able to connect.

Whatever kind of network you use, some care should be taken to keep your network address assignments in some kind of rational order, not just random and arbitrary. If you start out with a small network, you may choose to believe that the number of hosts is small enough so that it will never be complex. This is almost guaranteed to fail you eventually. Environments always grow, and having a sane and rational system for assigning addresses (and hostnames, too, for that matter) will save you from having to go back and reorganize your entire network in the future.

Standalone hosts and file servers

In today's networked and distributed environments, no host is truly a standalone host; almost every machine will depend on some other machine for some kind of service or resource. Modern distributed computers are dramatically intertwined in their dependence on one another. A standalone host is one that receives no direct, critical function from another host (as do clients that boot from a network boot server). If the machine can boot and run and let a user get useful work done even if the network is unavailable, then it can be considered a standalone host, since it contains everything critical to its basic operation.

Standalone hosts are usually file servers or compute servers that will reside in the computer room (or area where your "main" machines are kept). In a large organization, you might have some "public" workstations that are installed as standalone hosts. Of course, some public machines might also be clients of a server in the computer room.

The advantage of a file server is that all the data resides on disk drives connected to that one machine but accessible to many other workstations. This makes back up of these files a much simpler task than individually backing up each workstation in different offices, areas, or buildings.

Installing a standalone host usually involves no more additional planning than any other type of system, since no other systems or users are *already* depending on it for any services. You can install it and verify its proper operation before modifying the configuration of your other hosts to take certain services from the new host. If you are installing the new machine in a computer room, be sure you have enough power, air handling capacity, and floor space in the computer room for the new equipment (see the next chapter for more details about environmental requirements).

Client hosts and desktop workstations

Installing a new client system, most likely a workstation to be used by someone in their office, takes a bit more planning. The most important part is to schedule with the user involved, so you don't disrupt his or her work. It is often convenient to install the system while the user attends a meeting or goes to lunch.

The other potential conflict depends on whether or not any modifications must be made to the boot server to boot the new client. If the boot server has space for another client, then you can just add the new client. If the boot server must have a file system expanded or any other work that requires it be taken off-line, then you must schedule *downtime* for the server, either before or during the client installation. Since this will render all other clients unusable during this time, this is best done outside of normal working hours.

3.2.3 Storage devices

Installing storage devices, such as disk or tape drives, on a machine usually requires taking the machine down. Controller cards cannot be inserted into the card cage while the system is running (although companies are working on *hot-pluggable* devices to reduce downtime even when adding devices to a system). Most versions of the Unix kernel only probe the bus at boot time and load the appropriate drivers for the devices found. To add a device and have the kernel recognize it, it is usually necessary to reboot the machine. It may also be necessary to build a new kernel containing a driver for the device, if it was not already included in the kernel.

If the device is being added to a user's workstation, then it is only necessary to schedule the downtime with that user. If the device is being added to a server of any kind, then you should warn users well in advance about the loss of service during the downtime. A machine that is critical to normal operation of your environment, such as a file server, should only be taken down outside of normal working hours.

3.2.4 Input devices

Input devices like terminals, mice, light pens, or any number of other special devices, are usually going to be installed on a user's workstation (with the exception of terminals which might also be connected to a server). Many of these devices do not require taking the machine down (e.g., the terminal driver is almost always present in the UNIX kernel, although you might have to configure a new serial port to be active). If you are replacing a faulty device, then all the software drivers will already be present. If you are adding a new device that requires a special driver, then you may have to build a new kernel and reboot the machine. If the machine is a user's workstation, this is fairly simple to work out with the user.

3.2.5 Output devices

Output devices like printers or plotters are often installed on a server that is expected to be available constantly (as opposed to a user's workstation, which the user might be able to reboot as she pleases).

If the printer is connected as a serial device, then its installation will probably not require taking the machine down to add drivers. If a special-purpose output device requires a special driver, then it might be necessary to rebuild the kernel and reboot the machine. Again, since this is probably a server-type machine, downtime should be scheduled and the user community should be warned in advance so they can plan around the outage.

3.3 Equipment Maintenance

Your computers, even though they may have few moving parts, can fail from time to time. The devices connected to them, being mechanical in nature, are even more prone to failure than the computers themselves. We've discussed the sorts of devices you may already have or that you might later acquire. You may have purchased these through the same vendor from whom you bought the computer or from a third party.

Maintenance should be performed on your equipment in two circumstances. The most obvious is when you encounter a failure and you diagnose the problem and replace the faulty component. The other is when you make a regularly scheduled check of a piece of equipment to make sure it is functioning properly in hopes of preventing a failure. This is known as *preventive maintenance* [NSS89, pp. 214–215].

If you have a hardware support contract from the vendor(s) of your equipment, part of that contract should include regular preventive maintenance by a *field engineer* (FE) or other support person. This person is trained in the proper procedures for upkeep of the equipment. If you do not have such a contract, you should periodically check over your equipment yourself (see *Self-maintenance* on page 86).

3.3.1 Tools

It may seem obvious, but you might be surprised how many people try to do jobs without the right tools. The right tool for any job, technical or otherwise, can make a huge difference in your effectiveness.

Every system administrator who deals with hardware on any level should have a minimum set of tools available. How large a set will depend greatly on how much work you will do with hardware components (e.g., if you only replace components rather than attempt to repair them yourself, then you probably do not need a soldering iron).

Screwdrivers,[5] wrenches, needle-nosed pliers, and hex wrenches of various sizes make up the set of "most commonly needed" tools. With these, you have a fighting chance. A rubber mallet is often useful,

[5] But watch out for the magnetized type; you don't want to get them near magnetic media!

although the author refuses to officially recommend any specific use for one.

More esoteric tools and supplies that may come in handy, depending on your needs, are:

- RS-232, RJ-11, and/or RJ-45 cable parts and crimping tools
- RS-232 gender changers and break-out box for testing
- spare network transceivers and drop cables
- flashlight
- power strips
- ladder
- vacuum cleaner (wet/dry, reversible, and/or hand-held models
- fuses
- electrical tape
- drill and drill bits
- volt/ohm meters
- network cable scanners
- grounding strap
- headset ("hands-free") telephone, two-way radios
- calculator that converts between hexadecimal, octal, and decimal for debugging network addressing problems (the UNIX `dc` command can also do this)

3.3.2 Vendor maintenance

The obvious advantage of having a vendor support contract on your equipment is that the vendor's field engineering staff should know the equipment better than you. This is not always true, of course, but any vendor with anything near a good reputation for its customer support organization will be able to provide more information about the equipment than you could know on your own.

The obvious disadvantage is the continuing cost of maintaining the equipment. Often, whether or not you have a support contract depends heavily on how much your organization paid for the equipment. A high-speed file server that costs several hundred thousand dollars is a good candidate for a hardware support contract. If something were to go severely wrong with this machine, you would not want to have to pay the regular repair rate to the vendor or wait for them to come out whenever they could. The vendor is probably the only company you want attempting a repair on a highly specialized piece of equipment. With a generic workstation or PC, you can usually afford to risk a longer downtime, and there are many companies capable of repairing such a well-understood piece of equipment.

The cost of maintenance will depend on the amount of coverage and the response time you require. The ability to call for service twenty-four hours a day, seven days a week will cost more than "business hours" coverage.

> A major computer maker, with whom we had a hardware support contract, notified us that they had found a problem with the disk drives used in the machine (which they also manufactured). The drives were airtight, but over time the glue sealing the case flaked off on the inside of the drive. We scheduled a replacement for each drive and they provided new (modified) disk drives for us. Without our hardware support contract, we would have gone merrily along until one day our disk would have crashed and we would have had to buy another one (and the machine would have been unavailable until it could be installed and the backups restored).

In the modern computing environment, you often find components from several different vendors in use together. If you have vendor maintenance contracts from all of these vendors, you may think you have all your bases covered, but beware of finger-pointing by vendors. While most companies understand that people just don't buy everything from the same manufacturer the way they used to, some will try to shift the blame from their component to another one supplied by another vendor. This is where it pays to be as familiar as you can be with the equipment. If the FE tells you the problem is with some other component, you'll be better able to evaluate and act on that opinion.

The FE is just a person, like you and me. Although you are putting your faith in him to be the expert, you shouldn't expect everything he does to be perfect, either. He can make mistakes and not understand some facet of the machine, just like an ordinary mortal. This is another good reason for you to be as knowledgeable as possible about your equipment and its uses.

> We once had an FE come out to replace a CPU board in a workstation. He pulled the old board and installed the new one and the machine booted back up. That afternoon I received a call from the user complaining that the machine didn't run his applications nearly as fast as it had before. After a few minutes of head scratching, I queried the machine for the amount of memory in it. It turned out that the FE had switched the CPU board, but had forgotten to move the memory SIMMs (Single In-Line Memory Module) from the old board onto the new board. A machine that was supposed to have 32 megabytes of memory had 4 megabytes. If I had been paying closer attention to what the FE was doing, I might have noticed it before it became a problem!

Just as you must take care to move your memory to a replacement CPU board, you must also move any other board-specific component or chip. The most common problem encountered when swapping CPU boards is not also swapping the *hostid* PROMs. Some manufacturers store unique information to identify each specific host in these PROMs, and if you boot a machine with a new identification PROM, the operating system may be confused as to its identify and licensed software may not run.

3.3.3 Self-maintenance

The most important self-maintenance task is making sure that the paths for air flow are clear and the machine itself is clean. Dust and heat are the major enemies of any modern computer system (and the devices used in one). Air is used to cool the components and is pulled into the unit by a fan. The human body can separate out the dust and other contaminants found in regular room air, but the fan just pulls it all through. Often, the electrostatic charges found inside an electronic device will act as a magnet on the dust in the air, pulling it down onto the boards and casing inside the box. Dust settling on board components also causes them to heat up even more than normal. Vacuuming out machines will reduce dust problems like this.

> After a laser printer failed, we opened up the case to see if we could see any particular problem before calling it in for repair. We found about a $\frac{1}{4}''$ layer of dust in the case, and the screen covering the back side of the fan was completely encased in dust, greatly restricting the airflow. We cleaned the dust out and let the unit cool for an hour or so. When we put the case back on and powered the printer up, it worked just fine.

A failure in cooling often causes other mysterious failures. A computer that overheats may simply stop. All the devices continue to operate, but the CPU freezes up and appears to "hang." A cooling failure can happen in several ways. Usually, it is because of a restriction in air flow, due either to a buildup of dust or an internal fan failure. Sometimes a machine can overheat because of an air conditioning failure. If you have machines in a computer room with a large air handler to maintain temperature, then you will find that other machines have (or will) also fail if that air handler fails.

Many sites, however, maintain some or all of their equipment in regular office environments. No longer is it a requirement that *all* of the computer equipment have specially maintained environmental conditions (humidity and temperature). Only the most sophisticated computers need this today because of the kind of heat they generate internally. Many low-end machines can survive well in an air-conditioned office environment. If you have machines in such an environment, it is even more important to keep them properly cooled, since they still generate heat inside. Dust particles (and sometimes even smoke particles from cigarettes) are also present in higher quantities in an office than in an environmentally controlled computer room.

> We once had a server that would "hang" for no apparent reason in the afternoons. We felt the room was cool enough for the machine to operate, but apparently we were right on the edge of getting too warm since, as the building heated up slightly in the afternoon, the machine would hang fairly regularly. We took the cover off the machine and noticed that the CPU board and the tape controller board were in slots next to one another. We moved the tape board two slots away to provide more space for air to flow through the boards and the problem vanished. This, of course, was not the *final* solution, since we knew we were "on the edge," but it prevented failures over the next few days. We eventually got the air conditioning capacity increased for that room.

If you do your own maintenance, it is important to track the parts in more detail than you would if you just had someone come out and replace a faulty part. You will probably keep a stock of spare parts available from which to replace parts. Then you will have to send the faulty component off to be repaired, track its progress, and return it to the spare parts stock when it is returned to you. You should also keep a history of the board itself, so that if a problem comes up in the future, you know what it has been through in the past (in case that might give some clue as to what the problem could be).

Often, diagnosing a failure may be complex. What looks like a CPU board failure might actually be caused by a block of memory failing or a controller locking the bus so that the CPU cannot access it. Sometimes you may need to swap components, either with your spare parts or another working machine. If the problem disappears or moves to the other machine, you know more than you knew before.

> There used to be a joke about field engineers from a certain company (even though it could be told of field engineers from almost any company) that was popular with system administrators:
>
> Q: How does an FE fix a flat on his car?
> A: He swaps each tire out with the spare until he can drive the car again.

Your computer equipment is expensive. It is worth your time and the company's money to send you to classes on the maintenance of your equipment if the vendors offers some.

Even though your computer equipment is probably the most expensive equipment in your computer room (and thus you will be most concerned about it), do not neglect other equipment like tape drives. Tape drives are the core of your backup strategy and you already know how important backups are! You should clean the heads of your tape drives on a regular basis, following the recommendations of the manufacturer. The old 9-track tape drives were easy to clean because the head was accessible. Newer self-contained tape drives like 8mm and 4mm drives may require a head cleaning cartridge.

In addition to checking the equipment itself, you should do self-maintenance on your sensors and alarms. Test these on a regular basis, just as you test the smoke detectors in your home.[6]

[6] You *do* test the smoke detectors in your home on a regular basis, don't you? :-)

Chapter 4

Physical Environment

In order to house all this valuable software and hardware, you will probably have a computer room of some kind. It might be a closet with an air conditioning vent or a 10,000-square-foot room in a warehouse with raised floor, a fire control system, and a half-dozen air handlers and power conditioners. It is more likely something in between.

If you are like many system administrators, you were trained as a programmer, and you probably have little working knowledge of electrical systems, cooling systems, security systems, and fire containment systems. These and other devices may or may not be necessary for your environment, but it is likely that you will have to deal with at least a subset of these. This chapter will examine the most common aspects of physical computing environments.

Even though your organization will probably contract with local service companies to set up and maintain your power and air conditioners, you should become familiar with this information so that you are not totally dependent on them for help or in an emergency. These service providers can be a good source of information and are usually glad to help you improve your understanding. In addition to the references provided in this chapter, catalogs provided by the system manufacturers and service companies often provide valuable information. Don't be afraid to ask these folks questions about things you don't understand.

4.1 Your Computer Room

The computer room, machine room, lab, or whatever other term your site might use to describe it, is the central place where your largest computers and most delicate equipment reside. Workstations are usually found in offices, printers may be in hallways or public work areas (sometimes loud printers such as impact line printers are put in the computer room to minimize the effect of the noise). The larger, noisier, and more sensitive machines are maintained in a computer room where special security and environmental conditions can be maintained.

In addition to the computers, the computer room will house the power and air conditioning equipment. You may find it helpful to keep other items in your computer room. Tape racks and fireproof vaults can store tapes that need to be kept on site. A fireproof vault will increase the chances of tapes surviving some kind of disaster, but this alone is no guarantee. Off-site storage of critical material is still a must. If you have a patch panel as the hub of your twisted-pair connections into offices, this will most likely reside in the computer room. Tools, workbenches, manual racks, bookshelves, and key cabinets may make life easier. A single page, short document, or book (whichever is necessary) that describes emergency procedures for both the experienced system administrator as well as the user who happens to be around when an emergency situation arises should also be kept in the computer room.

Depending on the needs of a site, most of the following items will likely be present in a sophisticated computer room.

4.1.1 Raised floor

Most computer rooms have a raised floor. This is a false floor that sits above the concrete slab and functions as the room floor. The floor is divided into two-foot square panels that can be individually removed, providing easy access to the space below. Network and power cables can then be run underneath all the equipment and furniture in the room, so as to avoid damage to the cables or to people who might trip over them. The raised floor is usually positioned eight to twelve inches above the slab. If a raised floor is not possible because of physical restrictions or cost, cable trays at either ceiling or floor level may be utilized to organize and protect cables.

Some of the panels of a raised floor are ventilated to allow air from the air conditioning unit (see below) to pass into the computer room from below the floor. In this way, the air space below the raised floor is also used as a delivery vent for the air conditioning unit.

The raised floor panels usually have a tile surface and are removed by a suction device which can be attached securely to any panel. Panels are sometimes covered with a carpeted surface. While carpet is more aesthetically pleasing (and makes the room somewhat quieter), it has two distinct disadvantages. One is that the lifting tool for carpet tiles has sharp prongs rather than suction cups (suction cups would not "grab" carpet), which makes it harder to use and more dangerous. The other disadvantage is that it is much easier to build up a static charge in your body walking on carpet. Because of the delicate electronic equipment, the computer room is the place where you least want to build up such a charge. Even though this type of floor may be more pleasant, it is advisable to avoid it.

Under the raised floor, in addition to power and networking cables, there should be drains and water sensors, if there is any source of water (such as fire sprinklers or chilled water pipes for an air conditioning unit). The water sensors will detect any buildup of water under the floor (indicating a clogged drain). Of course, any collection of water underneath a raised floor where power cables run is a potentially disastrous situation. You should check these sensors (along with your fire alarms) on a regular basis.

Equipment vibration on a slab or raised floor can also be a problem [NSS89, p. 217]. If your building contains any kind of large mechanical devices, you should investigate the potential effect they could have on the delicate machinery in your computer room (such as disk drives).

> We lost a disk drive to a head crash while the city was building a new highway just off the property of our building. They were having to blast because the ground in the area was mostly rock. The rock in the ground carried the shock wave from the blast to our building quite effectively and everyone felt a slight tremor. Unfortunately, the disk drive felt it, too.

4.1.2 Air conditioning

Much like the air conditioner in your home, the air conditioning unit in your computer room is used to maintain a cool temperature. Many air handler units are capable of both heating and cooling. Usually, the computers generate the heat and the air conditioner cools the room, but in an extremely cold climate, it is possible for the equipment to be too cold. Most air handlers also regulate the humidity. If the air is too dry, static electricity can be even more of a problem; if it is too humid, condensation can be a problem [NSS89, p. 216].

Two methods are used to cool the air in a computer room. A conventional, electrically powered air conditioner (using freon) is the most common method. Some air conditioning units use chilled water from an outside source to cool the room. Chilled water is usually only available to sites where a chilled water plant is used for other purposes as well (you wouldn't build one just for your computer room).

If you do have a chilled water system, it is a good idea to have a conventional system as a backup to it. If your air conditioning fails, it will only be a matter of time before the temperature in the room increases and your machines will hang or crash (or worse). Usually, temperature sensors are connected to the Emergency Power Off (EPO) switch and at a certain level the entire room will just shut down (before the temperature becomes high enough to do real damage to the equipment).

> Late one night, a drunk driver ran a stop sign, jumped the curb, and slammed into the air conditioning unit of a building. The power to the computers in the building's computer room was unaffected, but the air conditioning system was out. The temperature in the computer room began to rise until about 5:00 a.m. when the temperature sensors triggered the EPO switch. The sad part of the story is, assuming "lightning" would not strike twice, it was decided not to move the power transformers to a safer location. About a month after the power transformer had been replaced, the same thing happened again (with a different driver, though)!

4.1.3 Power conditioning

Just as the term "air conditioning" is used to describe the process of maintaining a constant temperature in a room, maintaining a uniform level of power is called *power conditioning* . Electrical power supplied from a wall plug in your home or office, while delivered at a consistent level, is not always exactly the same. If you have ever sat at home watching television and noticed the picture blink for a split second when your air conditioner cuts on, then you have witnessed a brief sag in the power level delivered to your television. Typical appliances found in your home or office can usually deal with these slight changes in the power level, but computers often cannot [NSS89, p. 216].

Several different types of transient voltages can have an immediate or long-term detrimental effect on electronic equipment. The ones that are of the most concern to the system administrator are voltage surges, sags, and spikes.

Surges and sags can be caused by any number of devices drawing power from a source common to the one you are using to supply power to your computers. When an air conditioner, copier, elevator, or other large device is activated, its sudden demand for power can create a sag, by drawing power away, or even a surge, by causing an overcompensation for the sag by the power supply. Usually, these kinds of transient voltages do not cause a computer to fail immediately, but they do put stress on the electronics inside the computer and can contribute to its eventual failure.

Voltage spikes are often caused by lightning or other severe external occurrences (such as an accident during construction or electrical line maintenance). These spikes are often intense enough to damage one or more components of a computer and cause it to crash. Note that the "off" switch on most devices only disconnects the "hot" wire (the positive half of the circuit), not the neutral or ground wires. Power spikes (from lightning) can still hit a device that has been switched off but is still plugged in. Even modems and the serial I/O controllers to which they are connected can be affected by lightning strikes on phone lines.

A *power conditioner* (sometimes referred to as a *power management unit*, a PMU, or a *power distribution unit*, a PDU) can be used to prevent these kinds of power problems. On a PC, one might find a *surge suppressor* plugged into the wall ahead of the PC. The power conditioner is a much more complex (and much more effective) version of the same idea. The power conditioner, handles much larger surges and spikes and also regulates the flow of power, thus supplying a clean and level supply of power to the equipment.

The amount of transient voltage that can be limited by the power conditioner is the *clamping level*. Voltages below the clamping level can be stepped down or eliminated by the power conditioner and not allowed to pass to the equipment. The clamping level will determine what kinds of hits your power system can take and still protect your equipment. It significantly impacts what your power management system will cost.

Cables that extend from the power conditioner and run under the raised floor to the equipment are often referred to as *power tails*. These are terminated by an appropriate plug receptacle for the type of electrical plug connected to the device. Each tail is connected to a circuit providing the appropriate voltage for the device. Each power conditioner has a limited number of circuits and a limited number of tails that can be connected to each circuit to supply the necessary power.

If worse comes to worse, most computer rooms also have an EPO (Emergency Power Off) switch. This switch should only be used in an emergency where the continued supply of power is causing some danger, since the act of removing power from your equipment suddenly may, itself, cause damage.

UPS

A UPS (uninterruptible power supply) is used when you cannot tolerate downtime because of a power failure. A UPS is basically a complicated battery backup system for your computer system. A UPS for a PC might be relatively inexpensive, whereas a UPS that can keep an entire computer room of mainframe computers running for several hours could cost more than the computers.

The UPS is connected between the power source and the computer and routes power from the power source to the computer during normal operation. If the UPS detects a loss of power from the regular power source, it will provide power of its own to the computer until power from the main source is restored (or until the reserves of the UPS are exhausted). With a UPS installed, you will have time to do an orderly shutdown of the equipment before the UPS power runs out as well. Even if you cannot provide UPS protection for your entire computer room, try to buy small UPS units to protect strategic or critically important machines.

If you have enough UPS capacity, the air conditioning system for the computer room should also be on it. Losing power to the air conditioner is just as bad as losing power to the computers (although the damage takes longer to occur while the room heats up!).

4.1.4 Fire suppression

Halon is a colorless, odorless, inert chemical sometimes used instead of water to extinguish fire. Halon removes the fuel from the fire by displacing the oxygen without harming computer equipment. Halon is more expensive than other conventional fire suppression materials, like water or foam, since it leaves no residue and causes no damage to electronic equipment.

While halon itself is not toxic to humans, it does damage the ozone layer in the Earth's atmosphere. Because of this, use of halon is being phased out. In the future, refilling halon tanks will no doubt become more difficult, just as the use of freon in air conditioners is now being restricted. Though many sites are phasing out their use of halon, it still is one of the fastest and most effective methods of stopping a fire in an enclosed area (such as a computer room). Acceptable chemical substitutes that can be endorsed by the United States Environmental Protection Agency are currently being developed by several companies.

How do you decide what the best method of fire suppression is? How much can you afford to spend to replace equipment damaged by water or foam? Halon will not permanently damage your equipment the way water or foam will. If you can afford to replace the equipment, either through insurance or because you are leasing the equipment from a company who has it insured, then either water or foam is a viable option. (Be sure to check with the insurance carrier to see if the policy changes when using foam or water.)

Replacing equipment will cost you time as well as money. If you cannot afford any significant downtime, even after a major fire, halon may be your only viable option.

If you do use halon, deactivate or remove any sprinkler lines that might be in the ceiling above your computer room (if you are using halon because you don't want to risk water in your computer room, remove the possibility). You should also take a training course on emergency procedures involving the use of halon. Halon, while not toxic to humans, suppresses the fire by removing all the oxygen from the room. If a person is in the room when the halon is "dumped," suffocation is a major threat to the person's.

In addition to a fire suppression system, every computer room should have at least one hand-held fire extinguisher (rated for electrical fire) easily accessible. A large computer room should have more than one.

4.2 Capacity Management

One of the most important aspects of planning a computer room is making sure you have enough space, power, and air conditioning for the equipment you will be placing in the room. You shouldn't simply move equipment into the room until the room fills up.

Vendors of equipment that requires any special environmental conditions (such as mainframes or minicomputers and file servers) usually supply a Site Preparation Guide (this may be a chapter in the installation manual or a separate document). This guide identifies the special requirements of the equipment so that you can have everything ready when the equipment arrives.

4.2.1 Floor space

Everything takes up space, although today's most powerful machines have smaller *footprints* than ever before. A machine's footprint is the amount of space it takes up on the computer room floor. One must also consider the space needed in the front and back of the unit for service access (usually, the space needed is in the front and back and not on the sides, although this is possible).

4.2.2 Cooling

Electronic equipment generates heat; therefore, every device in your computer room will generate some amount of heat. Heat is measured in BTUs (British Thermal Units). Your air conditioning unit is rated to cool a certain number of BTUs. By maintaining a list of the total BTUs generated by your equipment and adding the values of any new equipment to the list (usually available from the Site Preparation Guide) you will be able to determine if your air conditioning capacity is sufficient to cool the room with the new equipment added.

The Site Preparation Guide should also provide the recommended range of temperature and humidity for the equipment. Most modern computer equipment functions well at temperatures between 60°F and 70°F (15°C and 21°C). Equipment such as workstations, intended for an office environment, can tolerate higher temperatures. The ideal humidity level is between 40-percent and 60-percent relative humidity. Again, equipment intended for an office usually has a wider tolerance.

Some guides may note altitude limits. The major factor here is that at higher altitudes, the air is thinner, and air is the critical element in cooling the computer. If the air is thinner, then more of it will have to be moved through the machine to achieve the same amount of cooling.

4.2.3 Power

In the Site Preparation Guide you should find information about the power required by the equipment and the type of plug needed (and sometimes even the length of the power cord used by the machine). Using this information, you can run the correct type of "power tail" from your power conditioner with the proper receptacle and connect it to the proper circuit in your power conditioner with enough available power to handle the additional load.

Input power

Input power is obtained from several different values such as *voltage*, *amperage* (or *current*), *power*, and a *volt-ampere rating*. Voltage is an expression of the amount of "electrical pressure" (potential for moving energy through a circuit) stored or available. The flow of this energy is the *current*, and the rate at which this flow takes place is measured in *amperes*, or *amps*. Power is the amount of energy being dissipated in a circuit and is calculated by multiplying the *current* by the *voltage*, yielding *watts* [Hew81, Chapter 21].

$$watts = amps \times voltage$$

Watts describes power consumption. The supply of power is described by the *volt-ampere rating* (VA rating). The VA rating is the maximum amount of power a circuit can deliver. No equipment turns 100-percent of the energy with which it is supplied into work. Some power is lost through electrical resistance, depending on the components included in the circuit. The relationship between the power needed by the equipment and this loss through resistance is called the *power factor.*

The required VA rating of a circuit for a piece of equipment can be obtained by dividing the amount of power needed by the equipment (in watts) by the power factor (both values can usually be found in the Site Preparation Guide for the equipment). Most power conditioners measure available power in KVA (kilovolt-ampere, or thousands of VA). To obtain KVA rather than VA, divide kilowatts (thousands of watts) by the power factor rather than watts.

$$KVA = \frac{kilowatts}{power factor}$$

Now that you have determined the KVA requirement of the new equipment, you know whether or not your power conditioner can provide enough power for additional load.

Plugs

Just like your appliances at home, each computer and device has an electrical plug used to supply it with power. Unlike your appliances at home, the types of plugs and amounts of power used vary depending on the device. Most home appliances use a standard, three-prong grounded plug (except for larger appliances like dryers and window air conditioners, which need to draw more current than other appliances).

Plug receptacles are referred to in terms of the numbers of poles and wires. The poles are the prongs extending from the plug. The wires are simply the number of wires connected to the various poles. Depending on how the grounding in the circuit is done, a plug can have the same number of wires and poles or one more wire than poles.

The type of receptacle you need to provide will, of course, depend on the plug used by the manufacturer of the computer. Plug and receptacle types and capacities are defined by the National Electrical Manufacturer's Association (NEMA) and assigned numbers to describe them. For example, an NEMA 5-15P is a type-5 plug that is rated to handle 15 amps. The "P" indicates a plug; an "R" would indicate a receptacle. Your Site Preparation Guide might tell you that your new computer has a plug of type NEMA 6-30P. This means you need to provide a receptacle on your power tail of type NEMA 6-30R (on a 30-amp circuit).

Some plug and receptacle pairs will lock so that they do not accidentally come unplugged. This is noted by an "L" preceding the plug or receptacle number. A locking plug of the same type as the previous example would be an NEMA L6-30P. The NEMA L6-30R receptacle is different than the NEMA 6-30R.

The manufacturer will also specify the voltage and amperage requirements for the equipment. You will use this information to make sure your PDU supplies the correct amount of power to the machine.

PDU configurations

If you have the need for multiple power distribution units in your computer room, don't make one common mistake. It is easy to think of the collection of power tails underneath your computer room floor as coming from a single power source. But PDUs, just like computers, can fail. You should take some time to map out which power tails connect to which PDUs and make sure you don't have much cross-dependence on PDUs. For example, if you have a big server system where the CPU cabinet plugs into a power tail from one PDU and the disk drive rack plugs into a power tail from a different PDU, then if *either* of these PDUs fails, this server will go down, so your chance of failure is higher. Try to configure your dependence for each system on a single PDU. If you want to get even more complex, you may want to put machines that are highly dependent on each other for resources (such as a network disk) on the same PDU as well. Machines that are totally unrelated and unnecessary to each other are good candidates to spread out across PDUs.

Grounding

Grounding your electrical circuits is very important in a computing environment. Grounding a circuit provides a path to ground for any current that you or some part of a machine might accidentally contact. The current will take the path of least resistance to achieve a connection to ground and if it happens to be through your body, you will receive a nasty shock. Having a machine grounded greatly lowers the danger of electric shock.

Most industrial sites have a building grid underground to which all grounded circuits are connected. Your PDU will most likely also be connected to this grid. When grounding is provided, it should never be bypassed (and only older homes and appliances now lack grounded circuits).

> A site once regularly experienced equipment failures, especially on its computer displays. The failure rate was noticed by the vendor providing maintenance (who was having to replace an unreasonably high number of displays and wondered why). After ascertaining that the problem was not due to neglect or misuse by the users, the vendor commissioned an electrical engineer to check the building's electrical system. His report indicated that the building ground was unreliable. When the structure was built, the extra expense of a true building ground was a casualty of cost-cutting. The company had moved to a new building before the recommended changes could be made, but did not experience the high failure rate in their new location.

4.3 Disaster Recovery

You don't have to look far to see that disasters can happen to any of us: hurricanes on the East Coast; earthquakes, fires, and mudslides on the West Coast; and floods in the South and Midwest. They all remind us how devastating Mother Nature can be to all of man's relatively fragile installations. The Los Angeles riots and the bombing of the World Trade Center, though caused by humans, were just as debilitating to computer installations and businesses. This was especially true in the case of the World Trade Center, where nearly every company has some dependency on computer systems. One well-prepared company had a "hot" alternate computer center available to which they switched their operation, losing only a few hours of productivity. Others who were not so well prepared lost weeks of work and business. A commonly held belief states that 50-percent of all companies that suffer a major disaster never recover and eventually go out of business, either because of decreased activity or from missing some window of opportunity.

In this new age of distributed computing, disaster recovery has become even more complex because of diverse physical locations and the dependency of systems on remote resources. Sometimes, this diversity in physical location can actually help (since not all of your resources may fall victim to the disaster). But even companies with diverse locations must recover their connectivity to remote resources, which is as important as recovering any data that has been lost.

Can't happen to you? You only run a small operation and your town could hardly be considered a metropolis? Don't try to fool yourself. Floods, fires, and other disasters befall computer installations all the time. Whether a construction crew cuts a power line to your building or someone at the other end of your office park carelessly stores some paint cans in the back of their warehouse, bad things can and will happen to good people. If you are prepared, you can survive.

How important your data is and how quickly you need to be back in operation will vary from one organization to another. If your site is a small college academic department and all your machines are used for projects by students, then the worst you would suffer from a long-term outage is that some people may have to turn in late homework or skip an assignment or two. If you're a multibillion dollar investment firm, you might lose millions per day of downtime. Your disaster recovery plan should be designed to get you back in business from any conceivable level of outage (from a network break or a user deleting a file by mistake all the way up to your whole building burning down). It does no good to have enough insurance to replace the computer equipment if the loss of the data and the time involved to get and install new equipment drives you out of business.

4.3.1 What you can lose

The risks you face are greater than just the obvious one: the loss of your computer. Your data and the productivity of your staff are probably even more valuable than the computers themselves.

Hardware

The most obvious risk is the loss of your hardware. A fire, flood, or earthquake could seriously damage or destroy your hardware. If you own it, it should be insured (self-insurance is fine, as long as you are prepared to replace lost equipment). If you lease your equipment, discuss replacement procedures and timetables with your lessor and the vendor.

Data

A less obvious but much more important risk is to the data you keep on your machines. As already discussed, the machines and the computing environment are just the tools. Your data is the heart and soul of your operation. Without your data, the equipment has little value. If some kind of disaster befalls your equipment, you can bet that your data will have been damaged or destroyed as well. If you have backups of your data but keep them on-site, the risk to them in a site-wide disaster is equally high. This is why off-site storage of at least some of your backup information is so critical. Fireproof vaults are somewhat helpful, but they are no guarantee of data safety.

Some of your data at risk may not even be contained on machines in the computer room, but on machines in offices. Not only are these machines at higher risk from day-to-day accidents, they are not as secure as the machines in the computer room. The more data you can keep on machines in the computer room (and have these office workstations access via the network), the safer it will be. Don't let the relatively small value of the office machine fool you into thinking that the data on it has an equally small value. There is usually no correlation whatsoever.

Time

The least obvious but nonetheless real risk is loss of productivity. The time involved to rebuild your environment to its present production level will not be small, even if you have equipment replacement options and backup data stored off-site. In the best of cases, it will still be days before new equipment can be delivered, set up, and data restored onto it. This is presuming there is a computer room restored to operating condition that can handle the equipment.

Time can be lost by seemingly simple occurrences. If the power to your building goes out, not only do you lose the time while the power is out, but also the time required to restart all the equipment, boot all the servers, and get everything back in working order. In a complicated environment, it might take several hours for everything to be back to normal.

> One company where I worked lost an entire day while the development staff moved machines around because the roof leaked during a heavy rainstorm. The building owners had chosen a time when "it never rains" to make extensive roof repairs.

Remote resources

If your network connection to the outside world fails, your internal machines will continue to operate, but anyone who is depending on this network will be stopped dead in their tracks. Any dependency your site has on outside resources is especially risky because you have much less control over maintaining their availability.

4.3.2 What you can do

So what can you do to minimize the risk of loss to your computing environment and your organization? The most important precaution you can take is to design a procedure for recovering from a disaster and rehearse it on a regular basis, because eventually, no matter what you do to try to prevent disaster, it will happen. You can also keep a constant watch for developing problems and catch them before they become disasters.

Monitoring

Fire alarms in a computer room, just like in the rest of the building, are a must. Often ion sensors are used in computer rooms because they can detect a problem even before smoke is apparent. These alarms will trigger the fire suppression system (whether it be water, foam, or halon) to stop a fire early.

Water sensors under the raised floor are essential. If any source of water in the building (such as overhead sprinkler pipes or chilled water pipes to the air conditioning unit) leaks, the water will collect underneath the raised floor, out of sight of anyone (and in the same area as power cables)! A clogged drain pipe under the raised floor, or a clogged condensation line in the air conditioner, can cause water to collect under the floor when no one would suspect a problem. A water sensor would alert someone to the problem in time to correct it.

Most power conditioners have over-voltage and spike alarms as well as capacity alarms. Air conditioners have temperature and humidity alarms, which sound when either is out of a specified range. All of these alarms should be checked and tested regularly.

It may be helpful to have a weather radio with an alarm on it in an office or open area. You certainly cannot afford to shut down your entire computer room every time a lightning storm comes around, but if one storm is especially violent, you might at least consider the option before it arrives.

Redundancy

The first and best step you can take to provide redundancy in your environment is to do your backups.

Depending on how damaging your downtime would be to your organization, you might consider maintaining a backup "hot" site. This would be another computer room in another building, or even better, another city, that you could switch to in a time of emergency. Some companies in the World Trade Center had such facilities, which saved them from being off-line for weeks after the blast.

Of course, this is an expensive prospect and the majority of sites cannot afford this level of protection. You might be able to reach an agreement with another part of your organization, or even another (probably noncompetitive) organization to share some duplicate hardware in each of your computer rooms. If disaster strikes, one of you can help the other by sharing the duplicated equipment and resources. In a case like this, backups or mirrored images of disks probably reside at the other site and can be brought on-line quickly.

Do what is practical and necessary, but try not to become obsessed with preventing every conceivable problem. You will only make yourself crazy. No matter how prepared you might be, something could happen that you did not prepare for. You can overplan for the amount of return you'll receive for your preparedness.

> My first job in the computer industry was as a summer operator at a site with an IBM 370 mainframe. One day, the operations manager decided we were not well prepared for fire. The company leased its computers from IBM, so IBM would replace any damaged equipment, but the operations manager thought we should make an effort to protect the machines from water damage that they would surely suffer when firemen doused the computer room with water. He ordered sheets of plastic from which we made covers for each piece of equipment. I wondered if the melting plastic might be worse for the machines than the water, and others wondered who would be unfolding these covers and covering the equipment when everyone was running for the exits. In any case, we were cutting the cover for the CPU (which, on a 370, was a separate cabinet with a vent in the top). To cut it accurately, we tossed the cover over the top of the cabinet and began cutting along the bottom. The plastic was effectively cutting off the airflow, both the incoming cool air at the floor and the outgoing hot air from the top vent. After a minute or two, the temperature alarm on the console began to sound, but the CPU shut itself down before we could get the plastic off of the cabinet. It took the IBM FEs the rest of the day to get the machine running again. Nothing more was ever said about plastic covers for the equipment.

4.3.3 Emergency procedures

You should know, practice, and document your emergency procedures. You hope you will be present when any procedure of this nature must be performed, but you may not be. You must provide enough information so that someone, probably not as familiar with the alarms and equipment, has at least a chance of taking appropriate action.

Emergency procedure information should contain a step-by-step procedure for each kind of situation, along with a list of people to be contacted in the event of an emergency. Home phone numbers and pager numbers should be listed here. Privacy should not be an issue, since in a real emergency, you *should* want someone to be able to find you.

Optionally, you may also want to include booting and halting information for various pieces of equipment. If your user community is more than just user-oriented, they might be able to reboot a machine that has crashed on the weekend if the procedure is spelled out for them. This will save you having to come in to do something that is fairly easy. Encourage users to call you if they are unsure of what to do or not confident that they can follow the procedure.

When developing emergency procedures, keep in mind what will usually cause someone to begin looking for a problem. Since someone is usually reacting to an alarm, your procedures should list what to do in the case of each type of alarm that might be triggered. You may wish to contact your local fire department to review your procedures and make sure you have answered all the right questions.

Drastic situations

If a flood, earthquake, or other time-critical event occurs which doesn't allow time for consideration of an action, about all you can do is hit the EPO (Emergency Power Off) switch and hope for the best. Be sure to state that the EPO is only to be used as a last desperate measure in any emergency, since it may result in other problems later.

Fire

If a fire is obvious, then the only recourse is to call the fire department. If the fire is in the computer room, the fire suppression system will take care of it. If it originated outside the room, the building sprinkler system will try to contain it. In either case, you want the fire department there as soon as possible.

If you are in a computer room where a fire alarm is sounding and there is no apparent fire, you may wish to investigate for a couple of minutes to try to find it. It is always possible that you have a faulty sensor somewhere. You can usually find a trouble alarm board that shows the floor plan of the computer room and indicates which sensor has been activated. If you have halon in your computer room, it is probably in a countdown to dump at this point. Most systems have a large yellow button near the trouble alarm board which can be pressed to reset the countdown and give you a little more time to look around or get out. You can hold this button down if someone else is in the room with you who can go look for the cause of the tripped alarm. If you find there is a fire, you can just leave the room and the countdown will continue and dump the halon. Most systems include a button to perform an immediate dump of the halon, but this should only be used for a quickly spreading fire. While halon itself is not toxic, the force with which it is dumped from its container and its effectiveness at removing oxygen from the room will be quite unpleasant on anyone in the room at the time. You would be risking injury or possibly even suffocation. Once halon is dumped, the doors to the room should remain closed. Halon is only effective at removing the oxygen and smothering the fire if new oxygen is not allowed into the room. Of course, if someone was in the room at the time the halon was dumped, the doors should be opened long enough to get them out.

Unless you are extremely confident that a faulty sensor is to blame, you should continue to look for any sign of fire and have the fire department come out. At the same time, you may wish to shut down some or all of the equipment as a precautionary measure.

Water

If a water sensor under the raised floor is triggered, consult the trouble board to locate the sensor. Remove a panel of the floor in the area and visually inspect the floor. If no water is found, begin checking for faulty sensors.

If you do find water pooling up, do not touch it. Even though nothing in the room has shorted out, the water still could be in contact with electrical current. Try to find the source of the water, and examine your drain to see if it is working.

If the water source is slow (such as dripping condensation from the air conditioner), then you may have some time to try to solve the problem. In this case, water probably has not risen to a level to contact any electrical components and you can remove it from the floor with a wet/dry vacuum. You may have to do this on a regular basis until the problem can be corrected (i.e., the drain unclogged).

> A friend of mine spent one Christmas day vacuuming water from beneath his raised floor and cleaning up a mess made by leaky plumbing in the restroom next door to the computer room. He swears by wet/dry vacs, but suggests you not use the same vacuum to clean up water that you use to vacuum toner out of laser printers.

If the water source is fast, you should shut down as much of your equipment as you can. You also want to power down your power conditioner as soon as possible, since it may be damaged when the water comes in contact with the plugs on the power tails. If the water is moving quickly, the EPO switch may be your best option.

Temperature

A temperature alarm should sound before any problem is so severe that it triggers the EPO switch. This will give you some time to find the cause of the problem. Unless you were operating right on the edge of what your air conditioner could handle, a rise in temperature will usually indicate a problem with the air conditioning unit. If resetting it does not bring it back on, you will be faced with shutting down all the machines in the room so they do not operate in too high a temperature.

If a user finds the room temperature rising and cannot get in touch with anyone else, he should be able to perform an orderly shutdown of the equipment until such time as someone can diagnose the problem with the air conditioner.

Humidity

The procedure for reacting to a humidity alarm is about the same as that for a temperature alarm. Unless some unique occurrence can be identified as the cause of a drastic change in the humidity level, it probably indicates a problem with the humidifier in the air conditioner. If the problem cannot be diagnosed and corrected quickly, the machines in the room should be shut down.

If your machines have been exposed to high humidity levels, even when you get the air conditioner working properly and the humidity level in the room back to normal, you should not power the computers back on immediately. Water may have condensed inside the machine on boards or connections. Once the room is back to a fairly dry condition, you should wait a couple of hours before powering on any of the equipment to give it sufficient time to dry out.

Over-voltages and under-voltages

If an alarm in the power conditioner trips and it is a problem that is continuing, the power conditioner will eventually shut itself down. This abrupt removal of power from your computers is at best hard on them; at worst, some will suffer damage. You would like to find the problem and correct it before the PDU shuts down.

Generally, a novice user is not going to know enough other than to call you or someone else who can take some action. A user's main option would be to shut down some equipment to prevent damage to it.

If you have enough time, you can find which circuit is out of range and shut down only the machines on that circuit. This should bring the PDU back into its nominal operating range and give you more time to find the real cause.

Once the PDU shuts down, it will stay off until it is manually reset. Under no circumstances allow a user to reset the PDU. All equipment in the room should be powered off before power is restored.

4.3.4 Recovering

Shutting down is the easy part. If you're not there, the equipment will do it for you (albeit with some amount of damage). The hard part is putting everything back into working order.

You may face relatively simple recovery measures, such as repairing damaged file systems and restoring a few lost files. A more complex recovery might include replacing damaged hardware. If you do your own maintenance, this can still be handled quickly. If some act of nature affected companies in your area and you have vendor maintenance, you might have to wait for a visit from your vendor whenever they can schedule it. Like the insurance companies, they will be pretty busy at a time like this.

If the damaged hardware includes a disk drive, then the process is more involved. Not only must you replace the hardware, you must also replace the data on the disk drive from your backups.

The greatest effort will be involved when you have to replace large amounts of hardware or move your computer operation to an alternate site to provide service until the damaged site can be restored to working order. The procedure for this will be extremely specific for each site, but since you have been practicing the procedure (right?), you should have it well in hand.

The most common type of recovery that affects your entire computing environment will be recovery from a complete loss of power. Whether this occurs because your PDU shuts down, your air conditioning unit trips the EPO switch because of temperature, or your local electric utility cuts through the wrong line, once you have power back, you still have work to do.

Whenever you completely lose power, you should go around to all of your equipment (including workstations in offices) and switch everything off. You can enlist the help of your users here by asking them to power their own equipment off and not power it on again until you direct them to do so. You can also get "drop out" surge protectors that stay powered off when the power fails.

When power is restored, begin turning on the machines in the computer room. File servers and mainframes, which the workstations depend on, must be operational before a workstation will boot up fully. If all the workstations are booting and requesting network services at the same time your file servers are trying to come up, your network will be jammed with unanswered requests and booting up will take even longer than normal.

Once the computers in the computer room are back in working order, instruct your users to power on their workstations (you may wish to tell blocks of users a few at a time so that the resource requests don't come in to the file servers at the same time).

Chapter 5

Networking

One of the most useful, and most complex, aspects of any computer environment is the network. Your local network binds all of your distributed resources together into an accessible whole. The external networks to which your site may connect provide access to information and communications with users all over the world. In many environments, the computer itself is becoming only a tool used to access remote devices, information databases, and users.

Connecting computers together began in an effort to provide an easy way to move data from one computer to another without having to write the data on magnetic media, transport it to the other computer, and read it back in. As networks became more flexible and provided faster data transmission, the applications invented to take advantage of them grew. Today, a computer that sits alone, not connected to any other computer, only processing data that is provided to it on tape or disk, is almost unthinkable.[1]

5.1 Networking Standards

The two major types of information networks are *circuit-switched* and *packet-switched* networks. In a circuit-switched network, a circuit is

[1] This is still done, but only in cases where extreme security is required, or financial constraints prevent a machine from being connected to any network.

built between source and destination and all the while the communication is taking place, that same path through the network (the circuit) remains established and cannot be used by anyone else. This is the way our phone system works. When someone on the East Coast calls someone on the West Coast, the path the call takes through the country may not be the same today as it was yesterday, but all during a single call, the path is open and the connection remains established. For analog voice connections, this works well.

Packet-switched networks work better for data since you won't notice if one packet shows up a few milliseconds later than usual (if the next packet of your digitized voice showed up late, the other end would hear the delay). In a packet-switched network, it is not necessary for each packet to take the same path through the network as the packet before it. In fact, this is what makes a packet-switched network more robust. If a path fails during a connection, subsequent packets can be routed via another path and still arrive at the destination (whereas if one node of the path of your phone call goes down, your call gets disconnected). As long as all the packets arrive in the right order (which is what the network protocols are for), the user doesn't care how they got there. This allows software to route around congestion and modify the path being used as another path becomes more efficient.

While circuit-switched networks are interesting and quite useful, for the purposes of computer networking they are rarely used (except in the case of dial-up).

5.1.1 Standards organizations

The International Organization for Standardization (ISO) was formed in 1946 to oversee standards in many areas [Tan88, pp. 28–29]. People were learning that defining standard attributes for items manufactured in this industrial age made life much easier. The wisdom of this adherence to standards is what lets us purchase replacement parts for items around our home, like batteries and light bulbs for our flashlights, cassette tapes for our stereos and VCRs, and thousands of other products. While there are choices within each group of standardized items, the choices are much more limited than if each manufacturer had developed its own version of an item. This also allows other manufacturers to compete by providing compatible parts (which is a big reason for the explosion of companies and advances in technology in the computer industry in the last decade).

The United States member group of ISO is the American National Standards Institute (ANSI™). ANSI is probably best known in the computer industry for defining minimum standard requirements for computer languages, but it also defines many other standards. Standards adopted by ANSI are sometimes adopted by ISO as international standards as well, but ANSI only has authority in the United States. ANSI is a private, nonprofit organization made up mostly of computer systems and network vendors.

The Institute of Electrical and Electronics Engineers (IEEE®) is a professional organization that has made significant contributions to the standardization effort in the computer industry. Some of the IEEE standards have been adopted by ISO.

Another international organization that oversees standards for telephone communications specifically is the International Consultative Committee on Telephony and Telegraphy (CCITT).[2] The U.S. State Department is the member organization for the United States. Since computer networks largely run over some kind of telephone line, CCITT and ISO are often both involved in the development of networking standards.

The Internet Architecture Board (IAB) oversees work done in the Internet community involving Internet Protocols, and the Internet Engineering Task Force (IETF) deals with Internet standards (for more information on the Internet, see page 138).

The reason for all these standards bodies (and there are many more than just the ones mentioned here[3]) is so that networking methods and architectures are fully described so that computers manufactured by different vendors will be able to communicate with each other. If a vendor developed its own communications architecture and shared it

[2] The acronym is from its French name Comité Consultatif Internationale de Télégraphique et Téléphonique.

[3] As the now famous quote of networking expert Andrew Tanenbaum goes: "The nice thing about standards is that you have so many to choose from." [Tan88, p. 254]

with no one (which was common in the past), then no computer except another made by that same vendor would be able to communicate with it. When sites purchased all their machines from a single vendor, this was not as much of a problem as it is in today's heterogeneous environments.

Having networking standards is like buying a clock-radio, taking it home, and knowing it will work because the 110-volt plug on the clock-radio fits the standard 110-volt outlet in your home.

5.1.2 The OSI networking model

The ISO subcommittee on OSI (Open Systems Interconnection) developed a general architecture for standard computer communications. This seven-layer[4] reference model has become the international standard for computer network architectures. Starting at the lowest level, the seven layers are:

1. physical layer
2. data link layer
3. network layer
4. transport layer
5. session layer
6. presentation layer
7. application layer

A protocol stack would be one or more protocols that perform the function of each layer, "stacked on top of each other" to form a coherent path from the bottom to the top.

Though not every protocol in use today adheres to the OSI network model (indeed, many of the most popular ones do not), it is considered an excellent model for describing the different functions provided by any networking protocol stack.

[4] It has always been a source of personal amusement that there are as many networking layers as there are "deadly sins."

Tanenbaum provides an excellent discussion of the particulars of each network layer in his book on networking, [Tan88], a book many view as the bible of computer networking. Chapter 4 of [Ste90] gives a solid introduction to networking issues, and Chapter 10 of [Com91] provides a detailed discussion of protocol layering. Since many of the protocols in the UNIX world do not adhere to the OSI model, it is used here more as an illustration of the concepts involved than as a strict set of guidelines.

5.2 Physical Networks

The physical network is the wiring, the routers, bridges, and other devices that create the medium across which your data can move from one machine to another.

Many different kinds of cables and configurations make up a network. Connecting a network to another network (creating an *internetwork*) may use one or more of several types of interconnecting devices (see page 133). While this section by no means contains an exhaustive list, even for today, it will give you an idea of how many different options are available and where to go to find out more about the various components of a physical network.

5.2.1 Media

The first problem is getting a signal from one computer to the other. Almost any kind of network connection to a computer involves some kind of cable running from one machine to another (and possibly on to others from there). While radio communication is an up-and-coming topic, it is not in wide use today because of the security problems inherent in its use. In an environment where security is not necessary and cabling is a significant obstacle, radio networks will soon be more popular. However, for the purposes of this overview, only cabled networks will be examined.

Twisted-pair

A *twisted-pair* cable is exactly what it sounds like: two pairs of wires, twisted to minimize electromagnetic interference, connected to a computer or other device at each end. Generally, you will find RS-232 connectors of some kind on the ends of such a cable (see page 71). These connections provide low-cost, low-speed, point-to-point connections, usually over a short distance. The wires are twisted to reduce the electromagnetic interference that might be caused by another pair of wires close by (a pair of untwisted wires constitutes a simple antenna; the twist eliminates this [Tan88, p. 58]).

Twisted-pair cable was probably the first networking medium, since it was cheap and easy, and in many cases already existed. As networking needs grew, capacity and distance needs grew as well, and twisted-pair cabling was unable to grow along with the need. Twisted-pair cables perform well in an office environment, and they are making a comeback, replacing coaxial cable for short-range, local area network cables.

Coaxial

A *coaxial* cable (also called *coax*) is like the cable that runs from your wall to your television. The solid copper wire in the middle of the cable carries the signal, and the shielding around it acts as the signal ground. Because it is shielded, it is less prone to data corruption due to electrical interference.

Coax cable can transmit multiplexed signals (multiple signals sent at once by sending each in a different frequency range). This increases the overall capacity of the cable, the *bandwidth*. Coax cable is more expensive than twisted-pair.

Fiber optic

Twisted-pair and coaxial cable both use copper wire to transmit the electrical signal from one location to another. A fiber optic cable uses strands of fiber to send the signal via light waves from one location to another.

Fiber optic cables have the advantage of being smaller than most shielded wire cables. Not only is the cable itself smaller, but the capacity for data is much higher; therefore many more signals can be sent in less physical space. Fiber also has lower error rates than wire cable. One of the biggest advantages of fiber optic cable is that it is not vulnerable to electromagnetic interference the way copper wire can be.

The major disadvantage of fiber optics is the expense. Compared to copper wire, fiber is extremely expensive. You really do get what you pay for. Another potential disadvantage to fiber is that it is much more delicate than metal wire. Fiber can be easily damaged by overbending, and splicing into it should only be attempted by someone with experience and the appropriate equipment.

5.2.2 Topologies

A network *topology* is the physical layout of your network [Nem92, pp. 47–50]. Computer networks may be built in several topologies. The most common are the point-to-point, bus, ring, and star topologies. Most others are variations or combinations of these.

Point-to-point

Figure 5.1 shows the simple topology of a point-to-point network. A connection like this would most likely be to a remote machine that is accessible via a leased or dial-up telephone line. Usually, the distance involved precludes your wanting to run a network cable of your own (such as in the case of a leased line). If a leased line is more than you want to pay for a seldom-used connection, a dial-up connection that is only active while it is being used may be more appropriate.

Bus

Figure 5.2 shows the topology of a *bus* network. The bus network is probably one of the most common network topologies. Hosts can

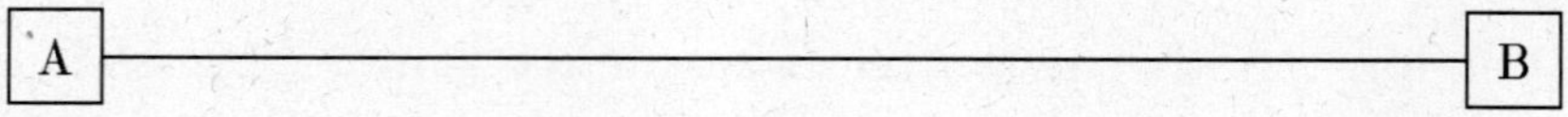

Figure 5.1: A point-to-point network topology

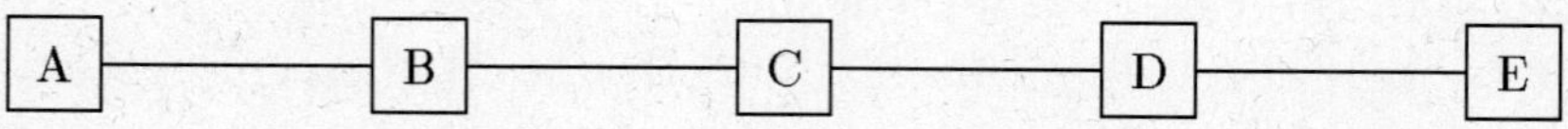

Figure 5.2: A bus network topology

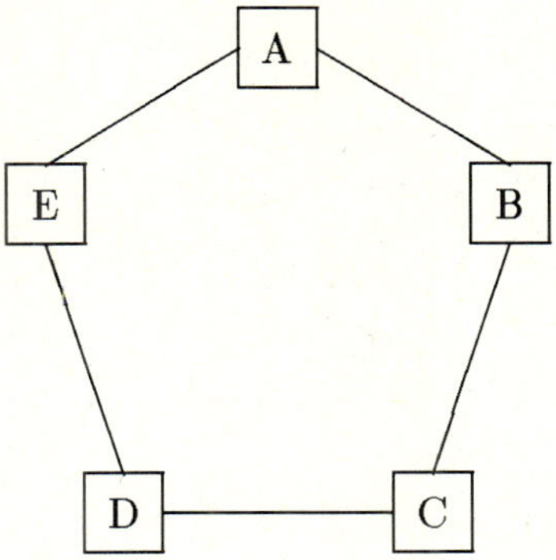

Figure 5.3: A ring network topology

be connected at any point along the cable[5] and can communicate with all other hosts on the wire. Communication is by *broadcast.* A host puts a packet on the wire to transmit it to another host. Embedded in that packet is a designation for the destination host. All hosts "see" the packet go by, but only the networking software of the intended host will copy the packet off the wire. This allows easy implementation of a real broadcast packet type that all hosts should pick up. Depending on the medium used, there will be length limits for the wire before repeaters or routers will need to be added.

Ring

Figure 5.3 shows the topology of a *ring* network. A ring network is similar to a bus network except that the two ends are connected together. The ring is not a broadcast network like the bus. It is really a collection of point-to-point links that form a circle. Each host then takes its turn putting a packet on the network and each succeeding host passes it along to the next host.

[5] Well, almost. Most standards specify minimum spacing distances due to signal wavelengths.

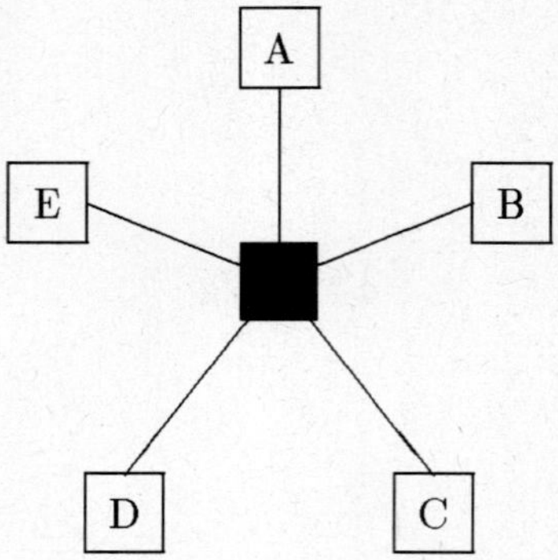

Figure 5.4: A star network topology

Star

Figure 5.4 shows the topology of a *star network*. The star differs from the bus or the ring in that all connections come in to a central location (or hub) for connection.

Note that with some of the newer multiple connection boxes for Ethernet™ networks (sometimes referred to as *wiring hubs* or *concentrators*), a local bus or ring network could appear to be a star network. Ethernet can now be implemented over twisted-pair wires run into a network box. The physical layout will appear to be a star (because all wires from all offices feed into this one central box); however, this is misleading. The bus network is now contained inside the box, but it is still a bus network. The connections from the offices to the network box simply act as very long *drop cables* (cables that are "dropped" from the network to, for example, a workstation in an office).

5.2.3 Implementations

A functioning network requires more than just connecting wires together. Once the medium is available, all participants must agree on how signals will be sent across it. The electrical specifications and data formats must be understood and agreed upon by all players to make the network function properly.

Packet-based services are most often used in networking computers together because of the ease with which packets can be transferred and routed. When the available bandwidth becomes saturated, it is usually a simple matter to add more connections and route packets via the new connection while keeping these facts from the end user, who simply sees a completed data transfer. As the use of wide-area networks increases and the world becomes even more distributed, these on-demand networking needs will increase. No one will want to pay for a high-capacity dedicated circuit when they only need it once in a while.

Some of these network implementations operate over the same medium but the specifics of the network traffic make them incompatible. It could be argued that some of these implementations are simply protocols. They are discussed here because they represent a major category of network type and, in most cases, multiple protocols can be run across them, making them a higher-level protocol at the very least. They are presented in approximate order of popularity in the UNIX community.

Ethernet

Ethernet[6] was developed by Xerox® PARC (Palo Alto Research Center) in the early 1970s. It was standardized through cooperation between Xerox, Intel®, and DEC® (Digital Equipment Corporation), and this standard was adopted by the IEEE as IEEE 802.3. Ethernet is explained in good detail in [NSS89, Chapter 14] and [Com91, pp. 20–28].

Ethernet is set up in a bus topology and uses the CSMA/CD (Carrier Sense Multiple Access with Collision Detection) scheme to decide what network node is allowed to transmit next. Each host listens to the carrier signal on the network and when it finds a "clear spot" it puts its packet on the wire. It also listens for a *collision* (where two hosts tried

[6] The term "ether" came from the notion that the network was some magical place "out there" (in the ether).

to send a packet at exactly the same time). If a collision is detected, it backs off for a random amount of time before retransmitting (the other host will back off a different random amount of time, so the two will not collide next time). This is analogous to a conversation between two people when both begin to talk at the same time. They stop and wait (probably different amounts of time), and one begins again. Should a second collision occur, the host will back off an exponential amount of time and retry until it can transmit its packet. This way, should the network become jammed because of some problem, this host doesn't add to the problem by continuously trying to send its packet. This is efficient with light to medium loads, but performance degrades quickly in a congested network. On an overloaded network, there is no guarantee when a packet may finally be successfully transmitted.

Three basic types of cables can be used to create an Ethernet network. The oldest type of Ethernet cable is known as *thicknet*. The official name for this is 10Base-5. This is $\frac{1}{2}''$ coaxial cable which is generally yellow in color [NSS89, p. 226], [Tan88, p. 142]. This is the most expensive type of Ethernet cable, but for years it was the only type available.

Not until *thinnet* was developed was there a cheaper alternative. Thinnet, officially called 10Base-2, was sometimes referred to as *cheapernet* because of its cost relative to regular 10Base-5 Ethernet cable. Thinnet is what most of you know as television cable ($\frac{1}{4}''$ thick, black coaxial cable). Being much cheaper, easier to handle, and less obtrusive to the surroundings, thinnet quickly became the choice in smaller environments [NSS89, pp. 226–227].

An even easier implementation for small offices is Ethernet over twisted-pair, 10Base-T. This is typically run to RJ-45 modular phone connectors in the office so that simple phone plugs can be used to hook up (and unhook) machines to (and from) the network. The twisted-pair wires run to a telephone room of some kind where they hook to a networking box (a hub) which provides the bus for the entire network. Moving people from one network to another is extremely simple in this case, since their wire in the phone room need only be moved to another location on the networking box (or possibly a different box). It is no longer necessary to string Ethernet cable through the ceiling or under the floor to make the correct network available in a particular office [NSS89, p. 228].

With 10Base-5 cable (thick Ethernet cable), a *transceiver* is connected to the cable to provide access to the network. The computer is connected by a *drop cable* to the transceiver and the network connection is complete. A *fan-out box* can also be used to create multiple connections at the same physical location on the Ethernet cable (replacing the same number of individual transceivers). These are useful in a computer room where many machines are connected in the same physical area.

The main method used to diagnose hardware problems on an Ethernet is called TDR (Time Domain Reflectometry) [Tan88, p. 142], [Nem92, Chapter 14]. A TDR device will give you an indication of breaks or bad spots in your physical network cable by reflecting a signal down and back on the wire. Ethernet cable is sensitive to bends. Bends that are too pronounced can cause failures. Ethernet doesn't always fail completely, however. It sometimes simply appears "noisy" (i.e., throughput is low because noise generated by faults in the cable appears to be traffic to the hosts). Some TDRs should not be used on a "live" network; the electrical signals used by the TDR could damage computer equipment connected to the network. Check with the vendor of your TDR about whether or not it is safe to TDR a running network.

> Sometimes a TDR won't inform you of a problem that is localized to a single workstation. I once spent the better part of a day trying to figure out why someone's workstation wouldn't "talk" on the net. The connection in the office looked fine, the Ethernet cable checked out, but monitoring the network from another workstation, we found that no packets from the user's workstation were appearing on the net. Only later did we discover that he had pushed his workstation all the way back on his desk and jammed the drop cable up against the wall, shorting it out (there must have been a bad spot in his drop cable for this to happen). As soon as we pulled the workstation away from the wall, everything worked just fine. We got him a new drop cable anyway. The slide connectors on Ethernet cables are notorious for having problems staying secure.

Token Bus and Token Ring

The Token Bus was developed as an alternative to the CSMA/CD behavior of Ethernet. The inability of Ethernet to guarantee a maximum delivery time was unacceptable for factories where networks controlled robots and assembly lines. The Token Bus (IEEE 802.4) is a bus network, but it passes a token around in a logical circle to determine whose turn it is to put a packet on the network. This guarantees that each host will get a turn to transmit within a finite amount of time [Tan88, pp. 148–153], [GK92].

The Token Ring (IEEE 802.5) is similar to the Token Bus except that the network is actually configured in a ring. Each node with a token passes the token and a packet to the next node in the ring. If no packet needs to be sent, the token itself is passed to the next host [Tan88, pp. 153–163].

Two types of Token Ring networks, 4 Mbs and 16 Mbs, allow each site to select the best tradeoff between capacity and cost (since, as usual, higher capacity comes with increased cost).

ARCnet

ARCnet is physically similar to Ethernet and Token Ring, but it does not strictly adhere to either standard. ARCnet is probably the most widely used method of physical networking that does not have an IEEE standard [CKM90, p. 11]. Originally developed by Datapoint, ARCnet uses coaxial cable and token passing protocols in one or more star topologies [CKM90, p. 5]. ARCnet can also be implemented using 10Base-T wiring, and is referred to as Lattisnet in this case.

ISDN

ISDN (Integrated Services Digital Network) is not quite like the other network implementations discussed so far, but deserves coverage. ISDN is basically a redesign of the worldwide telephone network [Tan88, pp. 90–110], [Gul91]. It is an attempt to bring the "primitive" (by modern computing standards) circuit-switched, analog telephone network into the age of packet-switched, digital signaling. Once this is done, computer networking will be able to take advantage of the existing network infrastructure provided by the telephone companies. So, while you personally will not lay down an ISDN network (as you might an Ethernet network), you probably will, at some time in the future, set up an ISDN interface to connect another host or network to your network.

ISDN provides multiple channels for voice and digital data along the same connection so that more and different kinds of information may travel across the connection simultaneously. In the current analog technology, you can send voice *or* data on a phone line, but not both. Other information (such as the call waiting tone telling you another call is coming in on your line) must be sent in the middle of the connection, interrupting the audio (or even worse, breaking the carrier signal on a modem and disconnecting you!). With ISDN, these different types of information will be sent independently of each other.

ISDN provides a completely digital, end-to-end connection over existing telephone lines. It is based on the CCITT standard and conforms to the ISO/OSI seven-layer model. The connection is made up of two

64-Kbps (kilobits per second) channels for voice or data (known as "B" channels) and a 16-Kbps channel for signaling and low-speed data (known as a "D" channel). This entire package (2 64-Kbps channel and 1 16-Kbps) is known as "2B plus D" and is the basic ISDN connection. ISDN also provides for a higher volume connection type called "23B plus D."[7]

Many PCs and UNIX workstations currently support ISDN driver boards. For a more in-depth discussion of ISDN and its future, see [Hel91].

X.25

X.25 is an OSI compliant protocol that is generally used over leased telephone lines and dial-up lines. The first X.25 Recommendation was issued by CCITT in 1976. X.25 comprises the bottom three layers of the OSI stack [Sch90], [Tan88, p. 254].

X.25 is mainly used in point-to-point dial-up and leased-line connections. Falling somewhere between the digital nature of ISDN and the high-volume capabilities of ATM (see below), X.25 will likely see less use in the future, although it is still popular in Europe.

FDDI

As mentioned above, fiber optic cable has several advantages over copper wire, most notably its high bandwidth and invulnerability to electromagnetic interference. Several networking architectures use fiber optic cable [Tan88, pp. 168–175], but by far the most common is FDDI (and its copper wire implementation CDDI).

FDDI (Fiber Distributed Data Interface) is a Token Ring implementation on a fiber optic cable [Nem92, pp. 197–199], [Nem94]. FDDI provides data throughput at rates in the range of 100 Mbps (megabits per second)[Tan88, pp. 166–168]. Its high bandwidth makes it suitable for use as a backbone network. Due to the relatively high cost of fiber cables, backbone and other "important" high-volume network segments see the greatest use of FDDI. Network segments contained in a single

[7] In Europe, 30B plus D is used.

building where the higher bandwidth is not required are usually built with one of the previously discussed cheaper alternatives.

Frame Relay

Frame Relay is a fairly new networking mechanism and is based on the Link Access Protocol D (LAPD), an ISDN signaling protocol [Smi93]. Data transfers via Frame Relay are connection-oriented, that is, a connection is established at the beginning of the data transfer and continues as long as the transfer is in progress.

ATM

The Asynchronous Transfer Mode is also a recent addition to networking and is emerging as an international standard. ATM is designed for large data transfers. Currently, only users with special high-volume needs are installing ATM networks, but it should become popular because of its ability to transport *any* type of data packet. Any networking protocol can be used across an ATM connection.

5.2.4 Coverage

Local Area Networks

Local Area Networks (LANs) are those networks that carry the bulk of your day-to-day traffic between machines under your control. Generally, this takes place within your group of offices, your building, or even between several buildings in your office complex.

Your LAN provides access to file servers, printers, tape drives, and other devices and resources needed by users or machines on a regular basis. Generally, you need high-speed data transfer rates for operations like accessing files from file servers. Typical LAN data transfer rates are in the range of 4 Mbps—2 Gbps (gigabits per second)[Com91].

LANs are usually built from twisted-pair and coaxial cable, often using fiber cables to connect buildings.

Metropolitan Area Networks

A Metropolitan Area Network (MAN) is a fairly new term. Until recently, LANs and WANs served most purposes, but more specific short-distance methods of networking are now needed. These networks only make sense for short distances, but don't make much sense for truly "local" networking (e.g., crossing a city street to another building where you do not control the property).

Fiber cables and telephone lines leased from the local phone company may provide your transmission medium in a MAN. A short-distance microwave transmission might also provide a good medium, depending on the application.

Typical speeds of a MAN are between 56 Kbps and 100 Mbps [Com91].

Wide Area Networks

Wide Area Networks (WANs) are usually implemented across some form of long-distance telephone line. Sometimes called "long-haul" networks, WANs connect sites separated by greater distances than do LANs and MANs. In these cases, speed is not usually the greatest asset because the sites are not closely coupled (i.e., depending on each other for information necessary to operate). Sites to which you connect on a WAN generally provide access to information that will be copied to a local file.

Some organizations may have remotely distributed collections of data upon which they are dependent for day-to-day operations. Even in these cases, however, speed is not usually the primary issue; access to the data is of primary importance; speed is secondary. Typical WAN speeds are between 9.6 Kbps and 45 Mbps [Com91].

These connections may be traditional dial-up lines, 56Kb digital leased lines (sometimes called *switched 56* lines), T1, or T3 lines. T1 and T3 lines are dedicated links that provide a higher bandwidth by providing multiple channels for data. A T1 provides 24 64-Kbps lines (8 Kbps is used for network control so each data channel is equivalent to a 56-Kbps leased line). A *fractional T1* can be purchased when the full T1 capacity of 1.5 Mbps is not required. A T3 connection provides almost 45 Mbps.

Not surprisingly, the increased capacities of T1 and T3 lines come with an increased cost. However, the increase is not quite a linear increase with capacity. Volume, as is often the case, will make a product more inexpensive per unit. Exact costs will depend on the long-distance provider and your local telephone company.

T1 lines are becoming more and more common, while T3 lines are still rare in all but the largest environments. Satellite links can also be used, but as you might expect, this is extremely expensive and usually only used in large organizations where high-bandwidth intercontinental connections are necessary.

5.2.5 Interconnection devices

A variety of devices can be used to *internetwork*, that is, connect one network to another. These are some of the most widely used devices.

Modems

For years, modems provided the primary method of connecting two remote computers together. Initially, modems were used to dial in to a computer system and obtain a connection for a terminal. Later, software was written to allow file transfer and other primitive networking functions to be performed over a dial-up connection (page 150).

Modem technology has changed drastically in the last decade, and this is sure to continue in the next. Once "connecting to a computer" meant dialing the phone, waiting for the tone, and then depressing the receiver into an acoustic coupler (two suction-cup fittings on a modem that allowed the analog signals to be sent through the receiver and speaker in the telephone handset). These were the days when someone could whistle in the room and generate random data on your teletype printout! These acoustic modems usually provided 110-bps connections (see page 76).

Once direct wiring of modems was available (bypassing the acoustic nature of data transfer), they became faster and more reliable. In the 1970s, 300-bps modems became common and 1200-bps modems followed soon thereafter.[8] Modems transferring data at 2400 bps arrived in the early 1980s and are about as primitive as anyone can tolerate today. The 1980s saw 9600-bps modems become common. In the 1990s, 28,800 bps modems are becoming the norm and some can get up to 57,600 bps.

The speed of current modem protocols is limited to 14,400 bps across ordinary analog telephone lines. To receive data at rates faster than this requires data compression. By compressing the data before it is transmitted, fewer bits are required to send the data. Modems with built-in data compression algorithms can send data at faster *effective* rates across analog lines. Digital lines have a much higher capacity.

Older modems were based on the Bell 103 and Bell 212A standards. Later, the MNP (Microcom Networking Protocol) Class 2 and 4 error detection algorithms and the MNP Class 5[9] data compression algorithms were later built into modem hardware.

Several CCITT protocol standards describe different speeds and types of modem communications. V.32 is a 9.6-Kbps protocol, V.32bis delivers 14.4 Kbps, V.42 adds error control, and V.42bis adds compression. A faster protocol standard is in the works, commonly referred to as V.fast, but it is currently in committee within CCITT. V.fast should bring modem speeds up to 28,800 bps (uncompressed). Experts believe this should be about the limit for speed of data across analog lines (though many believed 14,400 bps was going to be the limit). Fax modem protocols include CCITT V.21, V.27ter, and V.29.

Repeaters

A repeater is a device that is connected to two network cables that effectively makes them function as a single cable. Most cables have a physical limitation on their length before the signal begins to degrade

[8] To get a sense of the rate of change, a 1200-bps modem in the early 1980s sold for about $500 and represented the best you could do in terms of speed. Ten years later, that same modem sold for about $50, when anyone would buy it.

[9] MNP classes 1-4 are in the public domain, MNP 5 is licensed technology.

and delivery along the entire length of the cable cannot be guaranteed [Nem92, pp. 175–176].

A repeater simply copies bits coming in on one wire to the other wire and vice versa. It does no interpretation or conversion of the bits. The advantage here is that no matter what protocols are used, the repeater will simply repeat the information on the other wire. The disadvantage is that if there are bad packets or noise on the wire, the repeater will dutifully copy this corrupt information onto the other network as well, propagating any problem to the other network segment.

Bridges

A bridge is like a repeater except that it copies packets, rather than the raw bits, from one wire to another. A bridge can usually be set to copy a certain type of packet, thus blocking malformed packets and noise from "escaping" onto the other network [Nem92, pp. 178–183].

Some bridges, known as *smart bridges* can be configured so that they do not forward packets to the other network when they know they will not be needed there (i.e., a packet destined for a host on network A will still reach the bridge, but does not need to be forwarded to network B because its destination is on network A). These are also called *adaptive* or *learning bridges* [Com91, p. 27].

Bridges and repeaters are only good when length limitations require you to physically break up your network segments. They do little to decrease traffic on any single segment (although an adaptive bridge will help some).

Routers

Routers are used to isolate network traffic to only those machines that need to be involved. A router is set up between two or more different network segments. Packets destined for machines on the same network segment are not passed (as in the case of a repeater) to another network. Only packets bound for off-segment hosts are sent to the router, which then puts the packet on the appropriate segment [Nem92, pp. 183–184].

Routers work by understanding the networking protocol being used, and are therefore much more complex than bridges and repeaters. Routers also allow you to send a packet from your machine in your office to another machine across the country, simply because all the routers in between know about the existence of the various other network segments to which they are connected. Traffic that travels through routers is not generally "normal" network traffic but is destined for some specific remote host (such as an electronic mail message to a colleague in another department or at another institution).

5.3 Interconnecting Networks

So what good are all these different sorts of networks? Once they are in place, if your routing, bridging, and repeating are set up correctly, you will be able to use application programs or write your own application programs to run on a machine and access information on another machine in any part of your active network. This is known as interconnecting networks, connecting different networks to one another.

In order to interconnect your various networks, the hardware and software in your network must be configured correctly. This is far from a simple problem. In fact, proper network configuration is one of the more complex tasks facing the system administrator. Failures within a network that cut off access to other resources are a common problem for system administrators. Management of computer systems today includes management of the networks to which they are connected, for often these systems are useless without those networks.

5.3.1 Physical interconnection

The physical interconnection of networks is the process of getting the cables, repeaters, bridges, routers, modems, and any other necessary pieces of equipment set up and connected together to do the job.

In addition, some of these devices will require configuration and management on a regular basis. In general, repeaters and bridges are fairly simple devices which don't require much attention once they are set up correctly. However, routers vary in complexity and are more difficult to set up. At the very least, a router must know about the networks to which it is connected and the address ranges used on each network.

Take time to plan (and even draw) the physical layout and interconnection of your network segments. See [Per92] for all the information you will ever need to know about interconnecting networks.

5.3.2 Software interconnection

Interconnecting networks will require some software configuration, both on your routers and on your computers. Depending on the protocol used, you will probably specify some kind of default routing information so that each host knows where to send any packet destined for a physical network segment other than the one to which it is directly connected.

You may have several network segments in your local network as well as having access to remote network segments in other parts of your organization or even another organization. Having multiple segments in your own local network, you will need to provide access to some resources that you choose not to duplicate on every network (like printers or certain kinds of large or seldom accessed files). If you can afford the duplication of resources, or if only one group of people needs access to the resource, it is best to put the resource on the local segment where it is needed so access doesn't require routing to another network segment, especially if the resource is constantly accessed (like a user's home directory).

Try not to access resources like often-used utilities or home directory spaces through a router. Anything with a high access rate like this should be accessed on the local segment whenever possible.

Breaking your network into separate segments (called *subnetting*) may seem like a lot of work, especially if you don't really need to reduce the traffic yet. Unless you know your environment has a finite size, you can almost be guaranteed that eventually you will need to subnet. Don't wait until the last minute; it is much easier to do it before it becomes a necessity. You can monitor network traffic and deal with the problem before it begins to hinder your users' work. This also gives you some time to plan and schedule the work. Even a network with just a couple of heavily used servers could benefit from subnetting.

5.4 The Internet

Before diving into the various networking protocols and services that are in use today, it may be useful to talk about *how* these protocols and services are used by describing the "real world" that has been built using them.

Most of this "real world" revolves around the worldwide network known as the Internet. This network, which is really a collection of many smaller networks, had its beginnings in the research lab.

5.4.1 ARPANET

The ARPANET was developed and funded by ARPA (the Advanced Research Projects Agency of the United States Department of Defense, which changed its name to DARPA in 1972). BBN (Bolt, Beranek, and Newman, a networking company in Cambridge, MA) was contracted to provide the software. By late 1969, the ARPANET was born[10] [Com91, p. 33].

This network was originally intended as a testing ground for packet-switched networking research for government agencies, research laboratories, and a few educational institutions.

In 1983 the entire ARPANET completed a conversion to the then still new IP (Internet Protocol) suite of networking protocols (see page 147). IP and its component protocols had been developed and proven by this research network and were quickly accepted because DARPA provided the implementation free of charge to encourage its use. By the mid-1980s, there were thousands of hosts connected to the ARPANET. What started out as an experiment had evolved into a production network.

[10]For a humorous and poetic look at the birth of the Arpanet, see "The Big Bang!" in RFC 1102 [PKCB89]. See page 143 for more information on RFCs.

5.4.2 NSFNET

DARPA, seeing that their experimental network was now in production use by sites all over the country, wanted to discontinue its funding of the project. They could hardly experiment on a network that was in use by the public, nor did they wish to be in the business of providing network service.

In 1987 the National Science Foundation moved to establish a backbone network, known as NSFNET.[11] Over time, NSF took over funding and administration of this top level of the former ARPANET and independent organizations were formed underneath to administer geographically subordinate pieces of the regional networks. Many of these organizations are for-profit companies that sell network connectivity; some are educational institutions that oversee getting other local organizations connected to the Internet.

5.4.3 Usenet

Because of this capability to internetwork different networks together to form a single larger network, many of the smaller networks that were in existence at the time of the ARPANET now had the opportunity to tie themselves to the Internet as well.

Historical network names you might run across in reading networking lore are BITNET, CSNET, JANET, and Usenet. Though the pieces used in most of these networks are in existence in one form or another today, the boundaries between these networks are often unclear and sometimes have been totally removed. To all but the people who manage them, they appear to be simply pieces of the Internet.

Usenet is the most widely known of these other networks. It began when people used the UUCP protocol (see page 150) to allow UNIX machine to communicate with other UNIX machines over modems and telephone lines (which was cheap since almost everyone already had modems and phone lines to allow dial-in access). Because of its anar-

[11] It is a common error for people to transpose letters and confuse NSF (the National Science Foundation) with NFS (the Network File System). Since the two are vastly different entities, it is usually easy to figure out which was intended by the context in which it is used.

chistic nature, no one entity had any authority over this network. It was totally based on cooperating points of contact.

One of the more useful ideas that grew out of Usenet was the *newsgroup*. Netnews, as it is called today, is a collection of newsgroups (i.e., bulletin boards) where people can read and post messages in a public forum. The groups are divided up hierarchically by subject, so people may participate in discussions about topics they find interesting and skip those they do not.

Some of the newsgroups you may find worthwhile to monitor as a UNIX system administrator are:

- `comp.unix.questions`
- `comp.unix.wizards`
- `comp.unix.internals`
- `comp.unix.admin`
- `comp.sys.sun.admin`
- `comp.sys.sgi.admin`
- `comp.sys.next.sysadmin`

As may be obvious from their names, these groups cover topics involving UNIX computers in the areas of general questions, "wizard" topics, internals, and administration. You may find many other newsgroups interesting as well. Thousands of different groups are available, and more are being created every day.

Most newsgroups contain a regular posting of the FAQ for the newsgroup: the Frequently Asked Questions list. These are usually collected by some volunteer or group of volunteers during the life of a newsgroup, once people begin to ask the same questions over again. In the life of any newsgroup, there is a continuous flood of new members who want to know all the same "introductory" information that everyone else did the first time they started reading news. Reading the FAQ will bring you up to speed on many of the common topics that have already been covered in the newsgroup (and don't really need to be discussed again).

5.4.4 The Internet today

The Internet is an ever-growing expanse of connectivity between all different kinds of computers. Internet RFC 1462 [KH93] provides an overview to the beginning Internet user about what it is and what it is not. Whether or not it can be said that the majority of the computers on the Internet are UNIX computers is debatable. One does not have to look hard to find VMS™ hosts, IBM hosts, and even personal computers attached to networks on the Internet. The Internet may have originated on UNIX machines, but it is truly the network for everyone today.

It is no longer possible to do anything more than *estimate* the true size of the Internet. With the distributed management required by an entity of this size, there is never the opportunity for a snapshot of the topology with which to obtain a count of members. By the time the data for such a snapshot could be collected and interpreted, it would be out of date. As of early 1994, there are an estimated two million computers connected to the Internet worldwide, and this number is doubling annually.

Administration of the Internet

Though originally managed by various agencies of the United States Department of Defense, the Internet is becoming more of a commercial venture and must be managed as such. The function of the Network Information Center (NIC) has recently been divided into three sections: a registry service, a database and directory service, and an information service. These functions are now managed by agencies or companies with funding assistance from the National Science Foundation as part of the continued growth of the Internet. Together, the parts form the Internet Network Information Center, the InterNIC.

Being part of the Internet community

To complicate matters even further, not all hosts that are functionally members of the Internet community are necessarily connected to the Internet. What exactly does it mean to be "on the Internet?"

Each host connected to the Internet has a unique hostname (e.g., `catwoman.cs.utexas.edu` might be a UNIX workstation in the Computer Science Department at the University of Texas). Each user also has a unique electronic mail address (such as `jackson@cs.utexas.edu`). These two names sometimes point to the same machine; often they do not.

Electronic mail is a little different from other network services. Most network services require that you actually make a network connection to the machine from which you want service. Electronic mail does not make such a requirement. It is possible for electronic mail to be transferred in a *store-and-forward* fashion, that is, the message is sent though a series of hosts before reaching its final destination. This is the way mail was delivered in the early days of dial-up connections, since one had to specify exactly what route a message would take through the network to get to the destination. Of course, this required that the user know something about the topology of the network, which was an endless source of frustration for most users.

With the Internet addressing scheme, the network administrators can set up forwarding and routing information for mail messages that allow a user to simply use an address in the form `user@host` to properly address a message. Based on information in the host name provided, the proper "next hop" can be determined even if that is not the final destination.

The result is that hosts on dial-up networks or other networks that are not physically and constantly connected to the Internet itself can now send mail to and receive mail from hosts on the Internet. If these hosts register with the InterNIC and obtain an Internet domain-style hostname, others can send mail to them using a simple address.

So some hosts are *on* the Internet (connected to the Internet, allowing direct connection to the machine) and other hosts, although they are not directly connected to the Internet, can receive mail addressed to what appears to be an Internet host. Marshall Rose clearly describes the differences in the preface of his book on Internet mail [Ros93b].

Becoming part of the Internet community

If your organization would like to be directly connected to the Internet, or simply have dial-up access to exchange electronic mail with those in the Internet community (and thus become a part of it), where should you turn? Until recently, you had to know someone who was on the Internet, or who was doing some form of research or development that was at least partially supported by other users of the Internet, to get a connection.

Now that the ARPANET has been broken up into autonomous components (much like the break-up of the phone company), the end-user has several choices in terms of bandwidth, equipment, and cost, in becoming a user of the Internet. Many companies, called service providers, supply varying degrees of hardware, software, and consulting assistance to get you connected. Some supply you with the tools and let you manage your own connection; others provide you with an off-the-shelf Internet connection and support for a monthly fee. Before getting connected, you must decide what level of service you need and find out what service providers are available in your area. [Est93] is a valuable reference for this.

5.4.5 Internet information

Entire books can (and have) been written about the Internet [Kro92], [Ros93b], and [Keh92]. If you want anything more than a casual overview of the Internet, these books will be vital to you. The Internet itself can also be a good source of information, because as changes are made, the first place they are documented is on-line.

The best known source for on-line documentation describing various pieces of the Internet is the RFC (Requests For Comment). RFCs are written by the "movers and shakers" of the Internet community and describe proposed additions or changes to some specific piece of Internet technology, or a totally new idea that should be considered for use by the Internet community. Some RFCs are simply historical to help keep track of the evolution of the Internet.

RFC documents may be obtained from several hosts on the Internet ([Kro92, p. 317]) via the `ftp` command. The official repository for them is `ds.internic.net` which is the InterNIC Directory and Database Service server.

The files containing RFCs are in the `/rfc` directory and are named `rfc`*nnnn*`.txt` where *nnnn* is the RFC number. An index of all RFCs can be found in `rfc-index.txt`.

Some particularly valuable RFCs for those new to the Internet are:

- RFC 1462 – a description of the Internet [KH93]
- RFC 1594 – answers to common beginner's questions about the Internet [MRM94]
- RFC 1207 – answers to common experienced user's questions about the Internet [MMR91]
- RFC 1601 – the charter of the Internet Architecture Board [Hui94]
- RFC 1602 – the standards process in the Internet community [BG94]

For those sites not directly connected to the Internet, RFCs may also be obtained by sending an electronic mail message to `mailserv@ds.internic.net` with a message body (i.e., *not* a subject line) of "`file /ftp/rfc/rfc`*nnnn*`.txt`" (where *nnnn* is the RFC number); a copy will be mailed back to you. For more information, send the word "`help`" in the message body.

The information found in RFCs and other Internet documents eventually becomes outdated. As new protocols and ideas are developed, new documents are written which supplement or obsolete older ones on the same subject. All specific RFCs recommended in this text are current at the time of writing. Be sure to check to see if the RFC has been updated or obsoleted when obtaining it (a note is added in the document giving the number of the new document if it has been updated).

5.4.6 Internet services

Literally hundreds of different services are provided by different hosts on the Internet. Some services are accessed manually (like public access file transfer) and some are for automatic access (like network time service).

It would be impractical to try to list all of these services here. Ed Krol does a good job of this in his book on the Internet [Kro92]. What you will need, however, is a place to start.

Accessing files

The `ftp` (File Transfer Protocol) command is used to access files on a remote system. If you have an account on that system, you can `ftp` files from your own account or files that your account can access.

A popular subset of the `ftp` application is known as *anonymous ftp*. To perform an anonymous ftp is to `ftp` to a remote site as the user `anonymous`, supplying your e-mail address as the password. Many Internet hosts have an anonymous ftp directory set up which contains many interesting publicly accessible files and programs [Kro92, pp. 74–76].

Finding information

So once you know how to get information from another host, how do you find out *where* to look for the information? Until recently, you had to just *know* where to find what you needed or at least be able to find lists of places to look. Some introductory information about the best places to look for publicly available software and other kinds of data can be found in RFC 1402 [Mar93], along with information about getting connected to the Internet.

The amount of available information has exploded and manually consulting directory listings of well-known machines is no longer very useful. Several tools now exist to assist you in your search for information available on the Internet by searching databases of available information.

The first such tool was `archie`. Archie accesses an index of files from various anonymous ftp servers around the Internet. This indexed information is updated on a regular basis, so it represents a fairly up to date snapshot of files available from most public anonymous ftp servers.

Archie can be accessed via a `telnet` connection to an archie server, via e-mail, or via the `archie` program, which makes a direct connection to an archie server while running as a local program on your machine. If `archie` sounds like something you need, you should consult [Kro92, Chapter 9] for details.

Gopher, WAIS (Wide Area Information Servers), and Mosaic are other, more sophisticated applications for locating information and resources in the Internet. These, too, are discussed in [Kro92] in Chapters 11, 12, and 13, respectively. Gopher is defined in RFC 1436 [AML+93].

5.5 Networking Protocols

Even if two different vendors' machines adhere to the OSI networking model, this is no guarantee that they will be able to communicate. Many different communications protocols have been developed which fit one or more of the OSI model layers. To be OSI-compliant is to have a network architecture for which other OSI-compliant vendors could easily develop or port a protocol and thus communicate with you.

Many significant protocols do not adhere to the OSI model but are in such wide use that they influence present and future networking developments. Most of the protocols discussed here fall into this category. These by no means make up all the communications protocols available, but represent the group you are most likely to see in your job as a UNIX system administrator.

The OSI definition of how best to define protocols came after the need for standard protocols had already pushed people to develop them. So, while it might be nice to develop more OSI-compliant protocols (and work like this is currently taking place), many noncompliant protocols are popular because they are available now. Some of these protocols were developed by committees or corporations and adopted by standards committees. Some were developed by corporations for internal use and remain proprietary. A few were originally proprietary protocols but have evolved into open standards.

Entire books have been written about each of these protocols. For protocols about which you need detailed information, it is recommended you consult the included references (and, as always, the documentation shipped with your communications software). The following is intended to give you an overview of the architecture of each protocol and how the protocol is used. As with networking implementations, these protocols are presented in approximate order of popularity in the UNIX community.

5.5.1 IP

The most popular protocol used in the Internet community (as you might guess from the name) is the Internet Protocol. IP is a protocol itself, but when referred to in the plural, it describes the family of protocols that run on top of IP. IP was the grand experiment of the ARPANET and succeeded, perhaps too well.[12] Because of IP's importance in the Internet community, IP will be examined in more depth than the other protocols in an attempt to familiarize you with the "big picture" of how the protocols in the Internet suite of protocols work together. IP was originally defined by Internet RFC 791 [Pos81b], RFC 792 [Pos81a], and RFC 894 [Hor84]. Much more information than what is found here will be necessary to use and manage an IP network and can be found in [Fri91, Chapter 12], [NSS89, Chapter 14], [LMKQ90, Chapter 12], [Hun92], [Ste90], [Ste92b], and [CMQ93].

IP is not OSI compliant, but it performs many operations extremely well. IP itself is a datagram service, meaning it delivers packets to a destination, routing those packets from one network to another where necessary, but does not guarantee arrival of the packet. It does, however, guarantee the integrity of the packet if it does arrive. Other protocols[13] running on top of IP take care of acknowledgment, ordering, and retransmission on lost packets.

[12] While the author is biased in favor of IP because of history and experience, it is true that after IP was born, some realized it wasn't necessarily the best answer. However, by the time enough movement had started to try to replace it with something better, IP was too entrenched to be replaced by anything less than God's-gift-to-protocols. The world still awaits GGTP. :-)

[13] Many more than are mentioned here.

TCP

The most well-known protocol to run over IP is TCP (Transmission Control Protocol, defined by RFC 793 [Pos81c]). The two together make up the TCP/IP protocol stack, which is how you often hear TCP described.

TCP provides reliable transmission by creating a virtual connection between two application programs. The protocol guarantees the data will be received once, without error, and in the order the data was sent. It does this by keeping count of the packets sent and received, requesting retransmission of lost packets, discarding duplicate packets, and reordering packets that arrive out of order.

UDP

The second best-known protocol over IP is UDP (Unreliable Datagram Protocol, defined by RFC 768 [Pos80]). If you have not done much network programming, you may wonder what usefulness an unreliable protocol provides. Many applications wish to send informational (but not critical) messages to other applications (or remote pieces of a distributed application). This information may be useful if received, but not necessary, or it may change often enough to make waiting another minute for the update just as acceptable as requesting a retransmission in case of an error. In this case, the programmer designing the application has chosen not to be saddled with the extra overhead of a protocol like TCP (which uses more computing power to guarantee the proper arrival of packets). By not requiring reliable delivery, the overhead of the communication is much lower. The tradeoff is that each and every packet may not arrive at its destination. On a local network, this only happens in any significant amount when congestion is high. In sending a packet to the other side of the globe, however, any number of failures could result in the packet never arriving at its destination.

ARP/RARP

ARP (Address Resolution Protocol, defined by RFC 826 [Plu82]) and RARP (Reverse ARP) are used by IP hosts to obtain physical address information for themselves or for other hosts on the network.

RIP/OSPF/BGP/EGP

Four major routing protocols exist in the Internet community. Routing protocols are used to provide information about network topologies and paths to other routers so they may "aim" their packets properly.

RIP (Routing Information Protocol, defined by RFC 1058 [Hed88]) is usually used on a local network to route between the various local network segments. RIP's biggest shortcoming is it selects routes based on number of hops, which in this day of high-speed and low-speed network technologies in coexistence, is not always the best method for selecting a transmission path.

OSPF (Open Shortest Path First, defined by RFC 1583 [Moy94]) does more than RIP and is intended to eventually replace it. OSPF selects the best route available at the time, given more detailed information about the networks and routers involved. OSPF can better decide between the tradeoffs involving speed and cost of the link. OSPF requires more CPU power and manages more information than the older routing protocol, but with today's more sophisticated routers and cheaper memory, this is usually acceptable.

BGP (Border Gateway Protocol, defined by RFC 1267 [Lou91]) is used to pass routing information both to other local (same administrative network) machines as well as to other machines on the Internet.

EGP (Exterior Gateway Protocol, defined by RFC 904 [Mil84]) is used on the Internet to pass routing information to other sites.

ICMP

ICMP (Internet Control Message Protocol, defined by RFC 792 [Pos81a]) is used to send messages that perform control and error reporting functions [Hun92, pp. 17–18]. The best-known use of ICMP is by the `ping` program, which can be used to test the reachability of a remote host.

SNMP

SNMP (Simple Network Management Protocol, defined by RFC 1157 [CFSD90]) is one of the newest IP family members. SNMP provides a standard method for transmitting and receiving network management information on an IP network. See the Network Management Application section (page 165) for more details on SNMP.

SLIP

SLIP (Serial Line IP) provides a mechanism for sending IP packets over a dial-up or leased telephone line [Hun92, pp. 118–131]. Source code for SLIP is publicly available and is even shipped with some versions of UNIX. Its ease of access has helped it become popular. Although SLIP is losing its advantage to the superior PPP, as with many other older-but-popular protocols, SLIP has and probably will continue to hang around for the sake of backward compatibility. SLIP is defined by RFC 1055 [Rom88].

5.5.2 UUCP

One of the first, and most widely used, methods of networking in a UNIX system was UUCP. UUCP stands for UNIX-to-UNIX Copy [TF89, Chapter 8], [OT92], [Uni90b, Chapter 7]. Developed at AT&T, UUCP runs across phone lines connected to modems. This has the advantage of using an already-existing transport medium (phone lines) and is therefore inexpensive to implement. Today, many sites continue to run the UUCP protocol, but over other (faster) transport mediums because there are still some functions that are unique to UUCP. Few sites run UUCP exclusively over phone lines because of the low bandwidth this combination provides. UUCP is not OSI compliant.

In the System V Release 4 documentation, you will find UUCP called BNU (Basic Networking Utilities). For all intents and purposes, UUCP is the poor man's network.

UUCP provides mail and file transfer between two machines, as well as remote execution of commands. The transfer of electronic messages is by far the most widely used feature of the UUCP command set. This includes electronic mail and Netnews articles.

UUCP allows a temporary point-to-point link between two computers to be established via a telephone call. Configuration files contain information about other machines that are called. When the connection is made by the modems, the calling machine logs in using a preassigned username and runs the UUCP transfer program `uucico` (generally, this is the shell specified in the `/etc/passwd` file for the username). Each machine transfers all files waiting to be sent to the other, then the connection is terminated (the caller hangs up). You can imagine how connecting machines together in this way forms a conceptual network, even though at any one moment in time, there is no contiguous network in existence, but rather selected segments of the network are connected (by calls in progress). The path a message may take to get from one machine to another (passing through zero or more intermediate hosts) will make it appear that there is a network in existence, when in reality, each segment was only in existence as it was needed. This is known as a *store-and-forward* mechanism of information transfer.

This network of machines is sometimes referred to as Usenet[14] (although to call it a network at all is stretching the typical definition of the term). Today, it is simply one of many component parts of the Internet, and the machines that make up Usenet and other dial-up networks can be considered "loose" parts of the Internet (possibly not directly connected to the Internet itself, but addressable by hosts on the Internet).

5.5.3 PPP

PPP (Point-to-Point Protocol, defined by RFC 1331 [Sim92] and RFC 1332 [McG92]) had its origins in SLIP but improves on the older pro-

[14] Purists will be quick to point out that the term Usenet originally only described the collection of machines exchanging news articles via UUCP. Other machines could have dial-up UUCP connections without technically being part of Usenet. The definitions have become muddied over time and most common usage of the term Usenet often makes no such distinction. Usenet has always been a little hard to describe, anyway. :-)

tocol. Unlike SLIP, PPP supports protocols other than just IP. PPP is technically a collection of protocols rather than just one. This suite of protocols provides error correction and security features not present in SLIP. PPP is a generic solution to the problem of point-to-point links rather than only solving the problem for a single protocol. PPP should soon be the "official" standard for such connections (rather than simply de facto, as it is now).

5.5.4 SNA

SNA™ (Systems Network Architecture) was developed in the mid-1970s by IBM as a simple networking mechanism [Ste90, pp. 224–238]. The protocol defines logical entities or units (known as LUs), how they are related to physical devices, and the interaction between the two. SNA evolved from previous IBM networking products with backward compatibility as a requirement and thus it is more complex.

SNA LU 6.2, along with the Advanced Program-to-Program Communications (APPC) and Common Programming Interface Communications (CPI-C) architectures within SNA, represent the widely accepted current technology standard for SNA [Edm92], [Kap92].

SNA usually runs over Token Ring networks, but can run over Ethernet and X.25 links as well.

5.5.5 DECnet

Digital Equipment Corporation began developing their own communications architecture, known as the Digital Network Architecture (DNA) but commonly called DECnet™, in the mid-1970s [Han89, Chapter 8].

Major releases of DECnet are referred to as phases. In the first three phases of DECnet, an evolution took place from a simple networking protocol to that of a more robust, efficient, and OSI-compliant protocol. However, it remained proprietary until Phase IV when the proprietary nature was relaxed so that non-DEC vendors could offer DECnet compatible functionality in other operating systems. Currently in Phase

V release, DECnet is in the process of becoming fully OSI compliant [ML92].

If you have DEC equipment, you can purchase the DECnet product for it directly from your DEC sales representative. Many other UNIX vendors now offer DECnet products for their own platforms to enable communication to your DEC equipment on your local network.

5.5.6 AppleTalk

AppleTalk® , as you might imagine from the name even if you've never heard of it, is Apple's networking protocol developed to let Macintosh® computers talk to each other [SAO90].

The first media used by AppleTalk was twisted-pair cable, which made it simple and inexpensive. AppleTalk can also operate across a coaxial cable configured to either the Ethernet or Token Ring standards (known as EtherTalk® and TokenTalk® , respectively). This means the packets put on the cable by the computer can travel down the wire and be understood by another computer also using the AppleTalk protocol. It does *not* mean that any other computer on the network can understand the packet.

AppleTalk has its own proprietary coaxial cable standard known as LocalTalk™ . To date, two standards have been released for AppleTalk. AppleTalk Phase 1 was the original AppleTalk standard in 1983. In 1989, AppleTalk Phase 2 was released, which allows more interaction with more different kinds of networks and protocols.

On a UNIX machine, you should not have any need to deal with AppleTalk packets directly. However, if your organization's heterogeneous network includes Macintoshes, you may well find AppleTalk present on some segment of your network or encapsulated in your network packets. Several vendors do offer AppleTalk to IP network connectivity, and AppleTalk packets can be encapsulated in several other types of packets on other types of networks (Ethernet, Token Ring, PPP, X.25 to name a few).

5.5.7 Novell NetWare

Novell NetWare™ is really more of a network operating system than a single protocol or family of protocols [CKM90], but for the purposes of this discussion, only the protocol aspects of NetWare are of concern.

NetWare was originally developed by Novell to connect personal computers in a local area network. It usually runs over ARCnet, but also can run over Ethernet or Token Ring. In a UNIX shop, you may not have to deal with NetWare packets directly but rather through a NetWare/IP gateway (although some versions of UNIX do support NetWare protocols).

NetWare, either directly or through applications written to run under it, provides file access, printer access, electronic mail and office automation functionality, and accounting functionality. A NetWare server can also serve as a gateway to other types of networks.

NetWare uses the IPX (Internet Packet Exchange) protocol which was developed from the IDP (Internet Datagram Protocol) protocol in the XNS (Xerox Networking System) [Ste90, pp. 214–224] protocol suite. Another way a UNIX system administrator might experience NetWare use is through the encapsulation of IPX packets in IP packets for travel across IP networks [Pro91] or by using PPP to connect two machines speaking IPX. Routing via NetWare networks is accomplished by NLSP (Novell Link State Protocol). NLSP maintains link state information, much like OSPF in the IP world, and selects the best routing, as necessary.

5.5.8 MAP and TOP

The Manufacturing Automation Protocol (MAP) was developed by GM to standardize communications on the factory floor between terminals, robots, and other computing devices. It is now overseen by the North American MAP/TOP Users Group. MAP conforms to the OSI networking model and is implemented on the Token Bus architecture [Jon88].

The major requirement that brought MAP into being was that a factory environment could not accept the lack of a maximum delay time for packet delivery that was true of most of the major protocols of the time. An assembly line progressed at a regular rate of speed. It could be slowed to adjust for problems, but information had to be guaranteed to arrive where needed in some known maximum amount of time [Tan88].

The Technical and Office Protocol (TOP) was developed by Boeing Computer Services. The requirements leading to the development of TOP were similar to those that drove the development of MAP, except that they applied to office environments instead of a factory floor. TOP (like MAP) conforms to the OSI networking model and was implemented on Ethernet (since the minimum packet delivery time was not a requirement as it was in MAP).

5.6 Network Service Applications

Now that we have all these various protocols available and our network is connected through routers to all these other networks, what does it get us? We can now find all kinds of information and services in different locations on the network. If we have some unique information or service, we can provide it to others. These services may be a nationwide college information database or a local network time synchronization program. The variations are endless and new ideas are being developed every day.

Most services fall into one of several categories, however, and we can examine the categories and mention some of the more popular services being developed or offered in the area. Many more are discussed in [CMQ93, Chapter 2].

Many services use their own protocols that run on one of the previously discussed networking protocols. In the Internet community, most services use either TCP/IP or UDP/IP. However, at the level of the application itself (from where the user sees the operation) the protocol is unimportant. The user may or may not even be aware of where the connection is being made to obtain the service.

5.6.1 DCE

No discussion of network services would be complete without talking about DCE, the Distributed Computing Environment. DCE is an implementation of protocols, tools, and interfaces designed to provide a standard programming interface for remote operations in modern distributed networks [Blo91], [RKF92]. DCE is built on top of TCP/IP and UDP/IP [Shi92].

The DCE was built from software contributed to the Open Software Foundation (OSF®) by member companies and organizations. The core services of DCE include a global naming service, support for remote procedure calls to distributed applications (RPC), a distributed file system (DFS), an authentication service, and a time synchronization service.

The DME, Distributed Management Environment, is a subset of DCE designed to assist in managing the distributed environment.

Some DCE applications do exist and more are being developed. DME is in the process of being redesigned to include lessons learned from its original design. While many significant contributions to modern distributed computing have come out of DCE and DME, it remains to be seen if the tools themselves will become widely used.

5.6.2 Host database information

By the mid-1980s, the ARPANET/Internet (for it was going through the transition even then) had thousands of hosts. The host table for the ARPANET was managed at a single site and everyone on the net would `ftp` an updated copy on a regular basis. This form of management became unworkable as the size of the net grew. It wasn't long before the host table was out of date by the time you could pull down a new copy.

Clearly, a new method of maintaining host information was necessary. It was also clear that administrative responsibility must be pushed down a level, so that no one group had to maintain complete authority over the entire set of information. This is when the Domain Name System (DNS) was born [AL92]. The original conceptual and technical ideas for DNS are described in RFC 1034 [Moc87a] and RFC 1035 [Moc87b].

DNS provides a hierarchical method of naming hosts by defining "domains" where information below a domain level is the responsibility of a designated group. Thus, the responsibility and authority for information about certain subsections of the Internet was delegated to lower levels. Domains and zones were established, inside of which information for name to address resolution was defined and available to the rest of the network.

Top level domains were formed. A partial list of these is:

- `com` - commercial sites
- `edu` - educational institutions
- `gov` - governmental agencies
- `mil` - military sites
- `net` - Internet infrastructure sites
- `org` - miscellaneous organizations that don't fit other categories

Other geographically based top-level domain names exist as well. California, Texas, Finland, and the United Kingdom maintain top-level domain names of `ca`, `tx`, `fi`, and `uk`, respectively. RFC 1480 [CP93] provides a clear discussion of top-level domains and domain names in general.

Underneath these top-level domains are company, college, and other second-level sites. For example, under the `edu` domain is the `utexas` domain (the University of Texas). With this scheme, all subordinate hostnames (that end in "`.utexas.edu`") are the responsibility of the `utexas` domain administrator. He must either maintain information or delegate the management of subdomains to an even lower level. In any case, the management of the information ends at that secondary level. The rest of the Internet need not know about changes within the `utexas` domain. A (very simple) topology of the domain system is shown by Figure 5.5.

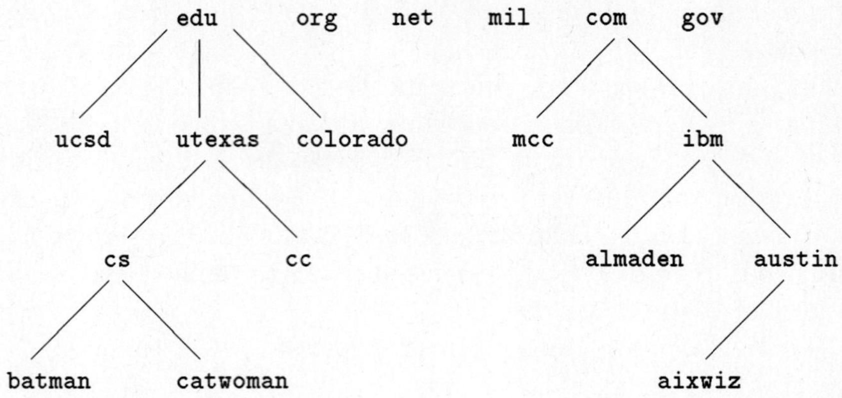

Figure 5.5: A *very* simple view of Internet domain hierarchy

With DNS, one can sit at a workstation and try to connect to a host (e.g., `telnet catwoman.cs.utexas.edu`). The local domain resolver realizes it doesn't know about this host since it is not in its own local domain, so it contacts the next higher level domain resolver. The request continues to be passed up to the top level (if the original requester is not in the `edu` domain at all), and it is then passed down to the `utexas` domain resolver. The `utexas` domain resolver may indeed pass the request to the `cs` subdomain resolver for resolution. Eventually, the requested address will be passed back along the same path to the requesting host. This may all sound like it takes a long time, but in reality it happens quite quickly.

5.6.3 Account information

Sun Microsystems' Network Information Service (NIS™ and the newer version NIS+) is the most common method used to distribute information about user accounts on a UNIX network. NIS is also capable of managing other types of information (like hostname and address information) [Ste92a]. NIS is available in most vendor's versions of UNIX and in previous releases was known as Yellow Pages® (the name was changed because British Telecom had previously trademarked the name in the United Kingdom).

One host is set up as the NIS *master server*, meaning that it is the definitive authority for the information in the domain.[15] Optional *slave* servers may be configured to store copies of the information distributed with NIS to protect against loss of access to the information because of network outages or to provide more direct access for each network segment.

5.6.4 Authentication service

Kerberos™ is an authentication service developed at MIT to satisfy requirements of users needing more security than basic UNIX provides. For a more detailed discussion of Kerberos, see page 210 in the next chapter on Security.

5.6.5 Global naming and lookup service

In a sense, the host database information lookup described above is a subset of a generic global naming and lookup service. DNS, therefore, does part of the job by providing information about hosts.

CCITT has adopted the X.500 standard (ISO has also adopted it as ISO 9594), which is a global directory service that can be used to look up any kind of information based on name keys.

5.6.6 Time synchronization

All modern computers have internal clocks. Timestamps on information in log files and during file modifications help humans track down events and know when information was accessed or changed.

In the UNIX (and therefore IP) world, the `rdate` command is often used to synchronize the time on various hosts on your network. Usually,

[15] This usage of the word "domain" has no relationship to an Internet domain as used with DNS. It is unfortunate that the same term was used because it often leads to confusion. You *may* use the same text string for your NIS domain name as you use for your DNS domain name, but it is *not* required and it can be confusing.

you will pick one host you will consider your *master* time server. This host is updated manually, connected to a device that obtains the time from some reliable source, or updates its time from a time server on the Internet or some other network.

Two popularly suggested time synchronization protocols in the IP community are NTP (the Network Time Protocol, defined by RFC 1305 [Mil92a], and RFC 1129 [Mil89]) and SNTP (the Simple Network Time Protocol, defined by RFC 1361 [Mil92b]). NTP is more reliable and accurate than `rdate` but requires a connection to the Internet or some other reliable external time source.

Since many files used on a local network today are maintained on a file server, it is important for the date of the server and the date of the workstation to agree. If you use commands to access a file that depend on knowing the modification time of a file and the server and your workstation disagree about the time, the commands you use may not behave as you expect. In cases like these, it is more important for all your hosts to agree on a time than for that time to be exactly correct!

5.6.7 Printer services

In any environment of any size, it is not practical for each user to have his own printer. Printers do not get constant use by any one person, and any printer that is relegated to serving a single user is being wasted.

In order to share the resource, each machine must be able to send files to a remote printer. Some printers actually have a connection to the network and behave as any other network hosts, accepting data from other hosts on the network. In most cases, the printer is attached to a single machine which has software that allows it to accept data from other machines to be sent to the printer. In this case, the machine to which the printer is connected manages the printer queue and sends the jobs in the proper order (usually, the order in which they are received).

On UNIX machines, the Berkeley `lpr`, `lpd`, and `lpq` commands or the System V `lp` commands are used to manage printers.

5.6.8 Remote file system access

Often a machine has a disk file system that needs to be accessed by other machines on the network, especially if it is serving as a file server (but even workstations can allow their local disk to be accessed remotely).

The most popular remote file system is Sun Microsystems' Network File System (NFS). NFS allows other computers[16] to remotely mount file systems and use them. The NFS protocol is specified in RFC 1094 [Sun89].

AT&T developed RFS (Remote File Sharing), which had several major differences from NFS, and for some time the two types of remote file systems fought it out for a standard. In reality, they solved different problems and could have coexisted, but RFS never caught on the way NFS did.[17]

Part of OSF's DCE will include a Distributed File System (DFS) (based on the Andrew File System).

NFS is by no means perfect; there are types of file access for which it is not well-suited. But like IP, it is here and it works and that probably has as much to do with its popularity as anything.

5.6.9 Electronic mail

Electronic mail (usually referred to as *e-mail*) is sometimes thought of as a network-related issue since a mail message may cross one or more networks to get to its destination. However, in its simplest usage, two users on the same machine may exchange messages without ever accessing a network [Kro92, Chapter 7], [CMQ93, Chapter 7].

Users rely on e-mail more today than ever before. Years ago, when it was a novelty, if messages arrived late or not at all, no one got very annoyed. It was a risk to send data in a mail message, but it could always be sent again. Today, a mail message is viewed like a telephone call by most people. They send the message (place the call) and expect it to get through to its destination. Unlike a telephone call, a mail

---

[16] Even PCs using PC-NFS can mount a UNIX file system as a letter drive (such as D:).

[17] This is largely due to the fact that Sun made the source code necessary to implement NFS publicly available, so many UNIX vendors and even some non-UNIX vendors implemented it on their own systems.

message does not always give immediate feedback of success or failure. In the event of a failure, the user will get a message back (sometimes called an *e-mail bounce*) containing information about why delivery failed (e.g., unknown user, unknown host, unable to connect to host).

A failure should always return some kind of notification to the sending user. If you send a mail message and get no error message back, you should be able to expect that your message was delivered correctly and the user will read it the next time he reads his mail.

Mail delivery and mail reading are two separate operations. The system administrator can choose the best mail delivery mechanism for the local environment and the users are free to choose their favorite mail reading programs.

The mail protocol for the Internet is SMTP (Simple Mail Transfer Protocol), which runs on top of TCP/IP. SMTP is a conversational way of specifying a sender and receiver and a block of message text. It is a simple protocol to do a simple job. The most popular mail delivery mechanism in the UNIX world is `sendmail`, though it is not the only one. RFC 821 [Pos82] and RFC 822 [Cro82] define SMTP and the standards upon which Internet mail tools are based. Consult [wEAR93], [CMQ93, Chapter 8], and [NSS89, Chapter 15] for excellent information about `sendmail`.

A newer protocol for reading mail is POP (Post Office Protocol, defined by RFC 1460 [Ros93a]). This allows an application to access a mailbox file in a central location from a remote system on the net. This is not a mail delivery protocol (since the mail had already been delivered) but more of a mail reading protocol, used when your mail is stored on a machine other than your own. It is popular with PC applications so that a PC user can read his or her network mail without having to login on another machine.

In the OSI world, the X.400 (ISO 10021) protocol is used to transmit messages between users [PLL+91]. Work continues to get the SMTP world and the X.400 world to coexist and be able to exchange messages between each other.

5.6.10 Remote processing access

Often in the course of using a computer, a user will need to run a process on a remote machine, either manually, or as part of a network application.

In the UNIX world, the `rexec` and `rsh` utilities can be used to manually execute commands on a remote machine within the same administrative domain.[18]

To perform remote processing from an application, you will most likely use an RPC (Remote Procedure Call) from within the program [Blo92]. RPC was originally developed by Xerox PARC and has been reimplemented by several companies. The version developed by Sun Microsystems is one of the more popular. As with NFS, Sun made their protocol definition available, defining it in RFC 1057 [Sun88], thereby making it popular and easy to implement for other vendors. While RPC implementations that do not follow Sun's protocol are similar, they are not necessarily compatible. For example, OSF will include an implementation of RPC in their DCE release, but it will not be compatible with the Sun version.

In the OSI world, JTM (Job Transfer and Manipulation) is used for remote processing.

5.6.11 File transfer

Sometimes it is sufficient to be able to get a copy of a file from a remote host. This is a simple procedure and may not require a lot of compatible protocols or even a compatible operating system between the two computers.

The simplest form of file transfer is the Internet method using the `ftp` (File Transfer Program) command. FTP stands not only for a command name, but also for a protocol (File Transfer Protocol) which, much like SMTP, is a conversational protocol used to specify a filename and destination to which to transfer a file [Kro92, Chapter 6].

[18] There's that word again! What this means is within a set of machines owned and/or managed by the same group of people where the user has an account.

In the UNIX world, a transfer between two UNIX machines, again in the same administrative domain, can be done with the `rcp` command (standing for **r**emote **cop**y).

In the OSI world, FTAM (File Transfer Access and Management) is used to move files between hosts.

5.6.12 Remote terminal access

Sometimes copying a file or starting a remote procedure on another host is not enough; sometimes the user actually needs to login on the remote machine.

For this, the generic Internet command is the `telnet` command. Telnet can connect you to any machine on the network, regardless of its operating system (no compatibility is required other than the remote machine must honor the `telnet` protocol) [Kro92, Chapter 5].

If both machines involved are UNIX hosts and both support the remote login service, then the `rlogin` command can be used and many of the features set for your terminal environment will be carried over to the remote connection.

In the OSI world, the Virtual Terminal Protocol (VTP) is used to gain remote login access to another host.

5.6.13 Remote display services

The X Window System is the most popular windowing system in use on UNIX machines today. It is designed around a client/server model where an application can run on any machine on the local network and display its output to any X server (workstation or bit-mapped display terminal running X server software; see page 74). The X Window System client and server processes communicate with each other using the TCP/IP or DECnet protocols.

Using the X Window System, applications can be run on a remote machine (e.g., a super computer at another site) and the text or graphics generated can be displayed on the user's local workstation screen [MP92].

5.6.14 Network management

Network management is probably the newest and fastest growing of all the network applications around today. While a network management station or system is a tool to help you keep your network running efficiently, it is itself a network application at the same time.

Two significant protocols have been developed to do network management. In the OSI world, CMIP (Common Management Information Protocol) was designed as the "right" answer to the problem of network management. At the same time, SNMP (Simple Network Management Protocol) was being developed in the Internet community because, as usual, something was needed immediately.

CMIP/CMOT

The OSI protocols and services for network management are used to manage objects. Objects are defined on the network and the protocol allows **get**, **set**, **create**, and **delete** operations to be performed on those objects.

Seeing how well thought out CMIP had been and how useful it would surely be in the OSI world, some tried to implement a version of it for the Internet community for IP networks. This was coined CMIP Over TCP (CMOT). While many have found it useful, it has not managed to displace SNMP and seems to be all but dead for future IP network management implementations.

SNMP

SNMP (Simple Network Management Protocol) was developed, partially as an answer to those claiming that CMIP was needed to solve the network management problem and partly because IP networks had no management protocol of their own. SNMP is defined by RFC 1157 [CFSD90].

Most of SNMP's capability is centered around the **get** and **set** operations used by SNMP agents and management stations. With these commands, any management station may query any agent for information. Because this is basically a polling mechanism, SNMP is not quite as robust as CMIP, which allows an agent to asynchronously send information to a management station. While SNMP agents can send *trap* messages to a management station, they are not guaranteed to be reliable so are mainly used as informational messages.

One difference between SNMP and CMIP is that in SNMP, the data space is not made up of objects, but a flat collection of data known as a Management Information Base (MIB). So far, two standard MIBs have been defined, MIB I and II [Ros91]. RFC 1156 [MR90] and RFC 1158 [Ros90] specify the standard MIB variables.

The growing popularity of SNMP, because of its success in the IP world, has caused it to be suggested as a solution to network management problems for other networks (e.g., RFC 1419 [MR93] discusses SNMP on AppleTalk networks).

The major drawback of SNMP was its lack of authentication and other security-related attributes. Now that the original concept of SNMP has proven useful, the designers are working to add security features to the protocol to make it more useful in different types of computing environments. SNMPv2, version 2 of the SNMP protocol, is introduced by RFC 1441 [CMRW93] and defined in further detail by succeeding RFCs.

UNIX tools

Without a network management application to help you manage your network, you still have some tools available to you to do more manual network management (RFC 1470 [Eng93] provides a list of many of the network management applications available).

The UNIX commands `ping`, `netstat`, and `nslookup` are shipped with almost all versions of UNIX and will help you find out if hosts are up, if routing and connections are set up the way you expect, and if your DNS name resolver is getting the correct information about your local hosts or remote hosts.

Other commands available on the Internet are `tcpdump` and `traceroute`. You can use an Archie server to locate these programs [Kro92, Chapter 9]. The `tcpdump` command lets you print out TCP packets as they travel on your network so you can debug addressing or other problems. If you have Sun Microsystems machines, the `etherfind` program which is included as part of Sun's software distribution is similar in function to `tcpdump`. The `traceroute` command can help you determine the path a packet takes during its journey on the network to help you verify if the route is correct.

Chapter 6

Security

The term "computer security" conjures up images of mystery, covert access to information, and stories of espionage worthy of James Bond. The truth, while every bit as lethal to an organization that falls victim to a disaster or an attack, is rarely so intriguing.

Computer security has different meanings for different people. To some, it is as intriguing as a James Bond novel because it means keeping West German *crackers* out of your computer system (as described by Clifford Stoll in his highly entertaining and informative novel [Sto90]). To others it simply means that your system works, nothing goes wrong, and your data is always correct. Three main categories represent the kinds of protection required for data security [Cou90, p. 49]:

- confidentiality
- integrity
- availability

Confidentiality is the assurance that only authorized people or programs will have access to data. Integrity is the guarantee that the data that was originally stored has not been altered, either accidentally or maliciously, and still retains its original meaning. Availability means that the data is always accessible to authorized users.

This topic, as with so many others previously discussed, can easily fill a book. By far, the most popular references on UNIX security issues are [Cur92] and [GS91]. Many papers are available from hosts on the Internet covering more specific topics, and references will be given for these later. A good look at the field of computer security in general can be found in [RS91] (and it is useful even if you have never heard of UNIX). RFC 1244 [Hol91] is also an excellent guide in security matters.

6.1 Why Be Secure?

Why all the excitement about computer security? To see the importance you must first define what it means for a system (or network of systems) to be insecure. If your system is insecure, you cannot trust the information you have entered into it and you cannot trust that the information you get out of it is reliable. Since managing information is the whole reason you have a computer in the first place, you begin to see the problem. Any violation of security in your computer environment has the potential to render useless this information upon which your organization depends.

6.1.1 What you could lose

Most people think of a *cracker*[1] or viruses when they hear the phrase "computer security." These two classes of security problems seem to get the most attention in the press because of the intrigue that surrounds them. This is truly the stuff of which movies and best-selling novels are made [Sto90].

As interesting as they may be, however, crackers and viruses are not the most significant threats faced by computer installations [Bak91,

[1] The controversy over the words *cracker* and *hacker* is, to put it mildly, a dead horse, and it does not need to be beaten further here. By way of explanation, traditionally, a *hacker* was someone who was involved in technical programming and could accomplish almost anything on a computer, often in the wee hours of the night (a night spent "hacking" code). This originally came from the real meaning of the verb "to hack": to cut with irregular blows or chop. One who hacked code often did so with no real plan and often made more of a mess than anything else. In the 1980s, the movie *War Games* (1983, MGM/UA) showed teenage, computer-literate, mischievous pranksters who were using personal computers and modems to break into various computers. As the public's awareness of this sort of electronic attack grew, they usurped the term *hacker* to describe these not-so-honest-and-hardworking people. Purists insist that the correct term should be *cracker* (as in safe-cracker) and that *hacker* be used only in its traditional and law-abiding (although sometimes disorganized) sense.

p. 3]. Many other, far more mundane risks threaten most computer sites. This is not to say that you should discount the possibility of malicious attacks. A common failing of a system administrator is to assume that no one could possibly be interested in the organization's information, so little or no effort is put into preventing even the *War Games* sort of cracker from gaining access.

The losses incurred by a breach of security, whether caused by a malicious human attack or a natural disaster, are generally measured in terms of money, but the cost often takes other forms. Information, employee time, and services rendered to employees or customers are all at risk. These risks are in addition to the more obvious risks of loss or damage of equipment due to theft or vandalism. Information can also be used for unfair competition or extortion, which can have hidden future costs.

In general, our legal system was not prepared for the onslaught of security-related cases. These have been increasing in the last decade and will, no doubt, grow at an ever-increasing rate. Computer crime does not fit the traditional model of crime [Par83]. As more cases of computer crime are tried and dealt with, this situation should improve.

> Early in the history of computer-related litigation, a case came to trial where the plaintiff claimed that information vital to the company had been stolen by a competitor by dialing into the company's modem and copying the information. The judge in the case completely missed the significance of the crime and ruled that since the plaintiff was still in possession of the information, that it in fact could not have been stolen so no crime was committed!

6.1.2 What you can do

So, given that you have a computer, that the information you store and process with it is important to your organization, and that you want to maintain the validity of that information, as well as keep others from gaining access to it, what exactly can you do to protect it?

To begin with, accept that you probably cannot *prevent* someone from getting at it if they want to badly enough. You can make it difficult. You can set up access controls so you can find out when an unauthorized attempt at access is made. But like the determined burglar trying to get into your house, you can rarely *stop* someone if they want in badly enough.

Neither can you stop a hurricane or earthquake or other natural disaster from striking. You can, however, keep backup copies of data, and even backup computers, so that you can get back in the game quickly in the case of such an event. Once you accept that over the life of your computer site, you *will* experience at least one occurrence of loss, whether man-made or natural, your prevention and recovery plans will reflect a more realistic philosophy. If you truly believed you could prevent every single type of breach, there would be no need for recovery planning. Believing "it can't happen to me" is the most serious mistake anyone can make when planning security.

Just as you begin to accept that you cannot possibly prevent every sort of security breach, however, don't let yourself believe that your efforts are therefore wasted. Just because you can't stop the experienced professional burglar from entering your home, doesn't mean you can't stop the vast majority who are not so experienced and determined. There are crackers who can be stopped by actively taking preventive steps.

Some sites try to minimize malicious threats through what is typically called *security through obscurity.* By not telling users (who later become former users) how the system works and where data physically resides, the odds are much lower that they will actually be able to access it through some means other than the normal authorized channels.

While this type of security does work in many cases, its biggest danger is that you think you are protected right up until the moment they "steal you blind." As a long-term strategy and sole means of protection, "security through obscurity" fails miserably.

Along these same lines, many feel that publishing information about tricks, security holes, monitoring mechanisms, and the like, runs a dangerous risk of tipping off the "bad guys" to what is done to try to keep them out or catch them at their nefarious deeds. The common belief, however, is that the people trying to break into a system are already aware of most, if not all, of these sorts of tricks, and it is more important to make sure the system administrators are aware and have the tools to help prevent a break in. Major General John Paul Hyde of the United States Joint Chiefs of Staff is quoted in Clifford Stoll's original paper about his experience tracking crackers ([Sto88, p. 494]) as being in favor of publishing such information. He blames "inattention to established security practices" as a contributing factor in the success of Stoll's intruder (and no doubt, many other intruders).

Not only must you take as many active steps as possible to try to prevent breaches in your security, you must also be ready to identify and track occurrences when they do happen [PCF91]. How you handle a security breach or some other catastrophic loss is as important as trying to prevent the breach (possibly more important since, as previously established, something *will* happen eventually).

6.1.3 The Internet worm

The Internet worm is probably the most famous case of a breach of computer security to date [Cur92, pp. 1–4], [Spa91b], and [Spa88]. On November 2, 1988, a graduate student at Cornell University released a program that copied itself from one machine to another, all across the Internet. Unlike a virus, a *worm* does not depend on a host program to move from one computer to another. It can reproduce itself (see the section on viruses below).

The worm took advantage of several security holes in various versions of UNIX used by machines on the Internet.[2] All have now been fixed, in large part because of this incident, and mechanisms for notification of users and customers of security risks and dissemination of fixes have been established. The best known organization coordinating this type of information is the Computer Emergency Response Team (CERT) [Cur92, Chapter 12]. CERT collects information about vulnerabilities

[2] So much for security by obscurity! Had the system administrators been made better aware of potential security problems and had the ones who knew about them taken them more seriously, the magnitude of the Internet worm would have been much smaller.

and assists users and vendors in communicating effectively about problems. Except for the huge amount of bad publicity, a lot of good did come from this event. It's just too bad the Internet community had to be beaten over the head before seeing the potential risks.

Because of a bug in the worm program, it did not copy itself to a target machine once, but time after time. The result was that as more copies of the worm began running on a machine, the load on the machine increased, eventually to a point where the machine was doing nothing but endlessly scheduling and swapping processes around (also known as *thrashing*). Eventually, these machines were halted, and as word of the worm spread throughout the Internet community, the infected machines were cleared of the worm programs before being brought back on-line.

While the worm couldn't run on every machine on the Internet, it was written so that it could run on a great many of them. Had it not been for this propensity to overload a machine, it might have spread much farther and infected many more machines before being noticed.

It is true that the worm itself performed no intentional malicious actions (like deleting files or copying passwords), and it's author claims that his intention never was to do anything malicious. However, many sites lost computing service and employee time tracking down the problem. These losses translate into money. Even in an accident, the losses can be significant. Think what someone could accomplish if they were *trying*.

6.2 Types of Risks

So far, only a few of the myriad of risks that can threaten a computer installation have been discussed. The risks involve Mother Nature, our fellow man, and simple random chance failures and occurrences. In order to effectively plan for the risks you face, you must first acknowledge them.

In almost all cases, having a good set of backups will help you recover from just about any kind of disaster that might befall you [Bra90, pp. 24–25]. It may take time. It may take more time than you really want to spend, but recovery will be possible (which is better than the alternative). Backups won't return confidential information from a competitor that has copied it, but they will prevent the loss of information from a disk crash.

6.2.1 Natural disasters

Mother Nature is not very forgiving. It seems each time we begin to think we really might have her caged, she does something new just to put us in our place. The natural risks faced by a computer environment are not that much different than the risks each geographical part of our society faces together.

Three of the four traditional elements (air, earth, fire, and water) are foreign to the inside of a computer room. Even air, in the form of high-velocity winds (storms, tornadoes, or hurricanes) can prove disastrous to a computer (or more to the point, the building that falls on the computer!). See page 101 for a more in-depth discussion of disasters and recovery.

6.2.2 Hardware malfunction

Assuming Mother Nature is content to leave you alone (for now), your equipment itself can fail you. Computers are machines. Machines fail. This has been true since the first man[3] built the first wheel and broke it running over a rock. When you buy a computer or extra piece of equipment, you can look forward to the day when it no longer operates properly.

6.2.3 Software malfunction

Although the hardware has the greatest chance of a malfunction, in the traditional sense of the word, software can also fail. While software does not "break" (although sometimes it may seem like it) in the same way a hardware component can, it can fail in a "new" way for no apparent reason. No program of any significant complexity is perfect. Even

[3] How do I know, maybe it *was* a woman who built it. It did work, after all. :-)

worse, some are just plain lazy [Bak91, p. 267]. Software failures are usually due to a design flaw in the program where some circumstance was not believed to be possible (the infamous "this can't happen"). If a state believed not to be possible does occur, the software may behave unpredictably and therefore fail and/or cause other errors. Software failures of this sort can cause losses equally catastrophic as those caused by hardware failures, and they are often much less obvious. A bug in a program that adds the wrong value to all your outstanding accounts or completely corrupts a data file can be much more dangerous than any hardware failure, especially if it is continues undetected.

6.2.4 Human error

Users and operators can make mistakes in the daily use of equipment as well. A user can accidentally delete files. An operator with a higher privilege level can do even more serious damage than a user. On most UNIX machines, the `root` user has complete privileges to do anything on the system. In malicious hands, this is disaster. Even in well-meaning but careless hands, it can spell trouble.

Audit trails will provide some amount of accountability in some situations. It isn't usually as necessary to assign blame as it is to find out exactly what happened to be better able to fix the problem and prevent it happening again. Of course, if assigning blame is your thing, the logs will help with that, too.

6.2.5 Human abuse

Abuse by humans seems to be the most interesting risk faced by computer installations and system administrators. These attacks may take the form of a physical presence of a person or devious behavior of a program intended to access confidential data.

Vandalism and theft

The risks most visible and understandable to society are those of vandalism or theft. This type of risk has been faced by business owners for hundreds of years and moving into the Information Age has not stopped it. People are just a little more clever about it now, that's all. Tagging equipment (during your asset tracking procedures) and doing regular inventory audits will help minimize the threat of theft.

Crackers

Crackers usually attempt to gain access to a computer either by masquerading as a valid user or utilizing a bug in the system software to obtain a higher privilege level. A cracker may use a software ruse (below) to obtain passwords, privileges, or other information that could be used to fool or altogether bypass authentication mechanisms.

A cracker may be a hobbyist who likes the challenge of breaking into a computer site or a highly-paid techno-terrorist. The latter is, of course, more dangerous, since he will be more determined and have more resources. However, even the bored teenager or curious outsider, with no real malicious intent, can cause significant trouble for the computer support staff[4] [Sto88], [Sto90], and [Cheb].

Software ruses

The *virus* is probably the most famous type of software ruse used to undermine a system's security. Viruses run rampant on personal computers, in large part because the operating systems were originally designed with little thought to security. When only one person used a machine, the risks seemed minimal. However, personal computers have grown in popularity, use, and complexity. As the issues surrounding PC security become more complicated, the fallacy of the PC's early design becomes more clear.

A computer *virus* is analogous to a biological virus [Spa91a], [Cou90, pp. 267–269]. It is a small piece of code that "attaches" itself to another program (a "host" program) in such a way that when the host program is run, the virus code is executed. This generally occurs without the knowledge of the user. The code may or may not do anything

[4] Until the cracker is caught, you rarely know what his real motives are, so you must treat the threat seriously.

right away. Many computers check the date and perform as usual until some magical date after which they do something as harmless as print annoying messages on the console or as serious as deleting all the files from the disk.

The UNIX world does not have a serious virus problem [Cur92, pp. 8–11]. This is mainly due to the large number of different versions of UNIX in use and the number of different hardware architectures upon which they operate. No one binary (already compiled) program could run on all these machines. It is ironic that the very aspect of personal computers that makes them so attractive, their shrink-wrapped software which runs on all different makes and models, is the very attribute that causes their high vulnerability to viruses. One way to protect yourself from a virus is to know the source of your software and to not load software from "just anywhere" (you don't know where that software has been!) [RS91, p. 87].

The *worm* is also derived from its biological counterpart. Unlike the virus, the worm travels from one machine to another without the dependency of a host program. A worm program contains code that connects to another machine, usually via a network, and transfers itself to the target machine, where it starts the process again, transferring itself to any machine that the new machine can reach. Often, along with this process, the worm program either sends some information back to its originator or attempts to create some method where a user can later gain access.

The Trojan horse is one of the older methods used to gain unauthorized access to a computer. The term is taken from the story of the giant wooden horse used to conquer the city of Troy in Greek mythology.[5]

The mistake made by the people of Troy was trusting something about which they had no knowledge. The replica of the horse, in the

[5] For anyone who might not know the story: The Greeks had attempted many times to penetrate the walls of the city of Troy but never succeeded. Finally they devised a plan to construct a giant wooden horse and leave it outside the walls of the city as a gift for the people of Troy. Unknown to those inside the city walls, hidden inside was a group of Greek soldiers. Even though they were confused by the appearance of the horse and the disappearance of the army, the people of the city decided to bring the horse inside. That night, while the city slept, the soldiers emerged from the horse and opened the gates of the city. The remainder of the Greek army entered and took the city.

software world, is a program that looks and possibly acts like a legitimate piece of software, but has some darker purpose [Cur92, pp. 6–8]. One example is a program that mimics a command used to list the contents of a directory, but also assigns some privilege to a user. Once such a program exists, the user has only to trick a privileged user into running it (either directly or because it is in the privileged user's command processor's search path). Once the program is run, the user has been granted a higher privilege and the system administrator is probably unaware of the change. Another popular form is a program that puts a login prompt on the screen. An unsuspecting user will attempt to log in to the fake login program which will collect the user's username and password and write them to a file, print out a message that the login failed because of an invalid password, and exit. In most cases, the user accepts that he must have mistyped and logs in again, successfully this time, and goes about his business, completely unaware that he has just given away his account and password.

> A real-life version of a (very expensive) Trojan horse occurred recently when someone built an exact copy of an ATM (Automatic Teller Machine). They installed the ATM in a shopping mall and just sat back while the machine accepted cards, recorded the information on them, collected the PINs (Personal Identification Numbers, equivalent to passwords) from the customers, and then reported an error and returned the card. The customer, believing the machine was malfunctioning, continued on their way, stopping later at another machine to get cash. Meanwhile, the perpetrators used the information collected to manufacture duplicate ATM cards, and knowing the PINs associated with each card, went on an ATM rampage! Fortunately, they were caught quickly.

A *back door* (sometimes called a *trap door*), is a mechanism, usually used by a programmer, to leave a way to obtain access by bypassing whatever standard mechanism is built into the program. This may be as benign as misguided logic of the programmer to give herself an easy way to fix a problem later, or it may be as insidious as a way for a disgruntled employee to return at a later date and bypass security and copy or alter data.

Radio emissions

Computers and network cables emit small amounts of electromagnetic radiation, also called *electromagnetic interference* (EMI) [RS91, p. 254]. Shielded network cables are less vulnerable to this risk, but it is possible to pick up residual signals from equipment and reconstruct the data contained in the signal. Data being written to a disk or sent across a system bus to another device, or even across a network wire, could be picked up and decoded.

The FCC (Federal Communications Commission) certifies equipment for acceptable EMI levels. Class A is a commercial classification in which more radiation is acceptable since private users are not close by where their home appliances would be affected by the unwanted signals. Class B is used for residential equipment where the concern for interference is higher. In a sense, these are backwards for security concerns since the home machine is probably less vulnerable to attack by virtue of the "uninteresting" information found there (besides, anyone wanting data from a home machine could just break into the house and take the whole machine). Using Class B equipment in your business will decrease the possibility of someone eavesdropping on the airwaves to pick up information.

Wiretaps

Much like a wiretap on a telephone line, it is possible to physically attach a device to a network cable and listen in on the traffic. In fact, with some networks, like Ethernet, for example, a tap is simply the way any device is connected to the network. Therefore, a tap might appear as any normal device and in some cases, normal computers can be used to tap the network wire.

On a Token Ring network, a tap is more difficult, since the token ring protocol requires each device to actively participate in the passing of the token from one node to the next. An illegitimate device must do more to not be noticed.

A tap on an Ethernet network, however, could easily go unnoticed [Nem92, pp. 362–363]. To detect a passive listening device on an Ethernet, one might use the TDR (see page 127). The graph produced by a TDR will vary depending on the number and position of devices on the Ethernet cable. If a graph appears significantly different in a certain spot, it indicates a newly connected device. With `root` access on a known or unknown device, it is possible to listen to the Ethernet in *promiscuous mode*, that is, where *every* packet is shown, not only packets destined for that particular computer.

Optical network cables, because of the difference in the way the signal is carried (by light rather than electrical signal) are harder to listen in on, but not impossible.

Garbage

Many sites do not consider their trash to be of any consequence. A single scrap of paper probably is not a threat by itself, but a concerted effort to collect and sort through a company's trash could allow someone to put together a pretty good picture of what goes on inside the company. Information someone might find could include authorization codes and locations of data. Fewer terminals print on paper these days, so being able to find login passwords is far less of a possibility than in the past, but there is still much interesting information that is simply discarded.

Visual access

Unauthorized observation of confidential material seems like an obvious possibility. It may be so obvious that we forget about it. This sometimes seems to completely slip the minds of the people involved.

The key to preventing unauthorized visual access to information is simply to be aware to whom, where, and for how long you expose it. Just as you wouldn't let someone look over your shoulder at a pay phone while entering your phone card number, or at an automatic teller machine when entering your PIN, don't let someone look over your shoulder when typing a password. Don't leave confidential material out on the table in the lobby or cafeteria (for example). Some companies are so paranoid that no one in a window office is allowed a whiteboard or chalkboard on their wall for fear of competitors getting a look with a telescope!

> I once visited a company whose two business partners were strictly confidential during the beginning of their relationship. While being toured around the facility, I noticed brochures for one company's benefits packages in the library that strongly implied one of the partner's identity. I also saw a memo on the kitchen bulletin board that named the other one. In ten minutes, I knew all the big secrets. Not that it mattered since I kept it to myself, but it seemed silly to make such a big deal out of information that was treated so casually!

Disgruntled employees

By far the most likely of all these risks is the disgruntled employee or former employee. The unhappy employee accounts for over 80-percent of all serious security breaches [Bak91, p. 49]. The psychology of such a person is not like that of the typical criminal. In fact, it is not like any criminal at all (and in most cases, the person does not consider himself to be capable of criminal acts).

Usually, such a person is much more enamored with technology than with the company itself. He is more impressed with what he can do *to* a machine than with a machine. He usually feels underutilized or unappreciated by his employer. He would never steal from or hurt "real" people, but this uncaring monstrosity he works for wouldn't be hurt by a little dishonesty here and there (especially since it's for a good cause—himself).

> Sometimes a former employee can be just plain mean. One such employee at a large software development firm was so upset at having been fired that he started a recursive delete of all files on the company-wide distributed file system (terabytes of data). Since he didn't have write access to everything, many of the delete requests failed, but many succeeded (partly because people are often not careful enough about how they protect their files). Eventually, someone noticed what was happening and the distributed file system service was terminated. It took most of a day to restore the missing files from the previous day's backup and to get the file system service back to normal operation.

6.2.6 Bad publicity

Not all risks are technical in nature. Negative press can often be worse than the actual damage done by a break-in [Cur92, pp. 136–137]. If the security breach undermines your customers' confidence in your ability to provide your service or protect information you maintain about their business, they may take their business elsewhere. For example, reading about a break-in at a software company that sold security-related software would not go far in making you want to purchase their software.

6.3 Security Planning

Without a coherent security plan, you cannot hope to present any more than a token obstacle to anyone attempting to gain unauthorized access. If you have never thought about security before, your first step should be to plan out your needs and how to satisfy them. If you have only been identifying and fixing problems in a haphazard manner, now is the time to sit down and map out everything you've already done and identify the holes that remain [RS91, Chapter 5].

6.3.1 Risk assessment

The first step in a good security plan is to assess your risk. The previous section discussed the major types of risks that any computer environment might face. Your organization may face risks unique to its type of business or geographic location and some of what is discussed here may not be significant for you for various reasons. Every site's security plan will be a little different. The key is, you need what you need and you must identify the needs before you can hope to satisfy them.

In assessing risk, you should completely describe each type of risk, the maximum effect (i.e., cost) that such a breach would have, and the probability you believe such an attack would be successful. It doesn't so much matter what scale you use for these values as long as they are all on the same scale for each of your identified risks.

By multiplying the cost by the probability you obtain a relative weight, which should be used to prioritize work done to minimize all of your risks. This helps you gauge the tradeoff between the cost (the loss) and probability of the loss taking place. A small potential failure with a huge cost will get approximately the same attention as a likely occurrence yielding a smaller cost. Depending on your organization, you may wish to add weight to the cost if the end result of minimizing cost is more important to you. In other words, the formula doesn't have to be completely linear, such as:

$$risk = cost \times probability$$

You may decide that a risk with a high cost should get somewhat more attention than a more probable risk with a low cost (i.e., your organization is more willing to "take the hit" for a smaller loss). In this case, you might modify the formula like this:

$$risk = (cost \times 1.5) \times probability$$

6.3.2 Requirements

Based on your list of risks and their probabilities, you now have the information necessary to define your requirements to make your environment secure.[6]

Another part of your statement of requirements is a definition of the authorization for your site. Who (either personally, or even better, by job function) needs access to what kinds of information and capabilities. For example, the secretaries in marketing do not need to be able to build new accounts on your main server, and your system staff doesn't need access to your personnel records. Of course, depending on your implementation of the various operations in your organization, it may be more difficult to provide the exact level of access you have defined for everyone. If it becomes necessary to deviate from your original plan, you can make exceptions on a case-by-case basis. At least start with a desired plan. Don't give up on it simply because you won't be able to implement it perfectly.

6.3.3 Recovery plan

Now that you know what your security risks and requirements are and how your system could potentially break down, you should plan how you will recover from each type of failure, be it natural or man-made, accidental or malicious.

If you have done a good job identifying your risks, then your recovery plan will almost write itself. Simply take each risk you have identified and assume it *has happened.* Then plan what you would do to recover from it.

As you develop your recovery plan, you should test each piece of it. In the middle of a crisis is no time to find out that it will take three days longer to get your tapes from off-site storage than your off-site storage provider claimed! Some parts are easier to test than others and still maintain normal operations. You may find it useful to schedule a weekend of downtime to do practice runs of some of the more complex recoveries. The system management staff will grumble and your users

[6] This is not to say *foolproof,* but such that your confidence level is fairly high.

will be annoyed that they cannot work, but this exercise is worth the trouble and should be done on a regular basis.

6.3.4 Levels of security

The NCSC (National Computer Security Center) is an agency of the United States government[7] that evaluates and specifies security requirements for computer systems used by government agencies [RS91, p. 254], [Cur92, pp. 176–180].

The specification published by the NCSC is the Trusted Computer System Evaluation Criteria (TCSEC), commonly known as "the Orange Book" [RS91, Chapter 6 and Appendix A]. The Orange Book specifies levels of security from D (low, as in a personal computer) up to A1. The NCSC also maintains an Evaluated Products List describing products that have met the TCSEC requirements [Cur92, p. 177].

The Orange Book is not a complete definition of security needs, however [RS91, p. 112]. Recently, there has been a proposal to replace the Orange Book with the Federal Criteria for Information Technology. This newer criteria list is put out by the National Institute of Science and Technology (NIST), a government agency that deals with private sector security issues [RS91, pp. 325–326].

6.4 Administrative Controls

Now that you have your threats identified and your recovery from a potential security breach all planned, you can set about trying to prevent the breaches from occurring in the first place. You will not be able to prevent *every* possible type of breach. Therefore, recovery is the first priority, since you must be able to recover from every type of breach. Once you know you can recover, you have limited the amount of damage that will occur.

Many preventive steps can be taken that do not involve highly technical issues. Most of these are simple, common sense actions that reduce your risk simply by reducing the amount of information that leaves

[7] The NCSC is part of the National Security Agency.

your control and by increasing people's awareness of the importance of protecting the information.

6.4.1 Policy and procedures

The establishment and strict adherence to security policy and procedures is critical for the environment to have any hope of being secure [Cur92, Chapter 10].

Your security policy should state what is at risk, what each person's responsibilities are, and what procedures should be followed to keep your organization secure. A good example security policy can be found in [Cur92, pp. 235–246].

Once you have a good policy in place, don't walk away from it and never really look at it again. All policies and procedures should be reviewed regularly and updated as your environment changes.

6.4.2 User education

Many users assist would-be crackers without intending to do so. They are simply unaware of the ends to which some people will go to gain access. One is to call an employee and pretend to be someone from the company computer center who is tracking down an authorization problem. The cracker asks the employee for his or her password to verify that the authorization is set up correctly. The user, feeling the request is reasonable and not really knowing what is involved, happily cooperates with the outsider and the cracker's work is done, no muss, no fuss.[8]

Education can minimize this problem. Tell your users a little about how your environment works, what you can do, what you can't do. If important security issues are involved, deal with them in person, not on the phone. Encourage a little questioning of authority on their part. The more they know about normal procedures, the lower the chances

[8] This is similar to a common occurrence where after losing an ATM card, a customer is called by a "bank employee" (who is really the person who stole or found the card) to verify the PIN so that it can be returned. As soon as the unsuspecting victim gives the caller their PIN, the crook visits one or more of the local ATMs and makes withdrawals from the victim's account with the victim's own card!

they could be tricked into giving away important information. This is one case where security through obscurity definitely does not work. Users already have important information, but if they don't realize it is important, they won't take steps to protect it.

Instruct users on the use of protection mechanisms (in the UNIX world, for example, file protections, the `umask` command, and data encryption commands). Teach them how to choose good passwords and that they should never write them down or share them.

A high degree of security can be achieved simply by having the cooperation and vigilance of your users. If you're fighting your users as well as the potential crackers, your problem is just that much bigger.

> I once overheard a student telling a friend how useful passwords were because he could just tell someone his password to let them use his computer account. He simply had no concept of the risk he was presenting to the entire system and if he had, he probably would have been more careful.

6.4.3 System administrator policy

The system administrator must follow an even more rigid set of rules than the users because the potential for abuse is so much greater. Whether through an accidental or devious action, the system administrator can cause a great deal of trouble because of the higher privileges that come with the responsibility.

Follow the same rules as everyone else

System administrators should follow the same rules set up for users. Just as the president of the United States is not above U.S. law, the system administrator is not above the law of the computer environment. Sometimes it may be necessary to act outside certain boundaries, but you should never expect to need to or in any way decide to do so lightly.

Delete old accounts

Old accounts of users who have departed should always be removed, especially in an environment connected to any outside network. The files belonging to the user should be backed up before being removed from the system (in case a coworker needs something related to the former employee's work).

Avoid default and null passwords

Always set passwords when creating new accounts. Do not let a vendor-default password or, worse yet, a null password remain [Cur92, pp. 30–33]. You may think the user will login right away, but that may not be true.

> One popular way to break into machines of a specific manufacturer was to use the account used by the Field Engineers doing preventive maintenance on the machine. Every machine was shipped with this account already established and with the same password set for it. The customer rarely cared about it and sometimes didn't even know about it, but it seemed every cracker knew about it, and this was one of the first ways they tried to break security.

Sanitize media upon disposal

One often overlooked procedure is sanitizing media upon disposal. This means shredding documents and punched cards or tapes.[9] It also means bulk erasing tapes (some companies even shred tapes). When sending a disk drive in for repair, you might consider erasing the data from it first. Erasing a disk drive does not just mean deleting all the files on the disk! To delete a file in most file systems only means to free the disk blocks being used by the file. Most, if not all, of the data remains until the disk blocks are reallocated to another file. Making

[9] Does anybody really still use this stuff? :-)

a new (empty) file system in place of the old one may not wipe every disk block clean, either. Even a complete reformat could leave some of the old data (unless a destructive write test is performed during the format).

To be sure the data is gone, you must write over the data in *every* block on the disk. Even disposing of a malfunctioning disk drive might be considered a security risk if the platters could be removed and inserted in another drive. With modern self-contained drives, this would be more difficult to accomplish, however.

Adopt a "least privilege principle"

Only increase yourself to the level of privilege you need to perform specific tasks and only for as long as you need it to perform these tasks [Cur92, pp. 35–36]. On a UNIX machine, this means only becoming the `root` user when absolutely necessary and for only as long as necessary. Don't get lost in what you're doing and continue to work as `root` when you don't need it. You may forget who you are and delete the wrong file or walk off and leave a command window open for anyone to come along and type into.

Do not execute unknown programs

Don't run unknown programs when you're running at an increased privilege level. If you have directories other than the standard system directories in your command search path,[10] you could unknowingly execute a Trojan horse program and give away privileges to another user. Do not read tapes from unknown sources as `root`, either. Some tape archive commands (like `tar`, for instance) will retain ownership and mode settings of a file when it is read from a tape as root. Someone could get a program installed in a privileged state if they could get you to read the tape as root and install the files and not check their status. Read the tape with your own user account first (so the files will

[10] The classic example of this is including "." in root's path. Although not having the current directory in your path is somewhat of an inconvenience, everyone agrees that it is safer to omit it.

be owned by you) and then move them and change the file modes if necessary.

Check for privileged programs

Check for programs that run at higher privilege. In the UNIX world, these are known as *set-uid* and *set-gid* programs, because they reset the user ID or the group ID of the user executing the program to some higher privilege value to legitimately access data needed by the program. Every UNIX machine has a few of these kinds of programs, but it is a good idea to know what programs are on that list and compare it to what is on your system on a regular basis. This way, if someone manages to get such a program installed on your system, you will be able to find it and deal with the problem [Cur92, pp. 55–62]. Do not allow shells to be set-uid or set-gid, even in your list of known-legitimate programs. Such scripts allow a window of vulnerability when the privilege is changed that can be used to gain `root` access [Cur92, pp. 51–52].

Minimize the privilege risk

Keep the number of people with privileges to a minimum. The larger the environment, of course, the larger the number of people you will have supporting it. The more people you have with privileges, the higher your potential for accidents, miscommunication, and chaos in general. It also increases the number of people an outside attacker could attempt to bribe or blackmail.

Sometimes, however, it is advantageous or even necessary to grant privileges to a user for some legitimate reason. Generally, these are users you know to be competent and who you feel will act responsibly (after you get to know your users, it is usually easy to see which users are good risks and which are not!). The user should have a healthy respect for the damage that could be done with the higher privileged account. Often such a user, possibly a former system administrator, can offer you much help and provide a good source of experience that you should take advantage of.

With the arrival of the desktop workstation, this happens even more frequently, since the machine actually does belong to the user instead of sitting in the computer room. Some users will feel since the machine is theirs and is in their office, why shouldn't they be able to do anything they want with it? Of course, since they're probably connected to the local area network, allowing them to do anything they want to that workstation often implies that they could do anything they want to other machines on the network as well. The environment can no longer be viewed as a collection of individual machines, each to be used in any way the user wants, but as a single collective of computing resource where everyone must behave responsibly in order to make it work.[11]

You can usually break your user community down into three types of users:

- those who don't know anything and know they don't
- those who know something
- those who *think* they know something

The first group is usually cooperative and happy to let you set down rules and regulations. You're the expert; you should know what is best for them (if you're wrong, they'll let you know!). The second group likes to be given the rationale for decisions, but is usually accepting of reasonable policies because they understand the risks involved in not following any policies. It's that last group you have to watch out for! They usually know just enough to be dangerous and not enough to be careful. They're so busy trying to get what they want out of the machine that they can break it for everyone else.

[11] Much like our society, although we see how well that works sometimes.

> While trying to diagnose a system that wouldn't fully boot, I booted it to the "single user" state and mounted the file systems and looked around. I quickly found that the machine had no /dev directory (on a UNIX computer, the files in /dev are the way the operating system communicates with all the external devices, such as disk drives). I asked the user if he knew anything about a problem with "slash-dev" and he said "Oh, yeah, we needed to free up some disk space... was that important?"

Examine logs

Your log files are your audit trails and tell you what's been happening on your systems. These should be examined on a regular basis. You may have a large volume of data that makes manual examination unreasonable. In this case, write or obtain tools that search for certain interesting strings and run them over the log files on a regular basis (of course, you will have to be familiar with the kind of information found in the logs first, so you may have to read them manually for a while). This information is out there to let you keep up with what has been happening on your system. Don't just delete these files as they grow, that's not what they're for!

Change passwords

Change privileged passwords on a regular basis and encourage (or force) users to do the same. Password aging mechanisms on accounts often prove effective in keeping users from using the same password for years at a time. A counter argument to this is if you make it too difficult for the user to keep up with his password, she will simply write it down on a piece of paper and carry it with her. This is even worse than not changing it!

In theory, regularly changing passwords will prevent a cracker from either having a long time to try to hit the same password, or from having access long before it is changed again [Cur92, pp. 20–23]. In practice, a cracker who is working hard to break in will be able to try most of the variations in his list over a period of a few days. With the speed of tools that can be used to test passwords, you can't do much to close the window down enough to cause a determined cracker any real problems [Bra90, p. 12]. This was more useful when crackers sat at terminals and manually typed password after password as they tried to break in. No serious cracker operates like this today.

Whenever a staff member with one or more passwords to privileged accounts or services leaves, all system passwords should be changed. Not only does this protect you from the former employee if she decides to exact some kind of revenge on her former company, it also protects the former employee from suspicion in the event some kind of security breach does occur shortly after she leaves.

6.5 Software Controls

Software can also be used to control access to your computers and networks. Even when the hardware and physical connections allow paths to your data, properly configured software will control and log access to the data so that unauthorized access is disallowed.

6.5.1 Authentication

The first step most software must do in determining access rights is to authenticate the user making the request [Cur92, pp. 148–150]. Many people confuse the words *authentication* and *authorization*. Authentication is determining the identify of the user or requesting agent (in the case of another piece of software) and insuring that he, she, or it is indeed who he, she, or it claims to be. Once the identity of the requester is verified, the request is processed only if the requester has the proper access rights to the operation or information (authorization). One common way to attempt to access information for which you do not have authorization is to bypass, or fool, the authentication mechanism. If you can convince the software that you are actually someone else (e.g., using an ID and password of another user) then you immediately have that user's authorization by virtue of having beaten the authentication scheme.

Passwords

Passwords are the most common form of authentication mechanism (not to mention the most abused and the easiest to undermine). Contrary to common perception, passwords are rarely a sufficient safeguard against unauthorized access to machines and information. Following a simple set of guidelines when choosing and using passwords, and simply being careful with them, can greatly increase their effectiveness [Bak91, Chapter 6], [Cur92, Chapter 2], and [Bra90, pp. 5–12].

Some of the more effective DOs and DON'Ts concerning passwords are:

- Don't write your password down
- Don't make a password a word found in an on-line dictionary
- Don't make your password something easily guessed by anyone who knows anything about you (like the name of a spouse, pet, a phone number, or a Social Security number)
- Don't share your password with anyone
- Change your password regularly, so at least if someone does guess it, they won't have it for long

Of course, this list could be expanded upon a great deal [Cur92, pp. 13–19, 30–33], [Kle90], and [Hol91, pp. 58–59].

If your site assigns passwords to guarantee they are nontrivial, make them pronounceable, or the first letter of each word of a well-known phrase, or something else that the user will be able to easily memorize. Otherwise, they will simply write the password down on a piece of paper and carry it with them, and that is almost as bad as a password that can be guessed. Some sites use password generators to generate random passwords. The fallacy here is if someone manages to get a copy or even back-engineer the algorithm used, they can generate their own set of passwords to use to try to break in to accounts on your system [Cur92, pp. 19–20]. Working humor into a word or phrase often helps people remember the password.

Badges and smart cards

Identification badges are one of the most common forms of authentication used today. Some have a simple photograph of the owner so that other users can verify the person by sight. Some have information magnetically recorded in a strip on the back (much like credit and bank cards). Some have their own printed circuit that has information recorded in it. Optically coded badges carry information in a pattern of spots on the badge that can only be seen under infrared light. These last two varieties are far more difficult to counterfeit than the magnetic strip or photo badges [Bak91, p. 131, 139–140], [RS91, pp. 244–246].

These latter badges, that can be read by electronic devices, can be used to provide automatic access to a room or building. They usually provide a log of who entered and at what times that can be useful when tracking down a security breach.

Smart cards look like badges, but are not passive the way ID badges are [RS91, p. 244], [Bak91, Chapter 6]. A smart card is a small computer that uses a random seed or a synchronized clock or some other common origin to generate a response code to an input code. The user is prompted with a code for which only the smart card will be able to generate the proper response. This is an improvement over the password since it is different with each use, but winds up being an awful lot like carrying your password around with you. The advantage is that if it is lost, it can quickly be locked out of the system so that its generated response codes will no longer function.

Biometrics

In reality, passwords, badges, and smart cards do not really authenticate the user. They merely authenticate who is in possession of the authentication device. The acceptance of this identity as fact is a leap of logic (faith in this case) which allows the access authorized for that user. If I loan my password or magnetic badge to someone, the equipment assumes the user is me. This isn't as much of a problem with photo IDs, although fake driver's licenses at night clubs are still used successfully.

The only way to authenticate the *person* is to identify something unique to that individual. Comparing biometric information, that is, information about the individual herself, not some device she carries or information she knows that can be passed on, is the only sure way to identify someone [RS91, pp. 246–252]. The sorts of attributes that are unique to each of us that can be used to authenticate an individual are fingerprints, voiceprints, signatures, DNA signatures, or retinal scans. The geometry of someone's hand can also be used [12] or even the intonations of keystrokes when typing a password [Bak91, p. 132–150], [RS91, Chapter 9]. Most biometric methods of authentication are still in limited use, mainly because of the inconvenience to the user and the cost to the organization to implement.

6.5.2 Access control

Once the identity of the user has been established beyond doubt, the next issue is to determine what level of access she will have to information [Cur92, pp. 157–160]. Not all users can be authorized to access all information. In most organizations, access to confidential or critical information is on a "need to know" basis. This is often called Discretionary Access Control (DAC) [RS91, p. 116] because the user can allow and disallow access to a user or group of users.

During your security planning, you mapped out what individuals and groups needed access to what information (and sometimes what groups you specifically wanted to keep away from certain information). Implementing these access boundaries may come in many forms. Information that is accessed through a software application will require the application to be configured in a way that it can look up access rights.

[12] Sometimes passwords *are* better, though. I remember a bad TV movie where the hero was refusing to open a security door for the "bad guy" since it required him to place his palm on a sensor for authentication. The "bad guy" told him that his hand would open the door whether or not it was connected to his body.

Relying on the operating system to allow or disallow access is simpler but less flexible. In the UNIX world (and indeed, in many other operating systems), the file protection mechanism is used to allow and restrict access to individual files by certain groups of users or all users. Some operating systems allow a more finely grained specification of access, even down to the level of the user and what time of day the access is being attempted. UNIX refers to the file protection settings as *file modes* (for details see Chapter 3 of [Cur92]).

A newer form of the more finely grained mechanism is the Access Control List (ACL). Several versions of UNIX, and no doubt other operating systems, are now implementing ACLs to provide users with more control over who can access their files [Cur92, pp. 49–50].

It is important to note that all the effort spent protecting files on your system from unauthorized access can be completely undermined if you don't expend equivalent effort protecting your backup media. Backup tapes and disks should be protected just as much as the original data. If someone can walk off with a backup tape, all your protection mechanisms on your computer are wasted.

6.5.3 Audit trails and logs

Audit trails only function as a control mechanism in the sense that if people know information is logged and there is some accountability for actions taken on the system, they may be discouraged from attempting any covert actions, where otherwise they might try.

Logging mechanisms are best suited for gathering information after a break-in or failure has occurred to allow you to piece together an explanation of how it happened. Only when you have determined how an unpleasant event took place will you be able to take steps to prevent it in the future.

6.5.4 Encryption

If you feel, either as a user or a system administrator, that you cannot prevent unauthorized access to some piece of information for whatever reason, you still have one recourse. You can encode the data such that it only makes sense to you or to software that can decode it with the proper key. This is known as *encryption* [RS91, Chapter 7] [GS91, Chapter 18]. Cryptography is an old art [RS91, pp. 166–169], but computer technology has altered it dramatically. Where once it took years for a human to decipher information, even knowing the encryption keys, a computer can do it in seconds (and hence can try thousands of different encryption keys repetitively until it finds the right one).

In a sense, encryption is merely another type of authorization using the encryption key as the password. However, this type of control allows the information to be moved around or even transmitted over public networks, without fear of revealing the meaning of the information to an unauthorized party. The access control is moved from the point of storage of the data to the point of usage.

`crypt`

Most versions of the UNIX operating system are shipped with the `crypt` command and system call to perform simple file or buffer encryption [Cur92, pp. 140–143]. When simply encrypting data for use on the machine, and to prevent the casual observer from seeing the data, this is sufficient. However, `crypt` is easily broken by a serious attacker.

DES

Other methods of encryption have been developed that can be used more universally, across different operating systems and architectures. The best known is DES, the Data Encryption Standard [Bak91, p. 183], [Han89, Chapter 11], [Per92, pp. 346–347], [Cur92, pp. 143–147], [RS91, pp. 179–187], [Cou90, pp. 259–261]. Some versions of UNIX `crypt` allow you to specify the use of DES as well. DES is described in National Bureau of Standards (NBS) Federal Information Processing Standard (FIPS) document PUB 46.[13] DES uses a 56-bit key and encrypts data in blocks of eight 8-bit bytes. It uses several varied processes rather than just a simple translation to achieve a more secure encryption. The only proof of its security is the fact that it has not been documented

[13] FIPS PUBs can be ordered from the National Technical Information Service (NTIS).

to have been broken in an actual attack (although some claim to have broken it in controlled tests).

Export laws currently restrict code containing DES algorithms to be shipped outside the United States (thus the newer versions of UNIX containing the DES-enabled **crypt** command do not include it when they are shipped to customers abroad). However, DES has been independently implemented outside the United States and is, therefore, available from other sources [Cur92, pp. 175–176].

Public-key encryption

While DES is reasonably secure, it is not very robust in who it will allow and disallow the ability to decrypt the data. If you have the key, you can decrypt the data, period (the same as if you have someone's password, you can login to their account). Passing keys around is about as dangerous as passing passwords.

The *public-key encryption* method provides a more interesting way of encrypting and decrypting real-world data ([Bak91, p. 183–184], [Cur92, pp. 153–154], and [RS91, pp. 176–179]). Two keys are used instead of just one. Each person has what is known as a public and a private key. Each person's public key can be used to encrypt data that only their private key can then decrypt. The reverse is also true, each person's private key can be used to encrypt data that their public key can then decrypt.

Public-key encryption can provide both authentication and secrecy. If I receive a file of data or a message from a user that I can decrypt with her public key, then I know it was encrypted with her private key. Conversely, if I encrypt a file with her public key and send it to her, only her private key can decrypt it so no one else can read it. To get both authentication and secrecy at the same time, both types of encryptions must be performed (although it is not as straightforward as that [Cur92, p. 154]).

6.5.5 UNIX tools

Many tools have been produced in the UNIX world and the Internet community[14] to help reduce the threats that most computer environments face. These packages can be found on many publicly accessible machines across the Internet [Cur92, Chapter 11], [CB94, Appendix A].

Passwords

In traditional UNIX, the `/etc/passwd` file contains the account information for users, including the encrypted password string. Although the critical information is encrypted, it is possible to write a program (such as `crack` [Cur92, pp. 172–173]) to compare test passwords against it and potentially figure out at least some of the passwords. If the encrypted strings are kept in a "shadow" password file that is unreadable to users, this threat is greatly reduced [Kle90]. Many versions of UNIX now include password shadowing. If your version does not include it, there is a version available on the Internet [Cur92, pp. 23–25, 174].

Password aging allows the system administrator to specify the length of time that can pass before a password must be changed. This guarantees that a user will not keep the same password indefinitely. As discussed before, the benefits of this are arguable. Any real cracker probably doesn't need a lot of time to do all the testing on the login ID that he will want to do. If nothing else, it will keep your users aware of the importance of password security.

Much effort is put into hiding the password, but if the user chooses an easily guessed password (like the username backwards) then hiding the data is irrelevant. The `npasswd` program, written by Clyde Hoover of the University of Texas at Austin, replaces the UNIX `passwd` command and examines the user's choice of password, testing it for easily guessed possibilities. Of course, there is no way `npasswd` can check for easy passwords like a spouse's name, since that name probably isn't available on the system, but it does check for passwords that are too short,

[14] For all intents and purposes, these two environments are the same since their overlap is so large.

passwords that are made from words in the on-line dictionary, and overly simple passwords [Cur92, pp. 171–172].

Logging `ftp`

Some versions of the `ftpd` daemon (that listens for connections from an `ftp` program) log users and what files are transferred, but some do not. If the version your vendor supplies cannot be configured to log connections, there are publicly available versions that can.

Network monitors

If you have a Sun workstation or server, the `etherfind` command will help you monitor network traffic. If you have other platforms, the publicly available `tcpdump` is a program similar to `etherfind`. `tcpdump` only works on Berkeley and some Berkeley-based systems, however [Cur92, p. 173].

The `nfswatch` program was developed by David Curry to specifically monitor NFS traffic on a network [Cur92, p. 173].

System monitors

The best-known UNIX system monitoring program (set of programs, really) is COPS, the Computerized Oracle and Password System [FS90], written by Dan Farmer and Gene Spafford. COPS detects and reports a multitude of insecure situations that it finds on your system, but it does not attempt to fix any of them. Fixing such problems should be a manual process. By running COPS on a regular basis, you will be initially notified of situations that should be corrected, and in the future you will be notified of new situations that develop without your knowledge.

6.6 Physical Controls

Controlling the physical environment and area of your computers is vital to their security. If someone can touch your machine, they can do just about whatever they wish. No software or administrative controls can help you if someone picks your computer up and walks away with it.

Physical controls come in two different flavors: those meant to protect the machine from accidents (fire, etc.) and those meant to keep people away from them (locked doors). All of the physical controls, as well as others detailed in [RS91, Chapter 9] and [GS91, Chapter 19] fit one of these two groups.

6.6.1 Environmental safeguards

You must protect the environment in which your computer operates. This means preventing contaminants like cigarette smoke and dust from entering or collecting near your computers. Not only do cigarettes raise your risk of fire, but smoke and dust clog filters and keep the air-cleaning systems from functioning properly. Ion filters on humidifiers can help keep the system clean, since many public water supplies have minerals that clog the humidifier filters. It should be unnecessary to point out the importance of regular cleaning and/or changing of all filters.

The high-temperature, smoke, water, and humidity sensors are also important parts of keeping your environment safe for your equipment. Environmental safety and recovery were discussed beginning on page 101.

6.6.2 Locks

Keeping the machine behind lock and key is the only way to guarantee its physical security. If you can't guarantee its physical security, you're wasting your time trying to protect it via software or procedures. Until recently, someone could boot a workstation in *single-user mode* (also known as *maintenance mode*) and get a `root` shell and do anything they wished. Many versions of UNIX now require the root password even to boot to single-user mode [Cur92, pp. 105–106].

The least sophisticated (and thus the cheapest) locks are the familiar mechanical keyed locks. Keys, like passwords, can be loaned or lost.

Electronic locks, controlled by keys, or more likely ID badges or biometric devices, not only have greater flexibility but can keep a log of entries and exits. Many exterior doors to corporate facilities are controlled by electronic locks in this manner. The biggest risk of this kind of lock is when another person "piggybacks" through the door with the person with the key. Educating employees in the proper use of lock mechanisms goes a long way to prevent problems. You can also find revolving doors that only allow one person through at a time by sensing weight on pads in the floor area.

A desktop machine poses a high risk. Valuable data may be physically stored on the machine, just there for the taking. When possible, remove sensitive data (if kept on removable media) and lock it up.

Loading docks are often less secure areas and have a higher potential for unauthorized entry into a building. This is not because there are no locks; sometimes the most sophisticated locks and doors can be found there. Problems occur because security procedures are not followed closely. The traffic in the area is higher and someone can get lost in the shuffle and sneak by. As large crates are being moved around, security doors are sometimes propped open to make access easier for the people moving the equipment. Someone trying to get into the building has only to look like they know what they're doing to walk through all this activity without being questioned.

One important consideration should not be overlooked when securing your computers with high-tech, sophisticated locks: does the wall of your computer room go all the way to the real ceiling or floor or only to the false one? It does no good to lock the doors and windows if someone can climb into the air-return area above and get over the wall into the computer room, or get under a raised floor that extends past the confines of the computer room!

6.6.3 Alarms and surveillance

In addition to the environmental alarms mentioned above, you may also wish to have alarms connected to doors of your computer room and possibly doors and windows of your building. Motion sensors in the computer room will alert you should anyone get past any of your precautions.

Security cameras and guards monitoring them and making rounds represent an even higher level of security precaution.

6.7 Network Security

If your computer is connected to a network, you have a problem [GS91, Chapter 11]. You cannot guarantee that data can't slip through the wire somewhere, sometime, or somehow. You can take several steps to minimize your risk, however.

6.7.1 Modem lines

The most common form of networking in use is via telephone lines. This form of communication is cheap, both in terms of resource costs and equipment costs. Most companies have at least one modem around somewhere and many home machines have one [GS91, p. 184].

Because of their ease of use and popularity, modems are also a high risk. All it takes to connect to a modem is knowing the phone number of the phone line to which it is connected. Nothing prevents someone from dialing that number.

Back when the movie *War Games* (see page 170) was popular, the same ploy to find modems was being used by crackers all over the country as was used in the movie (and it is still used today). With a personal computer and an auto-dialing modem, it is a simple matter to call every telephone number in a given exchange and make a note of where modems answer.

Do people really just try sequential numbers? Is it worth it? Let's say on the average it takes 20 seconds to dial and ring a telephone until a human, answering machine, or modem answers. At that rate, it would take less than 55 hours to dial every one of the 10,000 telephone numbers in a single telephone exchange. That's a little over two days to find every active modem in the exchange (and to greatly annoy thousands of people!).

Dial-in lines

A regular dial-in line used for remote users to access the machine present a large security risk. If someone can impersonate another user by finding out or guessing their password, they can get access to your systems from a remote location.

One way to decrease your risk is to have a *dial-back* system [Cur92, pp. 118–120]. When you dial in, you enter a code, either via the keypad on the phone or with your computer or terminal, depending on the system. Then the line is disconnected and the host computer calls you back at a predetermined phone number. In this way, the odds of anyone actually making a complete connection are low (since someone would have to be dialing in from an employee's home). This method does create some logistical problems for traveling employees, however.

Another way to increase security on a dial-in line is to modify the software that establishes the connection so that it prompts for another password in addition to the one you use to login [RS91, pp. 205–206]. Having a *double password* system on your lines helps, but has all the same weaknesses of regular passwords. The only advantage is now the cracker has *two* roadblocks to get past instead of only one. A variation on this is to use a modem that actually has a password mechanism built into it. Some vendors offer modems that are equipped to do encrypted *handshaking* (each authenticating the other modem by special password) before completing the connection.

As always, closely monitoring your modem logs will help you spot attempted attacks early, probably before anyone successfully gets in.

UUCP

If you run UUCP to connect your UNIX machine to another UNIX machine to exchange mail or transfer other files, your biggest risk is that you have a modem that someone could dial into and try to login on as a user [GS91, Chapter 10], [Sto90, p. 135], and [Cur92, pp. 121–126]. Monitoring your logs of failed login attempts will tip you off to someone attacking this way.

Rather than having a single UUCP login ID for all other hosts you connect to, the more accepted method is to have an ID for each remote host. This increases the accountability of each connection and makes tracking a little easier.

6.7.2 Network applications

No networking protocol is perfectly secure. Data flies up and down network wires, some of it encrypted, but the vast majority of it in the clear. Bugs in networking protocols (such as TCP/IP [Bel89]) and wire-taps on network cabling are more the exception than the rule. Other problems are much more likely and much easier to take advantage of.

If someone can connect an unauthorized host to your network, he can masquerade as another host by using the same network address, or he can redirect network packets by putting out fake routing information. Maintaining a list of hosts and verifying it against observed network traffic is the best way to find unauthorized hosts on your network.

File transfer programs

Most versions of the UNIX `ftp` daemon log accesses made to your machine (if yours does not, there are publicly available versions on the Internet you can get). If your access controls are not set up correctly and someone retrieves a file they should not be able to, you can at least find out about it.

Electronic mail

Electronic mail is not known for its security [Cur92, pp. 71–75, 153–155]. The risk is a subtle one, but you can lose confidential information just as if someone broke in and stole it.

> A department head at a company worked part-time there and part-time at a university on the opposite coast. When at each location, he forwarded his e-mail to his account at the other site. One day, while he was at the university, a confidential e-mail memo was sent to all department heads at the company. The next day, the sender of the memo received an e-mail bounce (a message returned to the original sender when the message is undeliverable for some reason) from the computer at the university because the file system containing the user's mailbox had no room left and the message could not be delivered. The sender was unpleasantly surprised that she had sent company confidential outside of the company without knowing it. The user had not realized what kind of information might be mailed outside the company by forwarding his mail off-site. The company adopted a policy where no e-mail addresses could be redirected outside the company unless it was obvious to the sender by adding `ext-` to the beginning of the alias.

It is also quite easy to spoof electronic mail (i.e., send mail to a user and make it appear to be from someone else). Currently, no authentication mechanism is required for electronic mail in the Internet community (however, this problem is being examined). Right now, the message header is the only indication you receive indicating the message's origin.

While these possibilities may not seem as threatening, they are a potential source of trouble, and with the world depending more and more on e-mail communications, it is a problem that needs to be solved. A proposal for Privacy-enhanced Electronic Mail (PEM) is defined by RFC 1113 [Lin89] using public-key encryption similar to those described previously. These and similar implementations are being developed and should become more visible in the near future [Cur92, pp. 154–155, 176].

Remote file systems

Remote file systems are classic security holes, not because of errors in the protocols, but because of mismanagement of the machines exporting file systems to other hosts [GS91, Chapter 12], [Cur92, pp. 87–98].

For example, the Network File System (NFS) can make your life much easier by allowing you to specify certain file systems to be mounted via the network on other machines, eliminating the need for you to copy that data to each machine where it is needed. By default, however, anyone that can connect to your machine can request that their machine mount that file system. If you take no precaution to limit what machines are authorized to mount your file systems, unauthorized machines, even at other sites, might be able to mount your files and read them (or worse yet, modify them!). Specify what hosts can mount your file systems and what access rights they have (restrict access to read-only whenever possible). Except in rare, specific circumstances, you should only allow access to hosts you trust and that are within your administrative control.

6.7.3 Window systems

The X Window System is a powerful tool which allows input and output to be performed from and to various workstations, rather than requiring the local workstation perform all the work. With all this input and output going back and forth across the network, it is possible for confidential information to be transmitted on the network (this is true of other network applications, too, but it is of even greater concern with the X Window System because of the variety of types of information that might be involved).

A discussion of the intricacies of X Window System security is beyond the scope of this book. For a detailed discussion, see [MP92, Chapter 4].

6.7.4 Kerberos

Kerberos is an authentication system developed at the Massachusetts Institute of Technology (MIT) as part of Project Athena [Cur92, pp. 150–153], [GS91, Chapter 13]. Project Athena was a real-life attempt to develop and manage a distributed network of workstations on a large scale (over 1,000 nodes). Inherent in a distribution of users and information on that scale is an increase in the possibility of security breakdown. It becomes much more important to be able to authenticate each host and each user on a continuing basis. In a network of this size, it is virtually impossible to guarantee that every node present is secure and authorized to take part. Kerberos, therefore, strives to authenticate the user and host at the time the service is requested.

Kerberos is based on having a ticket as a means of authorization to receive a specific service. Built into your ticket is authentication information that identifies the requester. The user application requests a ticket from the Ticket-Granting Service (TGS) by supplying a password known only to Kerberos. Once the user has been identified and approved, the ticket is issued. That ticket will only work for that user and only for a short amount of time (so copying the ticket and attempting to use it later in another request by another user would fail).

Kerberos makes it much more difficult for a user to impersonate another user or another service. However, it relies on passwords at a basic level, so still suffers all the potential problems of any password-based authentication mechanism.

6.7.5 Network firewalls

The concept of a *network firewall* is well understood and critical to maintaining good security [CB94], [Cur92, pp. 75–78], [GS91, Chapter 14], [Ros93b, Chapter 9], [Ros93b, Chapter 16], [Chea].

The basic idea is that you have a single host that filters your incoming network connections and only allows in connections of the type you specify (usually electronic mail, sometimes no others). This machine may be a UNIX computer but is usually a router whose whole job is to do nothing but filter packets.

Using a firewall, you can select what kind of connections are allowed into your network. Useful and low-risk connections like electronic mail[15] are usually allowed; sometimes file transfer is allowed (and logged); rarely are plain login attempts allowed.

6.7.6 Monitoring network activity

Monitoring the traffic on your network may help to alert you to breaches in your security [Cur92, pp. 80–84, 108–110], [Bel92]. Maintaining a list of devices and hosts authorized on your network and periodically comparing observed hosts against that will help you identify covertly connected devices.

Looking over your log files and searching for special error messages or unknown hostname or address references is another way to find evidence of unwanted activity.

6.8 Handling a Breach

Well, you've made your security plan, you've identified your risks, you've put policies and controls in place to try to stop as many of the threats as you can, but still you've suffered a breach in your security. Now what do you do? Included in your security plan should be a procedure for handling such a situation [Bra90], [Hol91, pp. 61–67, 78–81].

In the case of a malicious attack, your first decision is whether or not to try to catch the perpetrator(s) [Sto90], [GS91, Chapter 15]. If you want to try to catch them, you will need to leave yourself vulnerable while you track them; otherwise, they will realize they have been found out and will probably stop. If your information is too valuable to lose and stopping them is your main goal (which is probably the normal case), then your mission is to find their means of entry and plug the hole. Only in rare cases do you have the luxury of actually playing

[15] Okay, okay, in the case of the Internet worm it wasn't such a low risk, but that's been fixed now... really.

along with the cracker, feeding him false information, and luring him into a trap as in [Sto90] and [Cheb].

In the case of a natural disaster, your first contacts will be your insurance company and your vendor(s). Note that most general personal and business insurance does not cover computer equipment. Be sure to check yours *before* the disaster strikes. After that, rebuilding what you had from backup equipment and data will demand your full attention.

6.8.1 Examine audit trails and logs

If your breach was malicious, one of the first things you should do is check your logs and audit trails. If you have been checking these all along (like you should), you may have noticed an increase in activity somewhere and know where to look. If a cracker was able to compromise your security quickly, you may not have noticed anything in your regular reviews of logs since the damage was recent.

Your logs will provide you more information about where the illicit activity was and give you a better idea where to look for clues to the method of access.

6.8.2 Recovering data

If your data has been lost, recovering it is much the same as recovering after any kind of disaster (see Chapter 2 for a discussion of backups and disaster recovery). Everyone has their own stories about the best or worst experience having to recover from a complete loss of data or equipment [Bak91, p. 236–239].

6.8.3 Legal issues

Even a cursory examination of the potential legal ramifications of a break-in at your site is beyond the scope of this text, but a few hints will get you started in the right direction [GS91, Chapter 17], [Bak91, Chapter 13]. Security-related legislation is also summarized in Appendix B of [RS91].

Only your legal staff can really help you with the specifics of the legal issues as they apply to your organization. While it is possible to prosecute those guilty of attacks on your computer environment, this is a fairly new area and it is often frustrating when the law is not up to speed with the reality in which you are living.

Good relationships and cooperation with local, state, and even federal law enforcement agencies will help you should you ever need their assistance [Cur92, pp. 135–136].

One common preventive action taken is to put disclaimers in the login and file transfer banners displayed by your machines. Warning all users who connect to your computers that they are intended for use only by authorized personnel and that use by anyone else will be prosecuted often will dissuade the casual cracker from testing your resolve. It will also help provide proof of your desire not to have just anyone on your machine and provide grounds for legal prosecution. There have actually been cases (both in computer crime and regular trespassing offenses) where failure to post a "KEEP OUT" sign was considered tantamount to an invitation to enter.

6.9 Keeping Up

The security community has set up many mechanisms for ongoing discussion of security-related topics. Those available from the Internet take the form of Internet mailing lists; those on Usenet take the form of Usenet newsgroups.

On the Internet, there are many mailing lists [Cur92, pp. 186–187] which discuss networking and security issues. The Risks Digest, the TCP/IP mailing list, and the Sun-Spots, Sun-Nets, and Sun-Managers mailing lists are only a few.

The Usenet newsgroups also boast a fair number of security-related groups [Cur92, p. 188]. A few of these are:

- `comp.security.announce`
- `comp.security.misc`
- `comp.protocols.kerberos`

- `comp.virus`
- `alt.security`

Keeping in touch with other system administrators and vendors is the best way to make sure you are doing everything you can to prevent unauthorized access to your computing environment.

Chapter 7

Administrative Skills

Don't let the relative positioning or size of this chapter fool you. The administrative side of system management is the one that will make or break you. You may be a consummate wizard technically, but if you cannot prioritize the services you provide and emergencies you will encounter in your job, no one will be satisfied enough to notice. On the other hand, you may be little more than adequate in your technical skill, but the ability to stay organized, know what needs to be done and when, and make it happen (through your own talents or the talents of others) can make you the most valuable system administrator around.

Organization is the key to being a successful system administrator. Many aspects of the job are not technical in nature. You must track problems to some sort of resolution. You must maintain good relationships with vendors and service people who all help you do your job. You may be involved in charging for services within your company depending on how the computing resources are allocated and accounted for. You will most likely be the focal point for anything that has to do with the computer environment, technical or otherwise. This may be anything from drawing up the budget for computer equipment and staff expenditures for the next fiscal year all the way down to ordering new paper for the printer.

7.1 Information Management

Documenting local information is almost as important as doing backups. Writing things down seems like busy work and thus is usually left until one has the time. Unfortunately, no one ever has the time so it goes undone.

I finally made the time and was never so glad about having done so. Others system administrators and even users were able to find information when I wasn't around (including a couple of emergency situations). It turned out to be a valuable project. Of course, it was easier to justify the time after the need was obvious than it would have been beforehand.

In the document, we recorded information like:

- the history of the environment
- computer room equipment, sensors, and alarms
- networking and dial-in information
- hardware and software information
- security procedures and information
- purchasing and procurement procedures

Try to write down as much of what you carry around in your head as you can. In the worst case, if something should happen to you unexpectedly, all will not be lost. Even in ordinary circumstances, others can find information without having to interrupt you to ask, which is extremely useful if you have a staff of several system administrators.

You cannot hope to document everything immediately, especially in an environment with a previous history. Once you begin to keep your records, however, document everything as you do it. Try to fill in the history you know or can discover as you have the time. But don't put off starting just because you can't create the complete picture immediately. The longer you wait, the more information you will be missing.

7.1.1 Activity log

The advice here is simple: log *everything*. Keep track of your local modifications to hardware and software, problems encountered by your users, visits by vendors, repairs and preventive maintenance performed by vendors, or anything else that changes any part of your computing environment. This not only helps you find what you did to solve that problem you solved six months ago, it also helps justify raises and staffing increases, and helps you write regular status reports for management. Along with your log, you may want to keep track of the time involved to solve problems, install software, or make system upgrades as well. This allows you to show where your time is going [NSS89, pp. 454–458].

Keeping activity information on-line is a useful mechanism when possible. This makes searching for keywords or specific information fairly easy. However, on-line information is not always portable. If you choose to keep your logs on paper, you'll want to have a logbook with numbered pages so you can cross-reference topics to facilitate future lookup of information. You may also want to do some sort of topic indexing or margin notations of subjects to help find specific information again later.

7.1.2 Problem tracking

One of the most visible parts of your job as a system administrator is to track the problems encountered by your users. Whether you fix the problem or a vendor provides you with a fix, in your users' eyes, you are ultimately responsible for making sure the problem is fixed.

The classic problem system administrators face is prioritizing their time to work on these problems. The ability to separate the critical problems from the noncritical problems is essential to providing good service, but one that a surprising number of people either do not possess or choose not to use.

Don't let yourself fall into "fire-fighting" mode, where you are constantly servicing the last request, regardless of what it is or how important it may be. Once you lose sight of the overall activity of your computing environment, you lose the ability to prioritize and you have no choice but to run around randomly fixing whatever you can get to at the moment. Chaos will result and people will see it.

Another common pitfall is to service the simple requests first just to get them off your list. While there is merit in simplifying your ever-growing "to do" list, and a simple request deserves a quick fix so the user can go on, concentrating on the easy problems will relegate the complex problems to the bottom of your list where they will likely remain. Often, the only solution is to actually schedule time to work on some of your more complex problems. Sometimes bringing in outside resources (such as consultants) to work on well-defined, complex problems will help progress on the problems without requiring you to devote large chunks of time to them (and thus prevent you from solving a dozen smaller problems).

In a small environment, whenever someone has a problem, they simply contact you. The larger the installation, the more people you have working on the problems. A large site will need a problem distribution mechanism of some kind. You don't want someone stopping just any support staff member in the hall and asking about the problem. You want a formal system for submitting requests (probably by electronic mail), where the most appropriate staff member can be assigned the task. In this case, the distribution mechanism can also track and log the work done to solve the problem and the time required. This information can be used to generate reports for management about the resources used to solve internal problems (and justify more staff, when necessary). If you run a site by yourself, you must keep a list of what you work on so that you can convey what it is you're spending your time on to upper management.

Even when a problem requires action from a vendor, it will be up to you to track the vendor's progress and make sure they provide a fix in a reasonable amount of time. Simply passing the problem on to the vendor and then crossing it off your list may or may not get the problem solved for the user. The user is expecting *you* to see that the problem is fixed, one way or another.

7.1.3 Introductory new user information

When a new user arrives to begin work, the chances of his knowing how things work are slim. Unless this computing environment is exactly like the one where he worked previously, he'll be lost in yours.

Being able to provide a new user with an information document or packet of documents can go a long way towards making the new user feel less out of touch. The information should include general information (such as how to print, how to dial in, how to send e-mail, and how to report problems and ask questions). In addition to this, a software and hardware inventory and a one-page emergency procedures list would be helpful. Simplified versions of much of the information you document for yourself as the system administrator may prove helpful in a user's overall understanding of the local environment.

7.1.4 Local network information

Keep a map of your network. If your network is large, then of course a detailed map with every host shown is probably unreasonable, but a diagram of the network cables and their major connections (like routers and bridges) is useful. Keeping both physical and logical network information available in a single view can greatly help keep everyone's mental model of your environment correct. A map of office connections, whether they be twisted-pair or coaxial cables, is also useful.

In addition to local network maps, you should keep a list of all dial-in and dial-out lines and any other external network connections, the locations of any log files associated with them, and any dependencies for their proper operation.

If you ever build specialized cables (rather than order them in bulk), you should also document the procedure for doing so.

All network cables, twisted-pair cables, and even power tails and power cords under your computer room floor should be clearly labeled. Few things are as frustrating as having a cable in your hand and realizing you will have to follow it to the other end to find out where it leads.

It should be unnecessary to point out that keeping all this information up to date is critical. Having a cable in the computer incorrectly labeled is worse than not having it labeled at all! At least when it is not labeled, you *know* you don't know where it goes.

7.1.5 Equipment inventory

You should maintain an inventory of all computer equipment, tools, spare parts, and any other devices for which you are responsible. Depending on the paperwork required by your site, how detailed this list is may be driven by other departments (e.g., Finance). Even if you do not maintain a list for others, keeping track of workstations, printers, and other devices is important, especially where the equipment is in a public access area, or taken on trips, or to a user's home.

In cooperating with a finance department, you will probably assist them with *asset tracking*. Just as you want to keep up with the equipment you use and have responsibility for, the financial people in your organization must keep up with all assets belonging to the company.

Your list of equipment for your own use should include the equipment name and model, serial number, location, user(s), and hardware configuration and operating system version information.

7.1.6 Software inventory

Every bit as important as your hardware inventory is an inventory of your software. A list of software, revision levels, machines for which it is licensed, and any dependencies it has (in the way of hardware or other software) is indispensable.

Many software packages provide services to the local network (either by providing a function, like printing a file, or by providing access to specific data). Document any such services that are installed locally (i.e., that are not part of your standard operating system distribution), what hosts are involved in providing the service, any other resources upon which they depend, and where the software came from (either vendor information or an FTP site if it came "from the net").

Of course, all locally written and installed software should be accompanied by local documentation, even if it is something as simple as a short shell script. If any local user is an expert, include this information.

7.1.7 Procedures

Much of the job of system management involves establishing and enforcing procedures for management activities. Although creating policy may not seem like a "fun" technical activity, creating effective policy requires a good understanding of the issues involved, most of which are technical. A technically inexperienced system administrator may seem like a good person to put in charge of procedures, but often he or she is the wrong person for the job.

Policies are like the rules of the computing environment. They help the users know how they need to behave, and they provide information about what the support staff can and cannot do for them. Don't let crisis dictate your policy. Define policies ahead of time when you can think them through calmly and reasonably.

Backup

Fully document your backup schedule, tape rotation scheme, the location of your backup tapes and logs, and the software used to create a backup, along with examples of how to restore a file or entire file system. Having the best backup scheme in the world doesn't help your users if you must personally restore files and you're out of town.

Emergency

It is important to provide information about what should be done in the case of various possible emergencies. You will not always be present when some emergency occurs. When time is critical, no one may have time to read anything more than the emergency shutdown section of your emergency procedures, but if the information exists, it is at least possible that it will be used.

A separate emergency procedures list should be developed for each computer room or area where computer resources are concentrated. Each list should include the names of all staff members who could be called in the case of an emergency at that location (along with home telephone or pager numbers). Each procedure should also describe a specific course of action to take in the case of any likely emergency like fire, power failure, air conditioning failure, or water accumulation. If you have a complex environment, requiring several pages to describe even basic procedures, then a one-sheet summary should also be created that can be attached to the door of the computer room.

Software installation

Every environment has its own philosophy for installing local software. What directories are used, who has access, how licensing is accomplished, and how the software is upgraded are just a few of the things that can be done in any number of different ways. To a great degree, things that might seem arbitrary are configured in some specific way to take advantage of some local system modification or to provide a specific advantageous service.

Any special location for software or any special configuration process to make the software available in the local environment should be included in the description of your software installation procedures. You will not always be the person installing new software. Even so, you want it to be installed properly and be consistent with the local software installation scheme.

New system installation

Rarely can you install a new workstation, even if it is the same model as all the other workstations in your environment, just as it is shipped from the vendor. Every site makes some number of local customizations to make the machine part of the local environment. Adding users, making remote file systems available, adding printing capabilities, and adding the new host to the local host table or database are all normal parts of adding a system to a local environment. Maintaining a list of all tasks required (for each type of host) to add a host to the local environment makes adding new hosts much easier.

Purchasing and procurement

Your documentation about purchasing and procurement should describe your part in the procedure. In large organizations, this may simply be filling out a form. In a smaller organization, you may be the person actually shopping around for the best deal. If others in your organization are responsible for certain parts, list who they are and the parts for which they are responsible. This will save someone else untold trouble trying to figure out from whom they should get help with the process.

List any forms you fill out, what kinds of items you buy from which vendors, contacts for sales and support at the vendor companies, who in your organization has signing authority and for what levels of purchase, and what path the completed form should take within your organization. If you have already documented information about your vendors in your local documentation for your environment, the mention here could simply be a cross-reference to that.

Replenishing consumable supplies

The most inglorious and mundane task performed by system administrators is replacing consumable supplies like printer or plotter paper, printer ribbons, laser printer toner cartridges, or diskettes. If users are free to write tapes as they please, then you may also have a public store of tapes that will need restocking periodically.

While these tasks seem almost like chores, your users find it extremely annoying when resources they count on are unavailable. However, with more modern equipment, like the laser printer, it is fairly easy for the users themselves to do quite a bit of this replenishment. For example, just about anyone can be shown how to refill a paper tray in a laser printer and probably can even figure it out for themselves. Users should be encouraged to do simple operations like this that don't require the system administrator's technical savvy.

Instructions for replacing things like paper or even laser printer toner cartridges should be included in your procedures documentation, along with the locations where these supplies are stored. Not only can other new support staff members learn by reading instructions rather than asking you to show them how to change a printer ribbon, but interested users who don't mind doing for themselves every now and then can also take advantage of them. Even laser printer toner cartridges can be changed by your users (after all, many people have laser printers in their homes now).

Security procedures

Your organization may already have a set of security procedures that apply to the entire company. Even if this is true, you should document any procedures that apply to the use of the computing environment. In addition, there will probably be some procedures you follow that are above and beyond what is specified by a companywide policy, or that implement the details of a companywide policy. The relationship between the workings of your computing environment and any company-wide security policy should be pointed out in your document.

If you require any forms (e.g., for new user accounts or access to the dial-in system), these should be described in your documentation. Any rules and regulations to which you expect users to adhere should also be included. This "local" security policy should be distributed to new users and on a periodic basic to all users (possibly via e-mail) as a reminder of these important rules.

When new users read your security policy, they should understand what kind of access and data is available or can be made available, and what is necessary to be approved for any special access to data or networks. The more you can explain the rationale for restrictions, the more the user will have an appreciation for what is being protected and why. This will lower the chances that the user feels someone (probably you) is simply "playing God" in an arbitrary fashion.

7.2 Planning

Most computing environments are constantly changing. You may plan, one day, to reach some level of stability, where machines don't move and software doesn't require updates, but you will never live to see that day. Planning for the inevitable changes to your environment should be a part of your daily life.

These changes may be as simple as finding a location for a new software package someone has ordered or space for a new compute server for the computer room. They may be as complicated as moving the entire environment to a new building or even a new city.

Keep up with what is going on in the company. Go to as many of the meetings to which you are invited as possible (and encourage management to keep you "in the loop" with issues that concern the computing environment). Staying involved with the planning being done by management is the best way to have good information with which to do your own planning. You may also find that management makes invalid assumptions about technical issues and if you are participating in the discussion, you can correct any such problems.

> I thought the first manager who invited me to department meetings was wasting my time as well as his. I would go and sit and listen to people talk about their specific projects and feel that it all had almost nothing to do with my work. In one early meeting, I was listening to a project leader give the status of a project. He said they were about to place an order for a specific workstation. They planned to port their product to the new architecture and send it to a potential customer for evaluation. I perked up and asked why they purchased that workstation rather than what we already used. The answer was because the graphical display was faster and of higher quality and the customer needed a high-quality display. Then I asked if the software vendor had ported their graphics package to this other workstation (which I knew had not been done). The plan was to run the same software which ran on our workstations in house. The people on this project were former MS-DOS programmers and were assuming everything ran everywhere. After the meeting, we were able to get together and change the order so that everything would work together. By investing 30 minutes in a meeting up front, I saved myself weeks of headache down the line.

Unfortunately, this kind of information won't come looking for you. The only way you can keep up with what is going on in the company is to participate in meetings and show that you are interested in what is going on. The more interest you show, the more people will come talk to you about future ideas to get your opinion. The more you do it, the easier it becomes because everyone gets used to the process.

Downsizing

Lately, the buzzword in business has been *downsizing* or *rightsizing.* This sometimes means moving from mainframes down to smaller computers. It often means shrinking the size of your organization. Sometimes, as an organization shrinks, multiple support groups can be more efficient if merged into a single, larger support group. This is usually a nontrivial task since these different groups almost certainly have their own ways of supporting their users and those users have their own special needs (this is probably one reason they evolved as separate groups in the first place).

I have been directly involved in two such operations (and swapped stories with colleagues about others) and, as is the case with computing environments, no two are alike. Technical issues are the obvious problems, but personal issues turn out to be equally important. An attitude of cooperation and teamwork goes a long way to help; individualistic heroism is usually self-defeating. Hurt feelings because someone feels "their" world is being destroyed in favor of someone else's model can create stress for everyone in the new group. Usually, being sensitive to these kinds of problems is enough to make them manageable.

Even though many of the issues involved will be nontechnical in nature, planning and executing a merger like this can eat up a large portion of a system management staff's time. Often it will involve equipment and office moves, as well as reorganization of the affected groups. The biggest challenge is maintaining an acceptable level of support while finding the time to devote to planning and executing a successful merger.

Moving

Moving a computing environment from one location to another, or merging two or more computing environments together, are two of the most challenging projects one can attempt. In today's corporate climate, where many organizations are downsizing their staffs along with their equipment, it is often necessary to consolidate resources. Often, these resources are the computer support. In a large organization with several distinct working groups, similarly distinct support groups may have formed to satisfy the specific needs of each group. As the working groups are merged together, so the support groups must be merged. Merging environments that make different assumptions, operate differently, have different personalities, and provide different kinds of help to their user communities, is a daunting task, and no two such mergers are alike since no two computing environments are alike.

7.3 Financial Management

Most technically oriented people do not enjoy dealing with financial issues. Whether it is because it is not as interesting as dealing with technically challenging issues or because the perceived level of responsibility is higher than one is comfortable with, many run away at the first mention of dealing with money.

A larger organization will employ people whose job it is to deal with these issues. Hiring, purchasing, and budgeting issues may be handled outside of your responsibility and, at most, you may only be asked to give some input to the processes.

However, in a smaller organization, the system administrator may double as the computer center manager who has to deal with some or all of these issues.

7.3.1 Purchasing and procurement

In a large organization, your only exposure to purchasing equipment and software may be to fill out a form (usually, a *purchase requisition*, also known as a PR or a Purchase Req). The purchasing channels, the bids, the vendor lists, and the authority for the purchase may be far removed from you.

In a small organization, there may not even be a form. You may simply obtain "permission" from your company officer in charge of financial dealings and pursue the entire purchase yourself. In this case, you will be shopping for the best product yourself, maintaining lists of vendors and your relationships with their sales representatives ("sales reps"). When the bill arrives, with your name on it, you just forward it on to your friend in finance.

In many cases, your experience will be something in between. In either case, you may be given an annual budget and be expected to justify expenditures. If not you, then your manager may take care of this piece of the financial pie. Regardless of your personal level of participation in the purchasing and procurement process, the basic activities are the same. The only difference is who performs them.

Consumables

Consumable supplies like paper, laser printer toner cartridges, printer ribbons, diskettes, or tapes must be kept on hand and reordered. You may simply be able to notify someone (like the office manager, who may order regular business supplies as well) when it is time to order more, or you may have to make the order yourself. In a small office, the procedure may be to stop by the business supply store on your way back from lunch and submit an expense report with the receipt. In a large organization, it may be necessary to chart usage trends so that you stock the appropriate amount of supplies to fill the needs. Usage may vary in cycles based on company deadlines, like fiscal years and product deliveries.

Product evaluation

The system administrator should be involved in evaluating products, regardless of his future involvement in the actual purchase. Any significant purchase should not be made lightly, and this is especially true of computer equipment that you will be bringing into service in your local environment. Any good purchasing procedure should require that the system administrator be involved in decisions concerning what to purchase, in what quantity, and in what time frame.

Before blindly buying a new device or software, you will want to evaluate its behavior in your local environment. This means obtaining an evaluation version of the product and testing it in its intended use. If your users can do what they expected to do with it and you can manage it in a reasonable way (and it causes no other side-effects in the environment), then you can be reasonably confident about the purchase. Often, in testing a new product, some unforeseen side-effect will preclude bringing it into the environment for long-term use. In these cases, you can work with the vendor to correct the problem or find a work-around, but at least you've found the problem before the software becomes a resource upon which your users depend.

Choosing vendors

Sometimes you have no choice of vendor. If only one company makes a machine with the performance you need, that can support the number of terminal connections or amount of disk you need, you buy it. As the UNIX market expands, however, more companies are competing for each market niche, and being stuck with a single choice is now the exception more than it is the rule.

So how do you choose a vendor when you want to purchase a computer, printer, disk drive, or other piece of equipment. First and foremost, you will still narrow the field down to the companies that provide a piece of equipment that will perform to your specifications. If, after evaluating the product and the price, you still have more than one possibility on your list, consider the service reputation of each vendor. If you are buying a service contract along with the product, then how well they support their product is also of particular interest to you. Talk to other people you know, either personally or on one of many computer networks, who have purchased the same or similar equipment recently. Find out what their experience has been with the product and with the company itself. You may find a company whose product isn't quite as fantastic as another's, but whose service reputation is so good you want to go with them anyway. With the speed of advances in computer technology today, lagging a little behind the market may be quite tolerable, if you receive excellent service.

Find out how long the company has been in business. This is a measure of survivability. While there are certainly many fine companies that have not been in business long (and this in no way implies they won't live long and productive lives), a company that *has* been in business a long time has proven its ability to survive market changes in the industry. A lifetime warranty means nothing if the company is no longer doing business.

For some sites that need to remain on the "leading-edge" or "cutting-edge" of technology (i.e., always using the newest, most advanced equipment available), the tradeoff turns out to be the lack of ability of the vendor to support its own product. In this case, where an organization often winds up helping a vendor test their own product, the company is sometimes said to be on the "bleeding-edge" of technology.

If your site is an engineering shop that can stand a few days of downtime, then quick service may not be as important to you as it would be in a production environment where invoices don't get sent out if the computer isn't working.

If you already have a maintenance contract with a vendor and you are unsatisfied, shop around with their competitors. It is not unusual for third parties to offer themselves as qualified technicians for another company's products and compete as a service provider. Be sure to check out the reputation of a candidate for service, especially when it is service for equipment from another company. However, don't assume a company cannot service equipment just because they don't manufacture it. A number of reputable companies are quite competent at servicing other company's products these days.

Recycling

In an industry that has promised "the paperless office" but has delivered more information on more paper than ever before, you should try to recycle as much of your refuse output as possible. Old-style computer paper didn't recycle well, but since many people use laser printers now, the paper is regular business stock typing paper that can easily be recycled.

Most laser printer toner cartridges can be recycled (refilled with toner and reused) and the refilled cartridges are usually cheaper to buy. Many sites choose not to take advantage of this because the quality of a refilled cartridge is often not quite as good as one that is brand new. Even in this case, however, you should consider advertising some of your printers as "test" or "development" printers which can use the refilled cartridges, thereby keeping separate printers for "high-quality" output that is guaranteed to always have new cartridges. Even if you do not wish to deal with companies that refill cartridges and would rather just throw yours away, consider giving them to such a company rather than filling up a landfill with all that plastic.

7.3.2 Hardware and software support contracts

In a large organization, your purchasing department may take care of negotiating pricing and service for your equipment. If you are part of a smaller site, you may deal with these issues yourself.

A service contract is comparable to an insurance policy. Your organization pays a certain amount of money, possibly per machine, for the knowledge that the vendor will come to your site and make repairs when necessary. You may go months without needing service. In a run of bad luck, you may see your field engineer every day for a week.

Software support usually involves telephone support for diagnosis of problems and identification of ways to work around the problem, the ability to submit bug reports, and the right to obtain updated versions with bug fixes when they become available. Pricing is generally based on the number of licenses purchased.

7.3.3 Resource cost chargeback

Depending on the size and internal structure of your organization, you may need to gather usage information in order to charge other departments for the cost of resources. Often, the computing center bills back to departments for their use. Sometimes this is simply to gauge the use and allocate funds in budgets; other times real money is transferred to pay for services rendered.

If your company has a chargeback policy, it will be important for you to be able to produce reports on usage of resources like CPU time, printer paper, plotter paper, disk space, or network usage. The accounting subsystem of a computer running UNIX will provide these services. Your job will be to gather the information and create a report, by user or by department, detailing the use of resources in the computing environment.

7.3.4 Budget issues

One of the most important, regular jobs done in the computing center is to establish a budget. In an organization of any size, the system administrator will probably not be required to do this, but may be involved, at least peripherally, in the process.

The budget is an attempt to project where money will be spent in the following year. Some budgets may be made to cover shorter periods of time, but a year is typical. A year is a long time in the computer industry. Products change a great deal in a twelve-month period. Your users' needs change, too. Forecasting every possible need is not really possible, but forecasting most of the major ones is.

What kind of hardware, peripheral equipment, and supplies will be used in the coming year? If you know the directions of the projects and the changing market, you can probably make an educated guess at the needs. Many project leads and department heads can provide input into the budget.[1] After all, who better to describe future needs but those whose needs you're trying to satisfy?

How your budget totals out depends on how you pay for equipment and software. Some organizations choose to pay for software or equipment over a period of years, not all up front. These are known as *capitalized assets.* A fraction of capitalized assets is included in each budget every year until the debt is paid. Equipment is often leased this way. Sometimes at the end of the capitalization period you own the asset, and sometimes you must return it. You might compare it to paying rent on a house or making a house payment. At the end of the term, you either move out or you own the house, but either way, you did not pay the entire fee for living there all at once. You paid as you used the resource.

Small assets with short expected lifetimes (like software or supplies) are usually *expensed assets.* The full amount of the purchase price is applied to the current budget and the item is paid for at the time of purchase. Just as with a car, you don't want to be still paying on a capitalized asset long after you've lost the use of it. The value

[1] In fact, some organizations develop their budgets at this lower level, making the high-level budget simply a process of collecting and refining these individual budgets.

of computer equipment *depreciates* , or is reduced, over its lifetime. Since the advances in the computer industry are coming so quickly, computer equipment tends to depreciate at a rapid rate. A traditional five-year lease for cars or large equipment is much too long for computer equipment; it would be obsolete long before the lease period expired.

Staffing comes into play when creating a budget. A significant portion of recurring cost is people. In the long run, the amount of money an organization spends on a computer system, no matter how advanced, is never as much as is spent on support and service, either through service contracts or hiring a support staff (or both). Because such funds usually come from two different "pots," they usually aren't compared equally. If you are the senior system administrator or a computing center director and have employees under your management, your current staff and future hiring needs will play a significant role in your budgeting work.

Chapter 8

Personal Skills

Along with being administratively talented, a successful system administrator must also have good "people skills." A surprising number of people believe that a "wizard" will solve all the problems you might ever have in a computing environment. While a wizard can be valuable, if he is unable to impart his wisdom to "the masses," a valuable resource is wasted. Too many traditional Unix wizards sit in an office, late at night, and do things that no "mere mortal" would ever consider attempting to keep the systems running smoothly. The system runs, shrouded in mystery and fear of the day when the wizard moves on to a new job or gets hit by a bus. This is no way to run a computer center.

System administrators must keep in mind why they are there and what services are expected of them, and take pride in the service they provide. Maintaining a good relationship with users, management, and others outside the organization is critical to the system administrator's success. The system administrator is also entrusted with access to all the information on the system. That requires a high ethical standard as well. A good system administrator can be your best friend. A bad one can be your worst enemy.

8.1 User Services

Depending on your environment, helping your users get their work done may well be the most important service expected of you. In environments where your users are all expert programmers, this is less of an issue, but the vast majority of computing environments are filled with people who are barely computer literate. They have problems to solve and tasks to perform and the computer is their tool. They may not be completely comfortable with that, but it is probably their only choice.

Your users may ask for all kinds of help from you to assist them with their work. After all, you are the expert. They may want to know the best way to solve a problem. They may want a better explanation of a topic than what they found in the manual (they *did* look in the manual first, didn't they?). They may ask you to perform some task that requires the privileges of the operator or *super user*.

If you can help your users get their work done, they will be happy and their objectives will be met. They will love you. If you are perceived as an impediment to their progress, they won't like you so much.

8.1.1 Your users

Always remember, you provide a service. To paraphrase John F. Kennedy: "Ask not what your users can do for you but what you can do for your users." They are the major reason you have the job you have.

How well you deal with people is at least as important as how experienced you are technically. Many brilliant system administrators have been unsuccessful because of their inability to deal with the people they support, not because they were in over their heads technically. Just because you are a wizard programmer doesn't mean you can take care of a machine *and* the people who use it.

Some prefer the word "customer" to "user." The word you use to describe the people you help is of little significance, but your attitude towards them is of extreme importance. Working together, you and your users form a team of people with the capacity to achieve the goals of your organization. Neither half of that team should have dominion over the other half. A partnership is the most effective relationship you can have.

8.1.2 Your equipment

To say "your equipment" is a misnomer because it is not *yours*. It belongs to the company. While it is *in* your control, if you seem to enjoy that too much, your users will perceive you as a control freak.

In today's distributed environments, many users feel the machines are theirs, possibly because their departmental budget may have paid for them, but often because the machine sits on their desk. For you to act as if it's really your machine and you're letting them use it out of the kindness of your heart will only build a wall between you and the user.

Your opinions about how the machine should be managed are, of course, extremely valuable. Sometimes those opinions may have to be backed up with technical reasoning and presented to managers to get agreement from everyone involved on a certain issue. Rarely will you have a dictatorship, with yourself as the dictator. You will be lucky when you are in a democracy and you yourself have an equal vote.

8.2 Communication With Users

Since your users are usually the single most important aspect of your daily life as a system administrator, it makes sense that good communication with them is equally important. As in any interpersonal relationship, communication is the key to success. If you are open, honest, and helpful with users, they will appreciate it.

Your computing environment should not be a war zone. You should not look upon the situation as an "us versus them" conflict. Everyone is here to get a job done. At times it might seem to each group that the other is acting as an impediment, but this attitude can and must be overcome.[1]

[1] One of my pet peeves is people who don't return phone calls because they don't have an answer for someone (in any line of work). I would much rather hear back that someone is looking

8.2.1 Warn users of pending changes

The best way to make sure your users are aware of your plans for changes in the computing environment is to tell them. You should always notify them about new equipment such as printers or public compute servers, new software, or old tools that are outdated and are being removed or replaced. With any significant change in the computing environment, downtime is usually necessary. Warn users of scheduled downtime for machines and networks services. Always be sure to schedule sufficient downtime for an activity. It's better to be finished earlier than expected than to finish late. Even if the downtime is a simple reboot during lunch, let people know when it will happen and why it is necessary. Taking a little of the mystery out of the situation will reinforce the feeling that you know what you're doing. Operating in an air of mystery often leads to frustration and suspicion. Sometimes, in an emergency, you don't have any time to give warnings, but you should send out notification about what happened after the problem is fixed.

Many methods can be used to convey this information. On UNIX machines, the file `/etc/motd` is used to convey the "message of the day." Before everyone had a UNIX workstation on their desk, everyone had a terminal connected to a single large UNIX "mainframe."[2] The system administrator could edit the `/etc/motd` file and enter whatever message needed to be conveyed to the users. Anytime a user logged in, this message would be displayed on the screen. Today, with everyone having their own UNIX workstation, the `/etc/motd` file would have to be edited on each machine, a time-consuming task. Not only that, but the user only sees the message at login time, and since they often have their own machines in their offices, they don't always logout. Because it is less suitable in today's distributed environments, the `/etc/motd` file has fallen into disuse.

---

into my problem and will call me when they have time or something to tell me than not to hear from them at all!

[2] The term "mainframe" as used by many people today signifies a single, large computer system used by many people. In that sense, the older minicomputers that ran UNIX could be considered as providing mainframelike service; however, technically, these were not mainframe computers.

Electronic mail is a popular method of notifying users about changes to the local computing environment. Mail aliases that send a message to everyone (like `all` or `engineering`) can be easily defined to always reach the appropriate group. Some people object to having messages delivered to their mailbox when they don't believe they care about them. It is sometimes difficult to convince certain users of the importance of keeping up with planned changes to the local environment. Sometimes all you can do is answer a complaint with "Well, if you had read the mail I sent to everyone, you would have known about it." It seems harsh, and it should be a last resort, but usually even the most disinterested user catches on after an episode like that.

Local bulletin boards are an alternative to notification via e-mail. The advantage is that the user's mailbox is not cluttered with such mail. The disadvantage is that the user has to take the initiative to go read the bulletin board or newsgroup to find the message and might not do so on a regular basis. If you send your users mail, they are guaranteed to at least know about its arrival. Whether or not they read it is still up to them ("you can lead a horse to water..").

8.2.2 Be involved in users' plans

By maintaining contact with group leads, you will know what their future needs are likely to be. Train them to tell you in advance what they're buying. Try to be involved in the selection process so that they buy products that work together and that work in the local environment. One of the most frustrating things in the world is for someone to come into your office with a piece of software they ordered only to find that it won't run on your systems. If they will coordinate with you ahead of time, you can help them order hardware or software that will perform to their satisfaction.

If they are having guests or giving demonstrations, have them schedule with you so that you can provide equipment, disk space, accounts, documentation, or whatever else might be necessary. It is embarrassing for both you and users when they arrive in your office with a visitor who plans to give a demonstration and there are no resources available with which to do it. At best, you run around all afternoon in a panic to get it set up, pushing aside what you had planned to do, so someone else is likely disappointed. At worst, the demonstration is cancelled.

> A system administrator I knew used to have a sign on his door that read:
>
> YOUR lack of planning
> does not constitute
> MY emergency.
>
> In reality, in many cases, it does—but it shouldn't.

Situations like these are extremely frustrating. You want to provide good service and you probably hate disappointing people, which is one reason you're good at this job. So you jump through whatever hoop you can to try to make the best of the situation, and very often you pull it off! Sometimes, this only reinforces the idea that someone can come to you at the last minute and you'll work some magic and pull a miracle out of your hat. Pretty soon, people expect it from you and consider it a failure if you can't do the impossible! In a situation like this, you're set up for failure eventually. Try to explain the importance of keeping you involved in planning to management and users. Encourage them to work with you. You may find that sometimes you must stop yourself from *quite* pulling off "the miracle" and let something (relatively unimportant) fail. Only then will people realize the importance of notifying you of timely requirements in advance (just as you understand you should warn them of your plans).

Meetings

Depending on the organization, you may be involved in a number of meetings. Of course, meetings that directly impact your job, such as group meetings or meetings with department heads about what their group will need in the next year, are most obvious. Sometimes, people will pull you into a meeting just to give you the opportunity to learn something about their project and their needs. If you have the time, you should take advantage of these opportunities.

Most organizations should include their support staff in more of these kinds of activities. The few that do often have a support staff that is spread so thin that they cannot take the time away from problem solving. I have only worked for one company that included the support staff in these kinds of meetings on a regular basis, and it gave us good insight into the workings of the various groups. When you're sitting there, people will often ask questions of you while just brainstorming and you can discuss the issues concerning some idea they are considering. This is preferable to having them order equipment and/or software only to hear from you that it won't do what they wanted. Staying involved with your users will always help things run more smoothly down the line.

The 5:01 Phenomenon

A frequent specific occurrence of unplanned user requirements comes in what I call the "5:01 Phenomenon." It doesn't have to happen at 5:01, it can happen at just about any time during the day, but it typically happens "at the last minute."

A user drops by your office and needs a machine set up, a piece of software installed, or some other nontrivial action, and they need it *right now* because a vice-president is coming down in ten minutes to see it, or because they need it to finish a report that's due at 5:00 p.m., or some other critical reason.

You can ask if they knew about this deadline yesterday and why they couldn't have asked you to schedule it then, but it won't do you any good. They didn't warn you and here you are with an impossible deadline for something you don't have the time to do right now anyway. Often, these kinds of problems come up just as you're leaving the office for the day.

You have two choices. One is to tell them no. If the task truly is unworkable, even if you put your best effort into it, then this is the only fair thing to do. Convey to them the steps involved, the time it would take, and why it can't be done immediately. Offer to schedule the task as soon as reasonable. If you are cooperative, even in denying the request, the user will at least feel it is not an arbitrary decision on your part. During all this, impress upon the user the importance of planning ahead. Also, be ready to justify your denial of service to your managers in case the user does an end-run to complain.

Your other choice is to drop everything, risk missing deadlines on projects that are already scheduled, and attempt to fulfill the request. If it is at all possible, it is usually admirable to make the attempt, especially if this is the user's "first offense." Only attempt it if you believe you have a reasonable chance of success, however, because if you fail, it may or may not be perceived as a failure to plan on the part of the user (even though that's what it was). It does you no good to work on something that you know has no chance of success. But if you *can* pull it off, you will look like a miracle worker.

However, a bigger problem is hidden in all this. If you do manage to pull a rabbit out of a hat, you'll be a wiz. Next time, they'll expect you to do it again. So even if you manage to grab the ears of this rabbit, convey to the user, his management, and your management, through status reports or memos or whatever medium is appropriate, that you were *lucky* and that next time you might not be so lucky. Plead for more planning in the future. Think up a couple of variations on this scenario that could have made it fail to prove to them how easy it would be for it not to work out so well next time. With any luck, you can make your point without having to actually endure a failure, and never have to endure another 5:01 Phenomenon (but don't count on it).

8.2.3 Educate your users

You should be able to expect your users to stay interested in what is going on around them and to be able to help themselves to some degree. Some will insist they don't want to know anything except how to do their specific task, but an overall understanding about how the environment works, what services depend on what resources, and how to find out more information about a topic are essential to being able to accomplish any but the most mundane tasks. Most users understand that there is a certain amount of work everyone must do for themselves.

If you have a few users who insist that "ignorance is bliss," you may find it difficult to convince them of the value of staying informed. You can adopt a somewhat less helpful attitude with them to encourage them to be more self-sufficient. However, it is easy to go too far with this, which makes you appear uncooperative and unhelpful. Walking the tightrope between not doing everything for them while still helping them achieve their goals is sometimes difficult. Encourage any tendency they have to find out more for themselves. Anytime you do something for them, take them through the process as you do, so they will see that they could have done it themselves. Don't make it look like magic unless you want to keep doing it forever.

You can give your users the tools they need to keep up and learn more, but you cannot force the information into their heads. Show them that even *you* pull out the manual to look things up. [3] Users often come to you because it seems faster than looking something up for themselves. If it isn't any faster and they see they are capable of doing just what you do for them, they might do it themselves next time.

8.3 Communication With Management

Management (especially upper management) is not, by nature, a technically adept group of people. This is not a slam against management; it is simply not their job to deal with low-level technical issues. That's what you're for. Your job is to convey the important parts of the technical aspects of the computer environment to the managers who need the information so they can make reasonable high-level decisions.

Educating your management is similar to educating your users, but the information involved is different. Like users, though, you cannot force managers to take your advice, you can simply present them with it and with the reasoning behind it.

[3] There's always that classic advice: RTFM! Read The Fine (or other appropriate adjective) Manual.

> One company I worked for decided the electric bill was too high and, in order to bring it down, it was going to power all the computers off each weekend. Before asking anyone about this, they wrote up a memo and issued it to the company. Of course, everyone with any technical experience whatsoever went into hysterics. It took a meeting with two vice-presidents to convince them that if you turn 100 UNIX workstations off on Friday, only 99 of them are going to come back up on Monday, so turning 1,000 of them off was a "really bad idea."

Most managers like to receive reports, so that they can be better informed about what's going on. You may spend some time on a regular basis providing charts of system usage (from accounting data), disk, or other resource capacity, or even the amount of time you have spent on projects or servicing user requests. This will feel like busywork with no apparent benefit, but when asked, do it cheerfully. If it is resource information, you may be able to use it to justify new equipment. If it is information about your time, you might be able to justify additional personnel. At the very least, this is your chance to show those who have little concept of what you are really doing just what they get from you. Think of it as an opportunity, not a chore.

Often the system administrator sees things differently than a manager, and this can make life difficult. Managers are usually concerned about budgets, costs, and schedules. They are much more concerned about whether or not the network is working than the intricacies of what caused a failure.

Technical people usually think in terms of "the right answer," whereas management thinks in terms of profit to the company. This is a constant source of frustration to technical people everywhere. In the same vein, the system administrator's obsession with implementing the "perfect solution" is often frustrating to management, who see no corporate need for that level of perfection. Eventually, the two agree on a middle ground or management dictates the solution.

> While doing contract programming for a large computer manufacturer, I was speaking with a department manager who finally made me understand how managers and engineers differed. He told me that my job was to find the best technical solution to any given problem, without regard to cost or schedule, while his job was to do whatever helped the company make money. Because of this, a bug in a seldom-used utility reported by a small customer that required a redesign of an entire module was not fixed. You can argue the merits of "doing the right thing" forever, but from management's point of view, it was a simple equation of cost versus (immediate) return.

Pagers

The pager represents a controversial subject for most system administrators. Used properly, they represent a communication link between you and your management. Used incorrectly, they can represent a leash to which you feel tied twenty-four hours a day, seven days a week.

As with so many other issues, how you deal with this is up to each site. Some sites set hours of coverage, outside of which you don't have to answer a page. Some pass a single pager around between staff members to get twenty-four-hour coverage without any one person being inconvenienced all the time. Some sites consider it to be "part of the job," while others include compensation by the call or by the hour during a call.

The bottom line is, if your site needs to always have the ability to find someone responsible for the computing environment, then a pager (or in some cases a cellular phone) is going to be involved.

Who is allowed to call is another issue. Being called out of a movie to answer a question like "what's the argument to `ls` to make it sort by last file modification time?" is annoying. You don't necessarily want just *anybody* calling about *anything*. On the other hand, you don't want to make it difficult for a user to get help in a real emergency. Educating users about what is reasonable and what is not is the only real answer. One company had a workable solution. Only the building security guards had the pager numbers of all the system administrators for the various departments. If an environmental alarm went off, they could page us immediately. If a user had a real emergency, they went down to the guard and convinced him that it was indeed a problem. Of course, the guards were not always able to make such a determination, but often just the idea that they had to justify their need to page somebody eliminated the trivial problems.

If you have a pager, there will be occasions of (what you will perceive as) abuse. You can minimize it, but you cannot eliminate it. However, compared to the good it can do to free you to have a life (and not be tied to your office), it's usually worth it. It doesn't have to be a leash. It can be a device to free your conscience so you don't have to be afraid to run an errand or go out to lunch because you know if a *real* emergency comes up, they'll find you.

8.4 Communication With Colleagues

Your support staff may be the only group in your organization providing computer support, or there may be others in other departments. If there are others, you have resources and expertise inside your organization that you can use to supplement that of your own group.

In many cases, this supplementary talent is cultivated through contacts with the support staffs of other local companies. Through mutual cooperation and assistance, you can develop a base of knowledge that can be a valuable resource. Local and national user groups, for both technical topics and specific vendor platforms, provide a conduit for meeting other system administrators in your geographic area.

User groups can put you in touch with people all over the country and even the world. The Usenix Association sponsors SAGE, the System Administrators Guild, which is a special-interest group dealing with system management issues. Usenix sponsors two general conferences per year, and Usenix and SAGE sponsor the annual LISA[4]

[4] LISA originally stood for Large Installation System Administration, but now applies to both large and small sites.

conference. The Open Systems Conference Board in cooperation with SAGE also sponsors SANS, the Systems Administration, Networking, and Security conference.

Network mailing lists and bulletin boards (or newsgroups) are another source of contact. The SUN-MANAGERS mailing list on the Internet and the `comp.unix.sysadmin` newsgroup on Usenet are examples of these (see page 140 for more information on Usenet newsgroups).

8.5 Communication With Vendors

You will serve as the point of contact with vendors of your site's computer hardware and software. Users will come to you with their problems, which you will either solve or forward to a vendor for resolution. No vendor wants 500 users calling from a single site every time they have any problem. If you service a large site, this could mean maintaining working relationships with representatives from dozens of hardware and software companies.

Maintaining a good relationship with the vendors of your hardware and software is important. If you are cooperative and don't panic over every little problem, they will usually be happy to give that extra effort to help out when you *really* have a problem. If you whine and complain about small problems, they will lose their incentive to try to keep you happy because they will conclude that it's impossible. Your relationship with the vendor is similar to your users' relationship with you. You are usually happier to help the "reasonable" users, and you probably have less patience and, therefore, less enthusiasm, to help the "troublemakers." Vendors will deal with you in much the same way. If you deal honestly and reasonably with them, they are usually happy to help you solve your problems.

The people with whom you will develop a working relationship at a vendor company will be helping you with service calls and problems, as well as maintenance contracts. Many vendors also make pre-release or current versions of their newest products available to a few of their better customers for demonstration or evaluation purposes.

8.6 About Yourself

So far, we've looked at some of the valuable traits that you can develop, even if you don't already have them. What about inherent talents and tendencies that make you well-suited for the job?

8.6.1 How to know if you really want the job

While it is not as big a problem as it used to be, there is one frequent mistake that both candidates and hiring managers make that leads to unhappiness for everyone. If you want to be a programmer and see system management as an entry point into a company, stop. You won't do yourself, or your potential employer, any favors if you get the job and then leave it in a few months because you're bored. Be honest with them, tell them you have designs on another position and would take the job to get there. It might suit their purpose, and therefore be acceptable. Approach it honestly and you'll both be happier. If they are looking for someone who will dedicate himself to the job of system management for the long-term, you will both wind up frustrated.

If you want to be a programmer, you'll go out of your mind with boredom as a system administrator. You rarely get to sit down and write "real" code. You will write a little here and there to solve problems, automate tasks, or provide a special tool for some function, but most of your coding will be constantly interrupted by seemingly trivial user requests. Your main function will be to help others get their work done, not to write code of your own.

Many people have tried to be a system administrator rather than what they want to be, and have found it excruciatingly painful (with the possible exception of Cliff Stoll, who went from being an astronomer to a system administrator and wound up liking it, even though he still likes astronomy better [Sto90]).

Sometimes people take the job to satisfy a dream of being the one in power, the super user. This is a false aspiration. The responsibility that comes with being a super user is great. In truth, you are not all powerful, you work *for* all the users of the system. Many system administrators would tell you they sometimes feel like second-class citizens of the organization. The perception is up to the individual, of course. Many others (including this author) would argue that the system administrator is merely an integral piece of any high-tech organization.

8.6.2 Skills to develop

A system administrator is a generalist more than an expert on anything. His expertise is knowing a little something about just about everything. The price for this is probably not knowing everything about anything, but you will know where to find out more if you need to become an expert. Being able to find the answer to many questions is more valuable than knowing the answer to only a few questions.

Thick skin

When people are unhappy with a situation, they tend to try to blame someone. Any Psychology 301 student knows this. Human tendency is to lash out at "those responsible." Often, lashing out at *somebody* will do. That somebody is sometimes the system administrator. Don't take these attacks personally; most of the time they are not intended that way. People tend to adopt their positions and feel personally attacked when that position is challenged (both users and system administrators). Try to keep the technical disagreements technical.

> I will never forget the day that people witnessed a heated argument between myself and my co-administrator about a technical issue. We were (and still are) best friends and people were dropping their jaws watching the exchange, sure that we would never speak after the incident. At the end of the discussion, realizing that neither of us would be able to convince the other of our philosophical position, we agreed to disagree and then began discussing where to go to lunch. All those in attendance were dumbfounded. Of course, being best friends helped us not take it all personally because we knew nothing was meant that way.

Pride in your work, but not too much

Take personal pride in what you do; it will make your work better (this is true in just about any profession or anything in life; too few people take any pride in their work). However, pride for pride's sake is not good. Don't be so proud that you can't admit to a lack of knowledge about a certain subject. There is no shame in the answer, "I don't know." No one can know all the answers all the time; it's impossible. When you don't know, admit it, but follow your honest admission with a promise to find out. A user will respect you more if you admit that you don't know but then find the answer they need, than if you say you do know but never give it to them.

> Often someone asks me some strange, off-the-wall question, with little hope that I might know the answer. Every now and then, I can answer the question right then. They usually look at me with a wide-eyed look that can only be described as awe. They try to tell me I'm a real UNIX wizard. I explain that the only difference between a regular user and a wizard is that the wizard has made that exact mistake before and recognizes it.

8.6.3 Commitment

Don't get so enthused about keeping up with the latest and greatest in technology that you change the environment so fast that no one can keep up. Users need a stable, known environment in which to work. You may like toying with the newest and most wonderful tools, but most users who are trying to get "real work" done need reliable and predictable tools that they can understand [Jen90, pp. 123–124]. Set aside an area for experimental tools so that other users like you who want to play with the latest toys can do so without affecting the day-to-day productivity of the rest of the users.

Don't get "Babbage's disease"[5] and never finish any project before going on to the next. You want to build a stable environment, but something will always change; it's a fact of life. If you don't follow through on projects you start, even though your interest may be waning, you'll wind up with a collection of unfinished, and unusable, tools.

Of course, if you are working on the same project hour after hour because it must be fixed (I've spent a handful of sleepless nights with `sendmail` configuration files, for example), you get to a point of diminishing returns where you should stop and clear your head, eat, and/or sleep. Take a break, but throwing up your hands, exclaiming that the machine has beaten you, and going home for the weekend is not an option.

8.6.4 Don't-panic attitude

Just as Douglas Adams' fictitious *Hitchhiker's Guide to the Galaxy* gives its advice of "Don't Panic" on the cover [Ada87], the best advice for a system administrator is the same. Don't get desperate for a solution for the sake of the solution. If you are to the point of throwing in the towel on a problem, step back from it and approach it from a different angle. Get a "sanity check" from a colleague, either within or outside of your company (assuming the information involved is not confidential, of course). A fresh eye often sees the obvious where the weary eye cannot. The fresh eye can even be your own, if you're looking from a new perspective.

[5] Charles Babbage, famous first computer engineer, was good at getting caught up in the details of a project and then getting bored and going on to the next one without finishing it [Jen90, p. 30]

> When I worked in User Services at a university, faculty and staff would bring in problems they had dealing with the computer systems, usually programming problems they didn't understand. Someone once brought me a listing of a program that didn't work as he expected and he just couldn't figure out what was wrong. Since I knew nothing about the problem he was attempting to solve, he had to start from the beginning and tell me about the project, the data, and the desired result. About halfway through his explanation of the logic in his program, he stopped and looked closely at his code. With a stunned look, he exclaimed, "That's it! Thanks." I hadn't said a word the entire time. I just said "You're welcome" as he left!

Of course, if you really are in over your head, being stubborn about giving in can cause you just as much trouble. It's a balancing act to know when you really have exhausted your possibility of solving a problem, but giving up too quickly is worse than hanging on a little too long (although not as frustrating!).

8.6.5 You can't know everything

No one person can be "God's gift to system management." You can know a lot about many topics, but you cannot possibly know *everything*. Anyone who expects you to has unrealistic expectations. What they can ask is that you have the ability to learn about new topics. Through manuals, colleagues (friends or people you meet at conferences or "on the net"), and consultants, you have a huge pool of information that can be tapped when you don't already know the answer.

As a system administrator, don't be afraid to tell someone you don't know something. One of the biggest mistakes system administrators sometimes make is to fake knowledge and try to fool a user into thinking they know something when they don't. Sometimes, the user's need vanishes and they're off the hook. More often, the user becomes increasingly frustrated with the lack of results. When the user finally concludes that the system administrator didn't know the answer in the first place, he gets mad. "I don't know, but I'll see what I can find out for you" is a *much* better answer than "Sure, I can do that" and then never doing it.

Don't be afraid to ask for outside help, but don't depend on it. Consultants and temporary employees provide valuable services. Consultants usually provide highly specific, expert assistance or guidance for certain problems. Temporary employees may simply be "warm bodies" to fill a chair and get work done when the support staff is overworked or short due to layoffs or resignations. The hidden cost of overworking your own staff might be much more than the visible cost of hiring these kinds of temporary workers for short periods of time.

Consultants and other such resources are valuable and should be used to add to your knowledge and experience, but don't let critical information or expertise leave with a consultant (or any temporary employee) before having them document it. It does you no long-term good to hire someone to solve a specific problem for you, if once they're gone you have no idea how to solve the problem again.

8.6.6 Ethics

Ethics may not seem like an important issue, but it is critical in the UNIX world. Some operating systems have several levels of authorization for different functions. UNIX began with a single *super user* privilege. Either you could do anything or you were a regular user.[6] High ethical conduct is crucial to maintaining the trust of your users and management [Cur92, p. 164].

This means you don't snoop around in people's directories just because you can. You don't take advantage of your privileges to look at information in files and *never* read other users' electronic mail. You must respect the privacy of your users or they will not trust you. Everyone gets angry at parents, police officers, and even high government officials anytime they see the rules apply differently to them than to the rest of us. It's an abuse of power. The same rules that apply to

[6] Some versions of UNIX now implement multiple levels of authorization, and more are sure to come in the future, but many still have only `root`.

other users must apply to the system administrator, because after all, the system administrator is simply a special user. If you abuse your power, people will resent it.

8.6.7 Management style

Managing computer systems is not the same as managing people, but it is still an important factor in how successful you will be as a system administrator. Sitting back and waiting for problems to happen never works as well (in any form of management) as staying on top of activities and anticipating problems.

Proactive

Be **pro**active instead of **re**active in finding and solving problems. Anticipate problems rather than letting them surprise you. When your disk is 90-percent full, it stands to reason that it will soon be 100-percent full unless you take some action soon. Don't wait for that to happen. Look for trouble before it comes looking for you.

Many users may feel that a UNIX environment is inherently unreliable. Many UNIX environments *are* unreliable, but it is not because of problems inherent in UNIX, but rather the way the site is run. UNIX itself, while being somewhat unpredictable in its infancy, has developed and grown into a more mature and more reliable operating system. This is not to say it is foolproof; no operating system is. But UNIX gets more than its share of blame for problems, often as a way of diverting blame from the humans who are truly responsible. A UNIX site can be kept running smoothly with competent system administrators. If the system administrators are always in "fire-fighting" mode, planning for smooth operations will always take a back seat to the emergency of the moment, the "fire du jour," if you will.

Let knowledgeable users help

No system administrator can be an expert at every aspect of a system or environment. Somewhere there will be a user who uses some tool more than you, who has used it for years, and knows more about it.

"It" can be a type of system, a software package, or just about anything. If you have expert users at your site, don't be afraid to let them help you. Success at this job comes from your experience solving problems. Anytime you can use somebody else's experience (and gain some yourself for free at the same time), you win!

8.7 Stress Management

Stress is a normal part of the job of system management. When everything runs smoothly, it may be low, but even when this happens, it won't last long. You will also experience stress from other areas of your life. All these sources of stress may combine to hit you at once. You may snap at a user because of something happening in your personal life, or at your spouse because of something at work. The more you can learn about stress management to minimize your reactions, the happier you'll be all around.

8.7.1 Causes of stress

System administrators seem to have a higher incidence of stress than people in many other jobs. So many people depend on you, and generally you really *want* to help everyone.

Stress and illness are related, and the more you let it get to you, the more damage you'll do to yourself. Since your employers need you healthy, it is to their advantage to help you minimize the stress you encounter.

Stress isn't always negative. Even "good" changes in life cause stress (moving, getting married, changing jobs). These things can still add to your stress level. It is not the incident itself that causes the stress, but the individual's perception of the incident and its ramifications. You cannot always control the events around you, but you can control your reaction to them.

Diet and exercise also have major effects on your stress level. An old joke asks, "What's the definition of a programmer?" "A machine for converting Coca-Cola into code." The typical lunch of technical types was one or more soft drinks and a candy bar (high sugar, high energy). Of course, this is a stereotype, but as with all stereotypes, it has its origins in truth. Don't spend every waking moment in a cold computer room, eat out of vending machines, and get your extra energy from cup after cup of "high-octane" coffee. Not only will your health suffer, but whatever stress comes naturally from your job will have a more severe impact.

8.7.2 Controlling stress

The trick to managing stress is to recognize its causes and notice it increasing. Generally, stress comes on so slowly that you don't notice it from one day to the next and before you know it, you're dealing with a much higher level than what you would put up with if it hit you all at once. Some people don't see the symptoms because they've adapted and feel the level of stress they're experiencing is normal.

Symptoms of stress are like the lights on the dashboard of your car. You wouldn't continue to drive your car if you saw a warning light come on. Yet when one of our body's warning lights comes on, we often ignore it. Headaches, backaches, indigestion, are just some of the ways our bodies try to tell us something is wrong. Some people even try to one-up each other over how many aspirin they have to take just to get through the day! This is *not* something to be proud of; it's an indication of a problem.

Often, overcommitting to work is a source of stress. This is a source that can be easily controlled. If you don't believe you can provide a service in the required time, JUST SAY NO. If "no" is a problem, get with the requester and try to work out a solution. They may have to hire temporary workers or scale back their needs. Working an 80-hour week and getting it done won't help the user community in the long run when you make yourself ill and are out the following week.

Humor can help relieve stress. Certainly, it is a temporary relief, but every little bit helps. Embracing humor will help your general attitude, and there is a limit to how seriously you can take everything. As a popular saying goes: "Welcome to Earth. The deathrate here is

100-percent. Have a nice day!"[7] There just isn't any point in making yourself crazy over everything.

This is not to say that you shouldn't get excited or worked up about anything. From time to time, emergencies will happen. To some degree, they can even be exhilarating once in a while. However, this should not be standard operating procedure; it should be the exception.

8.8 Continuing Education

One of the most important aspects of the job of system management (or any job, really) is continuing your education. No job is ever complete; no mass of knowledge is ever enough. In almost any job (and especially jobs in the computer industry) you must keep up or be left behind.

Resources for continuing education may be simple, as in reading new books as they are published, or more involved, as in attending conferences and workshops. Your employer should see the value in this and be willing to foot the bill for you to keep your professional edge. If your employer will not (or cannot) help, don't let that be enough to discourage you. You are ultimately responsible for your own professional abilities and keeping them up to date.

8.9 Covering Your Assets

You are your best resource in your job. Your personal assets are all you really have available to do your job. If everything else were somehow taken away from you, your experience, knowledge, and resourcefulness would be your only tools. Use your other tools—colleagues, books, classes—but keep your personal abilities sharp, and don't be afraid to make sure people know what you have.

8.9.1 Toot your own horn

Management doesn't understand your job. It isn't their fault. Management understands status reports and milestone achievements. To

[7] A variation on this saying is "Don't take life seriously—you'll never get out of it alive."

really succeed, you have to make management aware of your successes, your failures, and what you need from them to eliminate failure in the future. Make them aware of problems you solve. Some of your users will pat you on the back. Many will not. Be appreciative when they do. Encourage them to "drop your name" when they feel they've had extraordinary help.

8.9.2 Don't try to be irreplaceable

Often it seems tempting to try to make oneself irreplaceable (a misguided attempt at attaining job security). Not only can you not make yourself totally irreplaceable, you don't *want* to be irreplaceable. If your user community and management rely on you too heavily, you'll never get another vacation or attend another conference. As the system administrator, your best biggest asset is your experience and your problem solving ability.

Document your local environment so others can find information in your absence. You'll never be able to address everything that can go wrong; only human adaptability can do that. But you can address the majority of problems that your users will face. Most of the other problems won't be emergencies, and they can wait for a few days. This won't make people think they can do without you, but it might make them able to do without you for a few days.

Make the environment so useful that your organizational ability is acknowledged to be a valuable part of it. Technical ability is common, but good organizational and interpersonal abilities are much more rare. It should never be necessary to *remind* users of your value; plenty will go wrong from time to time without help. If you are one of those few system administrators who runs an extremely smooth site, then it's your job to communicate to your users and management how much of an accomplishment that is.

> As unthinkable as it should be to most people, there have been cases of system administrators who actually *plan* little disasters that happen while they're away so that people are reminded of how important they are to the computing environment. Besides the obvious risk of being caught pulling this kind of stunt (and some have been!), they risk the productivity of their users and the integrity of their entire computing environment.

Cross-train with others on your staff, or even in other departments, and share responsibilities to cover for others during absences. If you're afraid of relinquishing your control, then you don't really have any. Don't forget, the point is to keep the environment running smoothly, not to make yourself feel valuable.

Chapter 9

The Career

If what you have read about system management up to this point still has you interested, then this might be the career for you. Now it's time to get you started in your new career choice. This chapter will help candidates and hiring managers better appreciate what is important to the other. It will help candidates better present themselves for consideration by identifying their important strong points. It will also help hiring managers recognize talented candidates and keep them interested and challenged, thus avoiding the classic system administrator burnout.

If you are already doing the job, you may think of it as a dead-end or as a stepping stone to a programming or management job. You may wonder, "Is there life after system management?" The potential career path of a system administrator will also be examined.

9.1 Hiring a System Administrator

Hiring a UNIX system administrator is more complex than simply bringing in a UNIX programmer from off the street to take care of your systems. Not only might you get someone who isn't well organized or good at dealing with people, you might also get someone who doesn't really want the job and is only using it as a stepping stone to another position within the company. If that happens, you'll wind up having to fill the position again in six months. It is not unreasonable to want to move on to new challenges after a time, but it is also not unreasonable to ask that the person do the job for more than a few months.

Often when searching for a system administrator, the hiring manager is in unfamiliar territory. As previously shown, the industry is only now beginning to understand what a system administrator really is, why he or she is necessary, and how to gauge his or her performance. System administrators are often hired as "programmers," for lack of a better title, but then performance evaluations are a problem since the job requirements are so different. Quantifying the productivity of a system administrator is difficult. If the job is done correctly and your machines run properly, the user community will wonder why they needed this person in the first place. The only time anyone notices the system administrator is when something is *not* working. **If the system administrator does his job PERFECTLY, he is INVISIBLE.** It is extremely difficult to call attention to performance when, by the nature of the job, the better it is, the less it is noticed!

9.1.1 Definition of need

The job of system management requires a person who is competent at many different aspects of computing, not expert at a few. An expert is a valuable member of a team, where the other team members are expert in a variety of different topics. But each area must be covered by someone. the bases are covered by someone.

Having only one system administrator is not an ideal situation (however, in a small shop with a small support budget, it cannot always be helped). A staff of two or more fosters teamwork. "Brainstorming sessions" can often lead to solutions that one person would not have thought of alone. And when skills are available from more than one source, the tendency of any one person to feel like a "czar" is lessened. Sometimes, the need is perceived as particularly small and an employee is split between two sets of duties. In a minority of cases, this may work. In reality, however, system management is hardly ever a part-time job. Much like the old adage that a user's files will grow to fill the available disk space, user's needs also grow to consume the available support resource. If you do attempt to hire a part-time system administrator, be equally prepared to expand that to full-time or augment the staff quickly.

A large staff can also be a problem. With many people, there is sure to be some overlap in their interests and skills, and they often wind up doing redundant work. Good communication between staff members helps minimize this, but past a certain point redundancy is inevitable. As Brooks pointed out in his classic, *The Mythical Man-Month*, one cannot draw a linear relationship between the number of people working on a project and the time it takes to complete the project. Brooks was talking about software development, but it is also true of system management. He goes on to say that as you add more people to a project, the time required to complete it not only slows its rate of decrease, but actually comes to a point where it begins to increase [Bro82, pp. 16–19].

As a hiring manager, it is important to select people not only because they are qualified, but also because they have an interest in performing the job. Hiring an experienced UNIX programmer to change tapes and string cable is a waste of money as well as potentially boring to the employee. By the same token, candidates should be honest about the types of work they find interesting as well as those they do not.

As previously discussed, the specific support needs of an environment depend greatly on the users and the type and use of computers in the environment. Therefore, it is impossible to provide a single, foolproof formula which can be used to determine the number of people needed in a support staff. However, it is reasonable to list factors that will increase the number of people needed to support a computing environment. Each of the following conditions that is true of a computing environment will significantly increase the amount of work required to keep things running smoothly (items that can be counted multiple times are cumulative in their effect):

- computers from more than one manufacturer
- external network connections
- multiple types of network implementations

- workstations with local disk drives
- users with privileged access (i.e., the `root` password)
- new software or hardware purchases on a regular basis (i.e., never reaching a "stable" configuration)
- self-maintenance on hardware or software required
- large and/or novice user community

9.1.2 Compensation

Salaries of system administrators are, for the first time, reaching levels equal to those of other technical professionals. For quite some time, system administrators were viewed as less technical than engineers, and so their pay was often lower. While adequate system administrators are available, highly experienced ones are still fairly rare and they command good salaries.

Since the cost of computer equipment has been falling, management sometimes feels that the cost of support should also be falling. This is a false assumption. When the cost of a computer was $500,000, paying a highly qualified system administrator $50,000 seemed reasonable. Now that the machine costs $50,000 (sometimes much less), paying that same amount to the system administrator sometimes seems unjustified. However, if you examine the skill level you are getting (the same as before, if not better) and the number of computers being serviced (usually several dozen or several hundred rather than just one), the comparison is not as one-sided as it first appears. Supporting a computer system always costs more than the initial purchase price, whether it is a PC or a supercomputer. Some costs are simply more visible than others.

Region of the country also affects the salary of a system administrator (just as it does any technical professional). East and West Coast locations tend to pay more for the same job, mostly because the cost of living is higher in those areas. Before moving, check the housing, utility, food, and transportation costs in the area. Don't just transfer from the Midwest to the West Coast and accept the same salary, because it may not go as far.

Many system administrators find that going into consulting is more satisfying. This increases the percentage of their time spent working on "interesting" projects (since one usually hires a consultant to solve a problem that can't be solved easily by internal resources). The day-to-day "firefighting" done by most full-time system administrators limits the amount of technical growth that can be experienced in any single work day. These highly experienced people can serve a valuable purpose by helping and educating a less-experienced, full-time staff member over a period of time. The company can wind up with a much more experienced employee without incurring the expense of hiring a senior employee who is not needed permanently.

9.1.3 Required skills

Often, because of the words "administrator" or "manager" in some job titles, the job of the system administrator is not thought of as a technical position (at least not as technical as, say, that of a programmer or engineer). The technical aspects of system management are critical and should not be overlooked. However, other, nontechnical abilities are also required.

The system administrator needs an informed and correct view of "the big picture" when it comes to a computing environment. She must understand the technical issues of many different components and their interdependencies, as well as the administrative and procedural issues faced by users of the computer systems. Being an expert graphics programmer cannot possibly prepare someone to deal with the environment as a whole. The system administrator is usually more of a generalist, knowing something about just about all parts of the system, rather than being an expert about any one component (for being an expert in one area often implies little or no knowledge about other aspects of the system).

In addition to being familiar with the technical aspects of the computing environment, the system administrator must also be competent with administrative and interpersonal issues, something rarely required of a programmer, who must simply produce working code. Disorganized programmers are more of an amusement than a problem, but a disorganized system administrator can spell disaster for a site. When a programmer doesn't "play well with others," he can be put on a project where interaction with other employees is kept to a minimum, but the system administrator must interact with the users constantly. System administrators truly deal with all aspects of the computing environment, with all the various types of users, and with all the different tasks for which the computer is used. This makes them fairly unique in the organization.

Communication is an equally important skill. As a system administrator, you will write thousands of pages of documentation and electronic mail messages over a period of years. The ability to convey what you mean effectively and to prevent misunderstanding will be extremely valuable.

These talents are difficult to gauge from a résumé. Evaluating technical candidates based on education and experience is easier because most of the information you need is there. Skills such as how well someone interacts with people and how organized they are do not appear on a résumé, but are every bit as important.

Many organizations require technical staff members to have college degrees or even advanced degrees. While college degrees are an excellent gauge for identifying the capable and ambitious, they should not be used as an exclusive or absolute metric. Many fine technical people and system administrators do not have degrees for one reason or another. To not consider someone solely because of a lack of a degree is to risk missing out on a highly capable employee.[1] If you are an aspiring system administrator without a degree, you should work schooling into your career plan. Having the degree *will* help your career, but you should not discount any possibilities simply because you don't have one.

9.1.4 Advantageous personal traits

The types of personal traits that the hiring manager will look for in a system administrator are somewhat dependent on the specific needs

[1] Plus, they may be cheaper. Since hiring is driven by the market, often these equally capable people can be hired for a little less money because of their lack of a degree.

and desires of the management of each organization. A site that has just fired[2] a particularly difficult person is likely to overcompensate and look for more specific personal traits than technical abilities. Another site that has had a friendly person as their system administrator, but one who is not very technical, is going to be more interested in technical abilities (again, overcompensating and making the mistake in the other direction).

In general, however, a good system administrator has the following traits:

- **initiative**
  someone who is a self-starter and who does not need to be told what to do at every step, but who can find what needs to be done and take care of it
- **independence**
  related to having initiative, someone who can work independently, with little supervision or encouragement, and not take the afternoon off just because the boss isn't around
- **awareness**
  someone who pays attention to the activity around him and can anticipate people's needs
- **adaptability**
  someone who can "roll with the punches" when needs and procedures change, as they will, and not become frustrated with the perceived instability of the environment
- **ethics**
  someone who will not abuse the absolute power entrusted to her
- **confidence**
  someone who does not need continual praise for a job well done ("atta-boys") because in this job, they often do not come

[2] Oops, to be politically correct, this should be "vocationally dislocated." :-)

9.1.5 How to find someone or be found

In the UNIX world, answering a classified ad is probably the most ineffective way to find a job. This is not to say that it doesn't work, because it does. However, knowing people and having a network of colleagues is the most effective way to keep up with what is going on in the industry and what kinds of jobs are available.

If you have lived and worked in the same geographic area for some time, then you probably already have a such a network, but if you are just starting out or have moved to a new city, you won't have one. In this case, classified ads in trade publications and local newspapers are another alternative.

Another widely used mechanism is the technical and executive search company, commonly known as a *recruiter* or a *headhunter*. Recruiters locate both regular employees and temporary employees (or contractors) to fill positions for companies. Often organizations have neither the time nor the expertise to sift through a large number of candidates. Or they may lack the resources to recruit nationwide for a highly technical position. Companies specializing in locating employees have the resources and (sometimes) the expertise to help organizations find just the right match for an open position. The term *headhunter* grew out of the way these search firms sometimes seem interested in the candidate only as a commodity to be acquired and traded. Don't let some derogatory images of headhunters frighten you away from using them. Just as some really are as sleazy as the worst used car salesmen, some are also extremely competent and honest. Finding a good recruiter is often an important step in finding a good job.

9.2 Job Descriptions

When posting a job opening, it is important to include a description of the position. This job description should include an overview of the computing environment (at least as much as would not violate any security policies), as well as a list of skills and qualifications the candidate should possess. Including a list of job duties is also helpful, although not always as easy to define. This allows the candidate to compare his or her skills and interests and better determine if the position is suitable. It also provides information for the interviewers and personnel staff so they are better prepared for the candidates that will be applying.

As with defining the need for support, the details depend on local peculiarities of the environment. However, it is usually much easier to write a job description after having read one.

This first example job description is for a system administrator at a smaller site within a large software development company.

```
Longhorn Computer Systems in Austin, Texas has
an opening for a system administrator.  The
responsibilities of the position will be to
provide system administration support for a
network of Unix workstations, servers, and
personal computers.  The active user community
consists of approximately 25 software developers
and project managers and is expected to double
in the next 18 months.

Present hardware consists of approximately 25
Sun workstations (and 3 servers), 10 personal
computers, and 4 laser printers on a local
network.  The local network is connected to a
local network in Dallas via a T1 link.  The
network in Dallas is approximately 4X the size
of the local Austin network.

The system administrator will be responsible
for the daily operations and long-term planning
for the entire Austin site, both hardware and
software.  In addition to regular and significant
growth, the company will be moving to a new
location within the next year.  The successful
```

```
applicant will be the primary planner and
executor of this move.

Regular job duties will include:

  + equipment installation and maintenance
  + hardware and software problem diagnosis
  + software and OS installation and upgrades
  + perform daily backups of all local disk
  + manage local area network and connection
    with Dallas site
  + user account administration
  + provide assistance with use of Unix and
    local software
  + supplement system documentation with local
    documentation
  + educate new users
  + coordinate new equipment acquisition
  + maintain Usenet news feed
  + maintain software and physical security
    of local environment
  + maintain accurate inventory of hardware
  + maintain necessary consumable supplies
  + perform software/hardware maintenance
    contract administration
  + provide interface with hardware and
    software vendors

Desired personal abilities:

  + good interpersonal and communication skills
  + good organizational skills
  + ability to be interrupted frequently
  + ability to reprioritize tasks in real-time
```

```
Desired experience:

  + bachelor's degree in Computer Science or
    Engineering
  + minimum 3 years user-level Unix
  + minimum 2 years system administration
  + shell and C programming
  + OS installation/upgrade
  + mail and networking
  + PC software and hardware a plus

This is a contract position for 6 months, when
it will become a full-time, permanent position
with excellent medical, dental, vision care, and
retirement benefits.
```

Many companies start new hires on short-term contracts rather than as regular employees. This is an alternative to a probationary period, often used as a "trial period." It also keeps the company's overhead lower since they won't pay benefits to a contractor.

This next example job description is for a system administrator in a university department with a larger user community.

```
The Department of Astronomy at The University
of Steamboat Springs has a job opening for an
assistant UNIX System Administrator beginning
September 1.  The department operates a
computing facility which serves its research
and instructional needs.  The active user
community consists of approximately 200 faculty
members and students.  The present hardware
includes 30 Unix workstations, 100 Macintoshes,
and 2 DEC VMS computers, all networked together
and to other campus systems.
```

```
The successful candidate must have experience
dealing with inexperienced users, knowledge
of general computer operations, user-level
knowledge of the Unix operating system, and text
processing experience with troff and FrameMaker.
Experience with shell script or C language
programming or user-level knowledge of VMS or
Macintosh is a plus.

The salary range is between $33K and $41K, depending
on experience.  This is a permanent staff position
with good medical and retirement benefits.  The
job is mainly 8:00 to 17:00 but may require outside
hours or weekend work occasionally.  U.S. citizens
only, students may apply.  The University of
Steamboat Springs is an Equal Opportunity Employer.
```

9.3 Keeping a System Administrator

Once you find the right people, you want to be sure you can keep them interested in the job they do, so they don't get bored and leave. Assuming they meet your expectations, as a hiring manager it is your job to meet theirs as well. Day-to-day job satisfaction and feedback about the job they do is as important as long-term technical growth. If someone feels their skills are being dulled because of lack of challenges, they will look elsewhere for experience and probably employment.

9.3.1 Expectations

Many problems that arise between system administrators and their users or management come from unfulfilled expectations. Users may expect someone more technical; they may even expect someone who can write code for them for small projects. Management may expect someone who can take care of the budget issues as well as the equipment. Often, technical people are not interested in management issues like these. Sometimes it is the system administrator who has the unmet expectations. Perhaps he or she expected to step into a programming position after six months or a year, and five years later they feel their career is at a dead end.

Avoiding expectation problems, on everyone's part, is extremely important to keep all these relationships running smoothly. None of these expectations is right or wrong. As seen with specific site needs, each set of needs is different. If your users need someone to write sections of code for them, then it is a reasonable expectation. Just make sure you acknowledge it and include it in the job description! If the hiring manager is truthful about what is expected of a system administrator, and the candidate is truthful about what he or she would and would not like to do, then unmet expectations will not be nearly as big a problem.

Whatever the specific requirements for support in your organization, the system administrator must be given the wherewithal to provide the expected level of support. If the system administrator is not expected to provide high-quality support, if the site can be run haphazardly, then what is the point of hiring a system administrator to begin with? The first and most important duty of the system administrator is to provide the best support possible for the users of the computing environment.

To balance that, no manager can expect such quality work from the system administrator without being willing to support his or her needs. Management must provide the funds and tools to adequately support equipment and software; otherwise, it is unfair to ask someone to do it. If the job can only be done half-way, the users will be unhappy because of the shoddy environment, and the system administrator will find his work frustrating and unfulfilling.

9.3.2 Performance reviews

Just as all other employees receive periodic performance reviews, the system administrator will want and deserve one as well. Having regular feedback about how one does a job is critical to maintaining or improving expertise. However, reviewing a system administrator is more difficult because of the nature of the job.

Unlike other kinds of positions, one cannot simply make a list of objectives and check off the ones that were accomplished a year later. It is possible to write a set of objectives for a system administrator, but to believe that, once written, the list will not change is unreasonable (unless one of the objectives states that you will deal with whatever unexpected activities come along, and that's a little open-ended).

Using a template, or objective list of other technical people, is unfair since the job isn't solely technical. Reviewing the system administrator as a member of the administrative staff is also unrealistic. This job is different from just about any other in the organization, and as such, should be treated with a unique style. The job of system management is a combination of technical and administrative skills and the review should reflect that.

Most reviews of system administrators acknowledge satisfaction of the user community as an important objective. If the users are happy with the job as performed, and it has allowed them to meet their deadlines and get their work done, then the system administrator has succeeded in his objectives. However, there will always be a handful of users who stick to their unreasonable expectations, or those who are just generally unhappy people and want to take it out on somebody. Unanimous approval of any system administrator is rare, but if the majority of the users are satisfied, then the system administrator has been successful. You may be able to use that few percent to modify the objectives for the following year.

9.3.3 Technical growth

Every system administrator wants to continue to learn and keep up with ever-changing technologies. Just as other employees are expected to "keep up" and continue learning, the system administrator should be expected to, also. Just as other employees are sent to conferences and training classes to continue their education, so should the system administrator. Claiming a system administrator is too critical to be gone is not a justifiable reason to deny her the chance to increase her knowledge (plus the organization loses by having someone whose expertise is stagnating).

If you hire junior-level system administrators, hoping to let them grow into the position, send them for training early in their careers and encourage their learning. More UNIX classes and books are available today than ever before. Don't fear losing them as they gain experience. A challenged and well-treated person is more likely to stay with her current employer simply because she enjoys her job and work environment.

9.4 The Career Path

If you do decide this is the job for you, where can you expect to be in five or ten years? Will you be filling printer paper trays and tracking the cause of system crashes for the rest of your life?

Certainly, if you still enjoy it, by all means, keep at it! But if you grow restless and want something different, you will have had many experiences upon which you can draw to figure out what to do next. You will have seen many new and wonderful things in your travels around to all the computer users both inside as well as outside your organization.

9.4.1 Within your organization

If you came up through technical ranks, you will have been exposed to just about every project in your organization at one time or another. Get to know the people in the groups that most interest you and express interest in the subject. When presentations are scheduled, make an effort to attend just to expand your knowledge. People will notice your interest.

In many organizations it is difficult to move from a support position into a workgroup position. Often, there is a perceived separation between the "thinkers" and the "worker bees" (secretaries, administrative support, etc.) that is hard to break through. Sometimes it's impossible. If you have to leave a company to find the type of job that represents the next step in your career, so be it. Once you've decided that you're willing to do that, you may wish to talk with management and let them know how important it is to you to move into another area of work. If they know you're serious and consider you a valuable company employee, they may be more helpful.

9.4.2 Outside your organization

If it is obvious to you that your current job is all your present employer will allow you to do, then you must look elsewhere for the next step in your career. If you have been going to conferences and attending classes and workshops, you probably know people from other companies in your area, if not all across the country. Talk to some of them and find out what interesting work is being done in their organizations. Keep up with discussions on the net and in trade journals to see where the action is in the field you wish to pursue.

9.4.3 Where you can go

Having been a system administrator, you have gained a unique insight into the workings of computer systems and users everywhere. The details will be different anywhere else, of course, but you will have experiences that no other technical or administrative person could hope to have, having only been exposed to one of the two areas.

If you wish to now become even more technical, you will be a more effective programmer or designer because of your understanding about how the computer system and associated devices interact with all of the other components of the computing environment. Too often, programmers know what happens inside their small application without having any concept of how it affects the rest of the system or how it can be affected by other system activities. The "top-down" perspective of a system administrator (or former system administrator) can be extremely valuable.

On the other hand, if management has become an interest, you will bring a technical savvy that is rare in management. Just as no system administrator can know everything, no manager can be a technical expert. The manager must depend on his technical staff to provide the technical information necessary to do the job. A technically literate manager can make decisions based on a much deeper understanding of the issues involved. Your biggest danger in this case is continuing to keep your knowledge up and recognizing when you've fallen behind, so that you don't try to make decisions on information that you no longer realize is out of date!

But what if you like supporting people and systems and playing with the latest and greatest in computer technology? Nothing is wrong with that. If you feel stifled and unchallenged in your current job, or perhaps you've set up the perfect environment and there's no fun in just sitting back and running it (you should be so lucky!), you can always find another organization out there with terrible support problems that desperately needs someone with experience in solving such problems. As more and more organizations embrace UNIX as a computing platform, the number of sites requiring your kind of expertise will grow even larger than it is already.

The possibilities are endless.

Appendix A

American National Standards Institute
1430 Broadway
New York, NY 10018
+1 (212) 354-3300

Computer Emergency Response Team
Software Engineering Institute
Carnegie Mellon University
Pittsburgh, PA 15213-3890
+1 (412) 268-7090
`cert@cert.sei.cmu.edu`

Internet Network Information Center (InterNIC)
+1 (800) 444-4345, outside the U.S. +1 (619) 445-4600
`info@internic.net`

MAP/TOP Users Group
1 SME Drive
P.O. Box 930
Dearborn, MI 48121
+1 (313) 271-1500

National Computer Security Center
ATTN: C11
9800 Savage Rd.
Fort George G. Meade, MD 20755-6000
+1 (301) 859-4458

North American ISDN User's Forum
U.S. Department of Commerce
National Institute of Standards and Technology
Gaithersburg, MD 20899

National Technical Information Service
U.S. Department of Commerce
5285 Port Royal Rd.
Springfield, VA 22161
+1 (703) 487-4650

NSFnet
Office of Advanced Scientific Computing
National Science Foundation
1800 G St., N.W.
Washington, DC 20550

The USENIX Association
2560 Ninth St., Suite 215
Berkeley, CA 94710
+1 (510) 528-8649
`office@usenix.org`

Glossary

ACL – Access Control List

AIX – Advanced Interactive Executive; the designation identifying the version of UNIX distributed by IBM

ampere – unit of measure of electrical current (also called *amp*)

ANSI – American National Standards Institute

ARPA – see *DARPA*

ASCII – American Standard Code for Information Interchange; standard character code used to represent characters in seven bits

asset tracking – keeping track of equipment and other valuables belonging to an organization

ATM – Asynchronous Transfer Mode

authentication – assuring that the user (or software agent) is who he (or it) claims to be

authorization – determining whether or not the requesting user has the privileges necessary for an operation

`automount` – program used to automatically mount remote file systems

back door – software mechanism put in place by a programmer to allow access without going through whatever authentication mechanism is usually used by the program

backing down – reverting to a previous version of software or hardware

backplane – an electrical interconnect where removable circuit boards fit so they may communicate with each other and with the CPU board; also see *motherboard*

`backup` – backup program provided with AIX

backup – the act of copying data onto another medium that can be stored in another place in case some disaster befalls the system disk; also see *full backup* and *incremental backup*

bandwidth – the number of different signals that can be sent along a network medium at different frequencies

baud rate – an expression of data transmission speed of a modem

BBN – Bolt, Beranek, and Newman

bit-mapped graphic display – display terminal where each point on the display can be manipulated rather than simply each character location

bootstrap – see *boot*

boot – the act of loading the operating system program into the computer so it can begin processing

bps – bits per second; transmission speed of a data connection, usually over a modem

broadcast – sending data to all hosts on a network

BSD – Berkeley Standard Distribution; designation identifying the version of UNIX distributed by the University of California at Berkeley

BTU – British thermal unit; a measurement of heat production

bus – network topology where devices are connected to a single line of network cable

bus – the communications medium used by hardware devices to communicate with the CPU

capitalized assets – items paid for over a period of years rather than all at once

CCITT – International Consultative Committee on Telephony and Telegraphy (from the French name Comité Consultatif Internationale de Télégraphique et Téléphonique)

CD-ROM – method of storing information on conventional Compact Disc and using it as a read-only medium

CERT – Computer Emergency Response Team

cheapernet – see *thinnet*

circuit-switched – network where a path is set up and continues through the life of the connection

clamping level – limit of transient voltage that can be limited by a voltage suppressing device

clerk – one who performs administrative tasks such as taking user questions and processing forms

CMIP – Common Management Information Protocol

CMOT – CMIP over TCP

coaxial – a type of shielded networking cable

collision – when two packets are put on the network by different hosts at exactly the same time

`cpio` – copy input to output; program to write disk files to another device

CPU – Central Processing Unit; the "brain" of the computer, which usually resides on a single circuit board in the computer

cracker – someone who attempts to gain unauthorized access to a computer system or other computing resource

crash – when a program (often the operating system) encounters some unresolvable condition and cannot continue processing. In the case of the operating system crashing, the machine must be rebooted to reset the fault condition.

`cron` – program used to run other programs automatically at a predetermined time

`crypt` – command used to encrypt data

CSMA/CD – Carrier Sense Multiple Access with Collision Detection

current – a measure of the flow of electricity, expressed in units of amperes

cycle – to reuse on a regular basis, especially with backup media

DAC – Discretionary Access Control

daemon – a program that runs in the background of a UNIX machine and waits to provide some type of service

DARPA – Defense Advanced Research Projects Agency

DAT – Digital Audio Tape

`dc` – desk calculator program

DCE – Distributed Computing Environment

DEC – Digital Equipment Corporation

depreciate – the act of something losing value over time

DES – Data Encryption Standard

DME – Distributed Management Environment

DNS – Domain Name System

downsizing – moving from mainframes down to smaller (and cheaper) computers or reducing the size of staff

downtime – a scheduled or unscheduled period of time when a machine is not functioning in the local environment

dpi – dots per inch; a specification of resolution of a display or output device, most often used when describing the clarity of laser printer output

drop cable – a cable that is "dropped" from the network cable to an individual computer

`dump` – backup program originally included with Berkeley UNIX

EBCDIC – Extended Binary Coded Decimal Interchange Code; character code originally developed by IBM to represent characters in eight bits. EBCDIC is primarily found in "mainframe" computing environments.

EIA – Electronic Industries Association

EMI – Electromagnetic Interference

encryption – encoding the data so that only someone with the key used to encode the data is able to decode the data

EPO – Emergency Power Off

`etherfind` – command used on Sun workstations to trace TCP packet traffic (similar to `tcpdump`)

expensed assets – items that are paid for in full from the current budget

FAQ – Frequently Asked Questions

FCC – Federal Communications Commission

FDDI – Fiber Distributed Data Interface

field engineer – customer support representative who performs engineering support in the field for customers of a computer maker (also known as an FE)

file modes – UNIX file protection settings

file system – area of disk space where files appear organized in a hierarchical directory tree

`find` – program used to search a file system based on certain search criteria

FIPS – Federal Information Processing Standard

footprint – amount of space taken up by a piece of equipment

`format` – program used to format a disk drive

freeware – software which is freely available but not necessarily placed in the public domain (may have restrictions on use or modification)

`fsck` – program used to check and verify the integrity of a file system

`ftp` – File Transfer Program or File Transfer Protocol

full backup – a complete backup copy of data

gigabytes – 1K megabytes, or 1,073,741,824 bytes of data

GNU – GNU's Not Unix

Gopher – distributed document search and retrieval application used on the Internet

guru – a term sometimes used to describe someone who knows a great deal about a specific computer system

hacker – talented, although possibly eccentric, programmer

halon – a colorless, odorless, inert chemical used to extinguish fire, especially where delicate electronic equipment is found

halt – the act of stopping the processing of a computer's operating system

handshaking – two ends of a network connection trading information in order to agree on the type or speed of transmission or to authorize access for the other

headhunter – slang term sometimes used to refer to job recruiting and locator services

heterogeneous environment – an environment with a mix of equipment and software from different vendors

homogeneous environment – an environment where all hardware and software is supplied by the same vendor

hot-pluggable – the ability to insert and remove components in a computer without requiring the machine be turned off first

IAB – Internet Architecture Board (formerly the Internet Activities Board)

IEEE – Institute of Electrical and Electronics Engineers

IETF – Internet Engineering Task Force

incremental backup – a partial backup copy of data which contains all data modified since the time of the most recent backup

`installp` – program used to install software in AIX

internetwork – many networks connected together

InterNIC – Internet Network Information Center

`iostat` – program used to gather input/output statistics in Berkeley UNIX

ISDN – Integrated Services Digital Network

ISO – International Organization for Standardization

Kbps – kilobits per second, or 1024 bits per second

Kerberos – security system developed at MIT

KVA – kilovolt-ampere rating

LAN – Local Area Network

LISA – Large Installation System Administration; annual conference on system management issues sponsored by the Usenix Association and SAGE

`lpadmin` – program used to manage printers in SVR4

`lpc` – program used to manage printers in Berkeley UNIX

`lpstat` – program used to obtain printer status in SVR4

`ls` – UNIX command to list the contents of a directory

MAN – Metropolitan Area Network

Mbps – megabits per second, or 1024 kilobits per second

Mbps – megabits per second, or 1024 megabits per second

megabytes – usually thought of as one million bytes of data, a true megabyte is 1K of 1K blocks (K representing 1024), or 1024 1024-byte blocks (1,048,566 bytes of data)

mirroring – when an exact, up to date copy of a file system is maintained so that if the primary copy fails, the system can switch to the secondary copy and continue

MIT – Massachusetts Institute of Technology

MNP – Microcom Networking Protocol

modem – a device used to communicate data across a telephone line

Mosaic – sophisticated search and retrieval application used on the Internet

motherboard – the main circuit board in a PC which houses the CPU and memory and has a built-in backplane

`mount` – program used to include a disk area as part of the overall file system hierarchy

mount – the act of connecting a file system at a point in the file system hierarchy

NBS – National Bureau of Standards

NCSC – National Computer Security Center

NEMA – National Electrical Manufacturer's Association

`netstat` – Berkeley UNIX command used to gather network statistics

network administrator – person who oversees the configuration and operation of the local network and any external networks that connect to it

network firewall – a method of limiting outside access to a network

NFS – Network File System; developed by Sun Microsystems

NIS – Network Information Service; system information lookup software developed by Sun Microsystems

NIST – National Institute of Science and Technology

node – special files in the `/dev` directory which allow access to physical devices via device drivers

NSF – National Science Foundation

`nslookup` – command to look up Name Server data

NTIS – National Technical Information Service

off-site storage – a remote location where backup media is stored to lower the odds of disaster befalling both computing equipment and data

operations manager – one who is responsible for the smooth operation of the computing environment

operations – the day-to-day running of the computer environment

operator – one who is involved in running the computer system(s)

Orange Book – see *TCSEC*

OSF – Open Software Foundation

OSI – Open Systems Interconnection

packet-switched – network where the path can change during the life of the connection, each packet possibly taking a different path from source to destination

partitions – physical areas on a disk in which file systems are constructed

password aging – a way of forcing the user to change their password after a some amount of time has passed so they do not keep the same password indefinitely

patch – small modification to a program or the operating system which can be added rather than having to do a complete reinstallation

PDU – Power Distribution Unit, see *power conditioner*

`ping` – program used to send an ICMP echo packet to a host (which is a rudimentary test to see if the host is operating)

`pkgadd` – program used to install software in SVR4

PMU – Power Management Unit

power conditioner – component in a computer room which provides a smooth flow of "juice" to all the computers

power conditioning – the process of providing a uniform level of power

power distribution unit – see *power conditioner*

power factor – percentage of power used by an electronic device and not lost through resistance in an electrical circuit

power management unit – see *power conditioner*

power tails – cables which run from the power conditioner to the computer

power – the rate at which energy is dissipated

ppm – pages per minute; used to describe the speed of a printer

preventive maintenance – checking over a piece of equipment to make sure it is in good working order in an effort to prevent a failure sometime in the future

PROM – Programmable Read-Only Memory

public-domain software – software which is publicly available at no cost and has no restrictions on use or modification

purchase requisition – a form used in larger organizations to request a purchase be approved and made

RAID – Redundant Array of Inexpensive Disk

rcp – remote copy command; used to copy files to another system

rdate – command used to remotely set the date and time (used to synchronize the date and time)

reseat – the act of removing and replacing a circuit board in a computer to assure it is making a connection

restore – program used to restore files backed up with the Berkeley **dump** command or AIX **backup** command

restore – the act of reading data from backup media and replacing it on a system from which it has been lost

RFC – Request For Comments

RFS – Remote File Sharing; developed by AT&T

rightsizing – see *downsizing*

ring – network topology where network devices are connected to a network cable in a circular fashion

rlogin – remote login command, used to login to another system

rm – program used to delete (remove) a file

RPC – Remote Procedure Call

RS-232 – common serial cable standard used with modems, printers, and terminals

SAGE – System Administrators Guild; special interest group sponsored by the Usenix Association

SANS – Systems Administration, Networking, and Security conference

SCSI – Small Computer Systems Interface; a popular standard for connecting peripheral devices to computers

security through obscurity – an often-used method of maintaining security simply by not giving anyone any ideas about how to break it

`sendmail` – a popular mail transport program

serial cable – a multiwire connection to a computer over which bits representing data are sent sequentially (as opposed to a parallel cable where the bits are sent in groups along different wires)

set-gid – a program that, when run, assumes the privileges of the group to which the file belongs

set-uid – a program that, when run, assumes the privileges of the owner of the file

shareware – publicly available software where the author does not sell it but offers it in return for a "donation" if you try it and decide to keep using it

SIMM – Single In-line Memory Module

single-user mode – when a UNIX machine is not fully "up" so that users can login, but when maintenance work can be performed; also known as *maintenance mode*

site manager – person with ultimate responsibility for the computing site

smart bridge – a networking bridge that can learn which packets should be forwarded and which should not be

SMTP – Simple Mail Transfer Protocol

SNMP – Simple Network Management Protocol

star – network topology where devices are connected to some central hub

store-and-forward – method of sending files or electronic mail via multiple "stops" along a route through a network

striping – equally spreading a file system across multiple physical disk drives to increase access speed

subnet – a physically separate segment of the local network which, when connected via a router or a computer capable of serving as a router, behaves as an integrated part of the local network

subnetting – breaking a local network into multiple segments

super user – the user with privilege to perform any operation on the computer, also known as the `root` user

surge suppressor – a small device used to reduce the chances of a power surge, usually used with PCs and workstations

SVR4 – System V Release 4; the designation identifying the version of UNIX distributed by Unix System Laboratories, formerly a subsidiary of AT&T, now owned by Novell

swap space – disk space used by the operating system to temporarily store a process which will not fit in memory while it runs another process

swapped out – refers to the state of an active process which has been moved out of physical memory and into the *swap space* so another process may run in physical memory

systems analyst – often another title for programmer and can be in varying degrees of expertise

T1 – dedicated communications medium providing a high-bandwidth connection over the public telephone network

`tar` – tape archive; program used to write disk files to another device (usually a tape)

`tcpdump` – command used to trace TCP usage

TCSEC – Trusted Computer System Evaluation Criteria which specifies levels of security for computer systems

TDR – Time Domain Reflectometry

technician – one who deals with repair of hardware components

`telnet` – command used to establish an interactive session on another host on the network

thicknet – the oldest form of Ethernet cable, also known as 10Base-5; made from $\frac{1}{2}''$ coaxial cable

thinnet – a newer form of Ethernet cable, also known as 10Base-2; made from $\frac{1}{4}''$ "TV" coaxial cable

thrashing – a state where so many processes are waiting to run that the system spends most of its time swapping processes in and out of memory and very little time actually running them. This is literally "going nowhere fast."

topology – the physical layout, usually of a network

`traceroute` – command used to trace TCP packet routing

trap door – see *back door*

Trojan horse – program that does more than it appears to do. It may collect information or perform tasks while the user is unaware of its activity.

tty – shortened version of teletypewriter, an old term used to describe a terminal `tunefs` – program used to adjust operating parameters of a file system in Berkeley UNIX

twisted-pair – network cable containing two pairs of wires, twisted around each other to minimize electromagnetic interference

`ufsdump` – SVR4 equivalent of Berkeley `dump` command

`ufsrestore` – SVR4 equivalent of Berkeley `restore` command

`umask` – command used to set default file permission

`umount` – program used to remove a disk area as a part of the overall file system hierarchy (the opposite of the `mount` command)

UPS – Uninterruptible Power Supply

`uucico` – UUCP program to transfer files

UUCP – Unix-to-Unix copy; an old protocol used for primitive networking over telephone lines

VA – see *volt-ampere rating*

virtual memory – a memory management scheme where the address space appears to be unlimited and the operating system maps logical memory into real memory space by moving other sections out to temporary storage

virus – program that copies itself onto other systems by attaching itself to programs that are legitimately transferred between systems, and "infecting" the new system when the transfer takes place

voltage – a measurement of the potential electrical energy

volt-ampere rating – the maximum amount of *power* a circuit can deliver

volume – logical collection of disk space representing a single file system which can be expanded by adding space from another source

WAIS – Wide Area Information Servers; used on the Internet

WAN – Wide Area Network

watt – a measurement of power used in a circuit

wizard – see *guru*

worm – program that copies itself onto other computers without assistance

WORM – Write Once Read Many; optical disk medium that can be written only once but read over and over

X.25 – OSI-compliant protocol used over leased telephone lines to form a point-to-point connection

Yellow Pages – see *NIS*

Bibliography

[Ada87] Douglas Adams. *The More Than Complete Hitchhiker's Guide.* Longmeadow Press, 201 High Ridge Road, Stamford, CT 06904, 1987. ISBN 0-681-40322-5.

[AL92] Paul Albitz and Cricket Liu. *DNS and BIND.* O'Reilly & Associates, Inc., Sebastopol, CA 95472, 1992. ISBN 1-56592-010-4.

[AML+93] F. Anklesaria, M. McCahill, P. Lindner, D. Johnson, D. Torrey, and B. Alberti. The Internet Gopher Protocol (a distributed document search and retrieval protocol), March 1993. Available via anonymous FTP from `ds.internic.net` as `/rfc/rfc1436.txt`.

[Bac86] Maurice J. Bach. *The Design Of The UNIX Operating System.* Prentice Hall, Englewood Cliffs, NJ 07632, 1986. ISBN 0-13-201799-7.

[Bak91] Richard H. Baker. *Computer Security Handbook.* TAB Professional and Reference Books, Blue Ridge Summit, PA 17294-0850, 1991. ISBN 0-8306-3592-0.

[Bel89] Steven M. Bellovin. Security Problems in the TCP/IP Protocol Suite. *ACM Computer Communication Review,* 19(2):32–48, April 1989. Available via anonymous FTP from `ftp.research.att.com` as `/dist/internet_security/ipext.ps.Z`.

[Bel92] Steven M. Bellovin. There Be Dragons. In *Proceedings of the Third Usenix UNIX Security Symposium*, September 1992. Available via anonymous FTP from `ftp.research.att.com` as `/dist/internet_security/dragon.ps`.

[BG94] Internet Architecture Board and Internet Engineering Steering Group. The Internet Standards Process—Revision 2, March 1994. Available via anonymous FTP from `ds.internic.net` as `/rfc/rfc1602.txt`.

[Blo91] Sumner Blount. The distributed computing environment. In Gary R. McClain, ed., *Open Systems Interconnection Handbook*, pp. 265–295. McGraw-Hill, Inc., 1221 Avenue of the Americas, New York, NY 10020, 1991. ISBN 0-07-044969-4.

[Blo92] John Bloomer. *Power Programming with RPC.* O'Reilly & Associates, Inc., Sebastopol, CA 95472, February 1992. ISBN 0-937175-77-3.

[Bra90] Russell L. Brand. Coping with the Threat of Computer Security Incidents: A Primer from Prevention through Recovery, December 1990. Available via anonymous FTP from `cert.sei.cmu.edu` as `/pub/info/primer/primer.ps.Z`.

[Bro82] Frederick P. Brooks, Jr. *The Mythical Man-Month.* Addison-Wesley, Reading, MA 01867, 1982. ISBN 0-201-00650-2.

[CB94] William R. Cheswick and Steven M. Bellovin. *Firewalls and Internet Security: Repelling the Wily Hacker.* Addison-Wesley, Reading, MA 01867, 1994. ISBN 0-201-63357-4.

[CFSD90] J. Case, M. Fedor, M. Schoffstall, and C. Davin. Simple Network Management Protocol (SNMP), May 1990.

Available via anonymous FTP from `ds.internic.net` as `/rfc/rfc1157.txt`.

[Chea] Bill Cheswick. The Design of a Secure Internet Gateway. Available via anonymous FTP from `ftp.research.att.com` as `/dist/internet_security/gateway.ps`.

[Cheb] Bill Cheswick. An Evening with Berferd In Which a Cracker is Lured, Endured, and Studied. Available via anonymous FTP from `ftp.research.att.com` as `/dist/internet_security/berferd.ps`.

[CKM90] Paul Christiansen, Steve King, and Mark Munger. *Networking with Novell NetWare.* Windcrest Books, Blue Ridge Summit, PA 17294-0850, 1990. ISBN 0-8306-3283-2.

[CMQ93] Smoot Carl-Mitchell and John S. Quarterman. *Practical Internetworking with TCP/IP and UNIX.* Addison-Wesley, Reading, MA 01867, 1993. ISBN 0-201-58629-0.

[CMRW93] J. Case, K. McCloghrie, M. Rose, and S. Waldbusser. Introduction to version 2 of the Internet-standard Network Management Framework, April 1993. Available via anonymous FTP from `ds.internic.net` as `/rfc/rfc1441.txt`.

[Com91] Douglas E. Comer. *Internetworking with TCP/IP, Volume I.* Prentice Hall, Englewood Cliffs, NJ 07632, 2nd edition, 1991. ISBN 0-13-468505-9.

[Cou90] National Research Council. *Computers At Risk: Safe Computing In The Information Age.* National Academy Press, 2101 Constitution Avenue, N.W., Washington DC 20418, 1990. ISBN 0-309-04388-3.

[CP93] A. Cooper and J. Postel. The US Domain, June 1993. Available via anonymous FTP from `ds.internic.net` as `/rfc/rfc1480.txt`.

[Cro82] D. Crocker. Standard for the format of ARPA Internet text messages, August 1982. Available via anonymous FTP from `ds.internic.net` as `/rfc/rfc822.txt`.

[Cur92] David A. Curry. *UNIX System Security: A Guide For Users And System Administrators.* Addison-Wesley, Reading, MA 01867, 1992. ISBN 0-201-56327-4.

[Edm92] John J. Edmunds. *SAA/LU6.2: Distributed Networks and Applications.* McGraw-Hill, Inc., 1221 Avenue of the Americas, New York, NY 10020, 1992. ISBN 0-07-019022-4.

[Eng93] FYI on a Network Management Tool Catalog: Tools for Monitoring and Debugging TCP/IP Internets and Interconnected Devices, June 1993. Available via anonymous FTP from `ds.internic.net` as `/rfc/rfc1470.txt`.

[ES90] Margaret A. Ellis and Bjarne Stroustrup. *The Annotated C++ Reference Manual.* Addison-Wesley, Reading, MA 01867, 1990. ISBN 0-201-51459-1.

[Est93] Susan Estrada. *Connecting To The Internet: An O'Reilly Buyer's Guide.* O'Reilly & Associates, Inc., Sebastopol, CA 95472, 1993. ISBN 1-56592-061-9.

[Fri91] Æleen Frisch. *Essential System Administration.* O'Reilly & Associates, Inc., Sebastopol, CA 95472, 1991. ISBN 0-937175-74-9.

[FS90] Daniel Farmer and Eugene H. Spafford. The COPS Security Checker System. In *Proceedings of the Summer 1990 USENIX Conference*, pp. 165–170, June 1990. Available via anonymous FTP from `arthur.cs.purdue.edu` as `/pub/reports/TR993.PS`.

[GK92] Hans-Georg Göhring and Franz-Joachim Kauffels. *Token Ring: Principles, Perspectives and Strategies.* Addison-Wesley, Wokingham, England, 1992. ISBN 0-201-56895-0.

[GS91] Simson Garfinkel and Gene Spafford. *Practical UNIX Security.* O'Reilly & Associates, Inc., Sebastopol, CA 95472, 1991. ISBN 0-937175-72-2.

[Gul91] Dale Gulick. ISDN and the global network. In Gary R. McClain, ed., *Open Systems Interconnection Handbook*, pp. 69–89. McGraw-Hill, Inc., 1221 Avenue of the Americas, New York, NY 10020, 1991. ISBN 0-07-044969-4.

[Han89] Bill Hancock. *Network Concepts and Architectures.* QED Information Sciences, Inc., P.O. Box 181, Wellesley, MA 02181, 1989. ISBN 0-89435-270-9.

[Hed88] C. Hedrick. Routing Information Protocol, June 1988. Available via anonymous FTP from `ds.internic.net` as `/rfc/rfc1058.txt`.

[Hel91] Hermann J. Helgert. *Integrated Services Digital Networks: Architectures Protocols, Standards.* Addison-Wesley, Reading, MA 01867, 1991. ISBN 0-201-52501-1.

[Hew81] Paul G. Hewitt. *Conceptual Physics.* Little, Brown and Company, 4th edition, 1981. ISBN 0-316-359696.

[Hol91] Site Security Handbook, July 1991. Available via anonymous FTP from `ds.internic.net` as `/rfc/rfc1244.txt`.

[Hor84] C. Hornig. Standard for the transmission of IP datagrams over Ethernet networks, April 1984. Available via anonymous FTP from `ds.internic.net` as `/rfc/rfc894.txt`.

[Hui94] C. Huitema. Charter of the Internet Architecture Board (IAB), March 1994. Available via anonymous FTP from `ds.internic.net` as `/rfc/rfc1601.txt`.

[Hun92] Craig Hunt. *TCP/IP Network Administration.* O'Reilly & Associates, Inc., Sebastopol, CA 95472, August 1992. ISBN 0-937175-82-X.

[Jen90] Karla Jennings. *The Devouring Fungus: Tales Of The Computer Age.* W. W. Norton & Company, 500 Fifth Avenue, New York, NY 10110, 1990. ISBN 0-393-30732-8.

[Jon88] Vincent C. Jones. *MAP/TOP Networking.* McGraw-Hill, Inc., 1221 Avenue of the Americas, New York, NY 10020, 1988. ISBN 0-07-032806-4.

[Kap92] Atul Kapoor. *SNA: Architecture, Protocols, and Implementation.* McGraw-Hill, Inc., 1221 Avenue of the Americas, New York, NY 10020, 1992. ISBN 0-07-033727-6.

[Keh92] Brendan Kehoe. *Zen and the Art of the Internet.* Prentice Hall, Englewood Cliffs, NJ 07632, 2nd edition, 1992. ISBN 0-13-010778-6.

[KH93] E. Krol and E. Hoffman. FYI on 'What is the Internet?', May 1993. Available via anonymous FTP from `ds.internic.net` as `/rfc/rfc1462.txt`.

[Kle90] Daniel V. Klein. 'Foiling the Cracker': A Survey of, and Improvements to Password Security. In *USENIX Security Workshop Proceedings*, pp. 5–14, August 1990. Available via anonymous FTP from `ftp.uu.net` as `/doc/obi/Security/Foiling.the.Cracker.Z`.

[KP84] Brian W. Kernighan and Rob Pike. *The UNIX Programming Environment.* Prentice Hall, Englewood Cliffs, NJ 07632, 1984. ISBN 0-13-937699-2.

[KR78] Brian W. Kernighan and Dennis M. Ritchie. *The C Programming Language.* Prentice Hall, Englewood Cliffs, NJ 07632, 1978. ISBN 0-13-110163-3.

[Kro92] Ed Krol. *The Whole Internet.* O'Reilly & Associates, Inc., Sebastopol, CA 95472, January 1992. ISBN 1-56592-025-2.

[Lau86] Leonard Laub. What is a CD ROM? In Steve Lambert and Suzanne Ropiequet, ed., *CD ROM—The New Papyrus*, pp. 47–71. Microsoft Press, 16011 N.E. 36th, Redmond, WA 98073-9717, 1986. ISBN 0-914845-74-8.

[Lib90] Don Libes. Choosing a name for your computer, August 1990. Available via anonymous FTP from `ds.internic.net` as `/rfc/rfc1178.txt`.

[Lin89] J. Linn. Privacy enhancement for Internet electronic mail: Part I—message encipherment and authentication procedures, August 1989. Available via anonymous FTP from `ds.internic.net` as `/rfc/rfc1113.txt`.

[LMKQ90] Samuel J. Leffler, Marshall Kirk McKusick, Michael J. Karels, and John S. Quarterman. *The Design and Implementation of the 4.3BSD UNIX Operating System.* Addison-Wesley, Reading, MA 01867, 1990. ISBN 0-201-06196-1.

[Lou91] K. Lougheed. A Border Gateway Protocol 3 (BGP-3), October 1991. Available via anonymous FTP from `ds.internic.net` as `/rfc/rfc1267.txt`.

[Lou92] Mike Loukides. *System Performance Tuning.* O'Reilly & Associates, Inc., Sebastopol, CA 95472, 1992. ISBN 0-937175-60-9.

[Mar93] J. Martin. There's Gold in them thar Networks! or Searching for Treasure in all the Wrong Places, January 1993. Available via anonymous FTP from `ds.internic.net` as `/rfc/rfc1402.txt`.

[McG92] G. McGregor. The PPP Internet Protocol Control Protocol (IPCP), May 1992. Available via anonymous FTP from `ds.internic.net` as `/rfc/rfc1332.txt`.

[McN82] John E. McNamara. *Technical Aspects of Data Communication*. Digital Press, 2nd edition, 1982. ISBN 0-932376-18-5.

[Mil84] D. Mills. Exterior Gateway Protocol formal specification, April 1984. Available via anonymous FTP from `ds.internic.net` as `/rfc/rfc904.txt`.

[Mil89] D. Mills. Internet time synchronization: The Network Time Protocol, October 1989. Available via anonymous FTP from `ds.internic.net` as `/rfc/rfc1129.txt`.

[Mil92a] D. Mills. Network Time Protocol (Version 3) Specification, Implementation and Analysis, March 1992. Available via anonymous FTP from `ds.internic.net` as `/rfc/rfc1305.txt`.

[Mil92b] D. Mills. Simple Network Time Protocol (SNTP), August 1992. Available via anonymous FTP from `ds.internic.net` as `/rfc/rfc1361.txt`.

[ML92] James Martin and Joe Leben. *DECnet Phase V*. Digital Press, 1992. ISBN 1-55558-076-9.

[MMR91] G. Malkin, A. Marine, and J. Reynolds. FYI on Questions and Answers: Answers to Commonly asked "experienced Internet user" questions, February 1991. Available via anonymous FTP from `ds.internic.net` as `/rfc/rfc1207.txt`.

[Moc87a] P. Mockapetris. Domain names—concepts and facilities, November 1987. Available via anonymous FTP from `ds.internic.net` as `/rfc/rfc1034.txt`.

[Moc87b] P. Mockapetris. Domain names—implementation and specification, November 1987. Available via anonymous FTP from `ds.internic.net` as `/rfc/rfc1035.txt`.

[Moy94] J. Moy. OSPF version 2, March 1994. Available via anonymous FTP from `ds.internic.net` as `/rfc/rfc1583.txt`.

[MP92] Linda Mui and Eric Pearce. *X Window System Administrator's Guide*. O'Reilly & Associates, Inc., Sebastopol, CA 95472, 1992. ISBN 0-937175-83-8.

[MR90] K. McCloghrie and M. Rose. Management Information Base for network management of tcp/ip-based internets, May 1990. Available via anonymous FTP from `ds.internic.net` as `/rfc/rfc1156.txt`.

[MR93] G. Minshall and M. Ritter. SNMP over AppleTalk, March 1993. Available via anonymous FTP from `ds.internic.net` as `/rfc/rfc1419.txt`.

[MRM94] A. Marine, J. Reynolds, and G. Malkin. FYI on Questions and Answers—Answers to Commonly asked "New Internet User" Questions, March 1994. Available via anonymous FTP from `ds.internic.net` as `/rfc/rfc1594.txt`.

[Nem92] Martin A. W. Nemzow. *The Ethernet Management Guide: Keeping the Link*. McGraw-Hill, Inc., 1221 Avenue of the Americas, New York, NY 10020, 2nd edition, 1992. ISBN 0-07-046320-4.

[Nem94] Martin A. W. Nemzow. *FDDI Networking: Planning, Installation, and Management*. McGraw-Hill, Inc., 1221 Avenue of the Americas, New York, NY 10020, 1994. ISBN 0-07-046322-0.

[NNM82] Elizabeth A. Nichols, Joseph C. Nichols, and Keith R. Musson. *Data Communications For Microcomputers*.

McGraw-Hill, Inc., 1221 Avenue of the Americas, New York, NY 10020, 1982. ISBN 0-07-046480-4.

[NSS89] Evi Nemeth, Garth Snyder, and Scott Seebass. *UNIX System Administration Handbook.* Prentice Hall, Englewood Cliffs, NJ 07632, 1989. ISBN 0-13-933441-6.

[OT92] Tim O'Reilly and Grace Todino. *Managing UUCP and Usenet.* O'Reilly & Associates, Inc., Sebastopol, CA 95472, 10th edition, January 1992. ISBN 0-937175-93-5.

[Par83] Donn B. Parker. *Fighting Computer Crime.* Charles Scribner's Sons, New York, NY, 1983. ISBN 0-684-17796-X.

[PCF91] R. Pethia, S. Crocker, and B. Fraser. Guidelines for the Secure Operation of the Internet, November 1991. Available via anonymous FTP from `ds.internic.net` as `/rfc/rfc1281.txt`.

[Per92] Radia Perlman. *Interconnections: Bridges and Routers.* Addison-Wesley, Reading, MA 01867, 1992. ISBN 0-201-56332-0.

[PKCB89] J. Postel, L. Kleinrock, V. Cerf, and B. Boehm. Act One—The Poems, September 1989. Available via anonymous FTP from `ds.internic.net` as `/rfc/rfc1121.txt`.

[PLL+91] B. Plattner, C. Lanz, H. Lubich, M. Müller, and T. Walter. *X400 Message Handling: Standards, Interworking, Applications.* Addison-Wesley, Reading, MA 01867, 1991. ISBN 0-201-56503-X.

[Plu82] D. Plummer. Ethernet Address Resolution Protocol: Or converting network protocol addresses to 48.bit Ethernet addresses for transmission on Ethernet hardware, November 1982. Available via anonymous FTP from `ds.internic.net` as `/rfc/rfc826.txt`.

[Pos80] J. Postel. User Datagram Protocol, August 1980. Available via anonymous FTP from `ds.internic.net` as `/rfc/rfc768.txt`.

[Pos81a] J. Postel. Internet Control Message Protocol, September 1981. Available via anonymous FTP from `ds.internic.net` as `/rfc/rfc792.txt`.

[Pos81b] J. Postel. Internet Protocol, September 1981. Available via anonymous FTP from `ds.internic.net` as `/rfc/rfc791.txt`.

[Pos81c] J. Postel. Transmission Control Protocol, September 1981. Available via anonymous FTP from `ds.internic.net` as `/rfc/rfc793.txt`.

[Pos82] J. Postel. Simple Mail Transfer Protocol, August 1982. Available via anonymous FTP from `ds.internic.net` as `/rfc/rfc821.txt`.

[Pro91] D. Provan. Tunneling IPX traffic through IP networks, June 1991. Available via anonymous FTP from `ds.internic.net` as `/rfc/rfc1234.txt`.

[Rei90] Glenn C. Reid. *Thinking in PostScript.* Addison-Wesley, Reading, MA 01867, 1990. ISBN 0-201-52372-8.

[Rit84] Dennis M. Ritchie. The evolution of the UNIX time-sharing system. *AT&T Bell Laboratories Technical Journal*, 63(8, part 2):1577–1593, October 1984.

[RKF92] Ward Rosenberry, David Kennedy, and Gerry Fisher. *Understanding DCE.* O'Reilly & Associates, Inc., Sebastopol, CA 95472, October 1992. ISBN 0-56592-005-8.

[Rom88] J. Romkey. Nonstandard for transmission of IP datagrams over serial lines: SLIP, June 1988. Available via anonymous FTP from `ds.internic.net` as `/rfc/rfc1055.txt`.

[Ros90] Management Information Base for network management of TCP/IP-based internets: MIB-II, May 1990. Available via anonymous FTP from `ds.internic.net` as `/rfc/rfc1158.txt`.

[Ros91] Marshall T. Rose. *The Simple Book: An Introduction to Management of TCP/IP-based Internets.* Prentice Hall, Englewood Cliffs, NJ 07632, 1991. ISBN 0-13-812611-9.

[Ros93a] M. Rose. Post Office Protocol: Version 3, June 1993. Available via anonymous FTP from `ds.internic.net` as `/rfc/rfc1460.txt`.

[Ros93b] Marshall T. Rose. *The Internet Message: Closing The Book With Electronic Mail.* Prentice Hall, Englewood Cliffs, NJ 07632, 1993. ISBN 0-13-092941-7.

[RS91] Deborah Russell and T. T. Gangemi Sr. *Computer Security Basics.* O'Reilly & Associates, Inc., Sebastopol, CA 95472, 1991. ISBN 0-937175-71-4.

[SAO90] G. S. Sidhu, R. F. Andrews, and A. B. Oppenheimer. *Inside AppleTalk.* Addison-Wesley, Reading, MA 01867, 2nd edition, 1990.

[Sch90] Sherman K. Schlar. *Inside X.25: A Manger's Guide.* McGraw-Hill, Inc., 1221 Avenue of the Americas, New York, NY 10020, 1990. ISBN 0-07-055327-0.

[Shi92] John Shirley. *Guide to Writing DCE Applications.* O'Reilly & Associates, Inc., Sebastopol, CA 95472, July 1992. ISBN 0-56592-004-X.

[Sim92] W. Simpson. The Point-to-Point Protocol (PPP) for the Transmission of Multi-protocol Datagrams over Point-to-Point Links, May 1992. Available via anonymous FTP from `ds.internic.net` as `/rfc/rfc1331.txt`.

[Smi93] Phillip Smith. *Frame Relay: Principles and Applications.* Addison-Wesley, Reading, MA 01867, 1993. ISBN 0-201-62400-1.

[Spa88] Eugene H. Spafford. The Internet Worm Program: An Analysis. Technical Report CSD-TR-823, Purdue University, Department of Computer Science, West Lafayette, IN 47907-2004, December 1988. Available via anonymous FTP from `arthur.cs.purdue.edu` as `/pub/reports/TR823.PS`.

[Spa91a] Eugene H. Spafford. Computer Viruses—A Form Of Artificial Life? Technical Report CSD-TR-985, Purdue University, Department of Computer Science, West Lafayette, IN 47907-1398, September 1991. Available via anonymous FTP from `arthur.cs.purdue.edu` as `/pub/reports/TR985.PS`.

[Spa91b] Eugene H. Spafford. The Internet Worm Incident. Technical Report CSD-TR-933, Purdue University, Department of Computer Science, West Lafayette, IN 47907-2004, September 1991. Available via anonymous FTP from `arthur.cs.purdue.edu` as `/pub/reports/TR933.PS`.

[Ste90] W. Richard Stevens. *UNIX Network Programming.* Prentice Hall, Englewood Cliffs, NJ 07632, 1990. ISBN 0-13-949876-1.

[Ste92a] Hal Stern. *Managing NFS and NIS.* O'Reilly & Associates, Inc., Sebastopol, CA 95472, 1992. ISBN 0-937175-75-7.

[Ste92b] W. Richard Stevens. *Advanced Programming in the UNIX Environment.* Addison-Wesley, Reading, MA 01867, 1992. ISBN 0-201-56317-7.

[Sto88] Clifford Stoll. Stalking The Wily Hacker. *Communications of the ACM*, 31(5):484–497, May 1988.

[Sto90] Clifford Stoll. *The Cuckoo's Egg: Tracking A Spy Through The Maze Of Computer Espionage.* Pocket Books, New York, NY 10020, 1990. ISBN 0-671-72688-9.

[Sun88] Sun Microsystems, Inc. RPC: Remote Procedure Call Protocol specification: Version 2, June 1988. Available via anonymous FTP from `ds.internic.net` as `/rfc/rfc1057.txt`.

[Sun89] Sun Microsystems, Inc. NFS: Network File System Protocol specification, March 1989. Available via anonymous FTP from `ds.internic.net` as `/rfc/rfc1094.txt`.

[Tan88] Andrew S. Tanenbaum. *Computer Networks.* Prentice Hall, Englewood Cliffs, NJ 07632, 2nd edition, 1988. ISBN 0-13-162959-X.

[TF89] Rebecca Thomas and Rik Farrow. *UNIX Administration Guide For System V.* Prentice Hall, Englewood Cliffs, NJ 07632, 1989. ISBN 0-13-942889-5.

[Uni90a] Unix Software Operation. *UNIX System V Release 4 Network User's and Administrator's Guide.* Prentice Hall, Englewood Cliffs, NJ 07632, 1990.

[Uni90b] Unix Software Operation. *UNIX System V Release 4 System Administrator's Guide.* Prentice Hall, Englewood Cliffs, NJ 07632, 1990. ISBN 0-13-947086-7.

[wEAR93] Bryan Costales with Eric Allman and Neil Rickert. *sendmail.* O'Reilly & Associates, Inc., Sebastopol, CA 95472, 1993. ISBN 1-56592-056-2.

[WS91] Larry Wall and Randal Schwartz. *Programming Perl.* O'Reilly & Associates, Inc., Sebastopol, CA 95472, 1991. ISBN 0-937175-64-1.

Index